Gay Su Pinnell
Irene C. Fountas

The **Continuum** of **Literacy Learning**

Grades PreK–2

A Guide to Teaching

SECOND EDITION

Heinemann
Portsmouth, NH

Heinemann
361 Hanover Street
Portsmouth, NH 03801–3912
www.heinemann.com

Offices and agents throughout the world

The Continuum of Literacy Learning, Grades PreK–2: A Guide to Teaching, Second Edition

ISBN 10: 0–325–02878–8
ISBN 13: 978–0–325–02878–1

Printed in Shenzhen, China

0912/12004804

3 4 5 6 7 8 RRD 15 14 13 12

Contents

Introduction

As the world of literacy changes, we also see some important changes in the acquisition of literacy and its increasing demands across grade levels. The second edition of *The Continuum of Literacy Learning* has been adjusted to reflect those changes.

First, the preschools of today are different and require different experiences from those of five years ago; so a prekindergarten set of continua has been added to the Prekindergarten–8 and Prekindergarten–2 versions of this book. This prekindergarten continuum does not represent "moving" the kindergarten curriculum down. Instead, it presents a rich array of understandings relative to oral language, story telling, and playful print and sound awareness to provide a strong foundation for kindergarten learning. The behaviors and understandings are goals for the four-year olds to achieve by the end of their school year, prior to entering kindergarten. Some of the goals may be achievable in three-year old classes, but be sure to honor the development and range in your children.

The basic detailed descriptions of behaviors and understandings to notice, teach, and support for grades K through 8 remain the same; but in this new edition of the seven continua, we have added new challenges such as the effective processing of graphic texts and novels. We have also examined carefully the National Assessment of Educational Progress (NAEP) framework and the Common Core State Standards and made changes in some of the ways behaviors and understandings are expressed. Additionally, we have strengthened the expectation to recognize and effectively process genres that are embedded within other genres (hybrid texts, for example, a letter, diary entries, or newspaper articles within fictional narratives).

The continuum has also been adjusted in response to current research as well as to a great deal of information related to the implementation of assessment in schools. Finally, the continuum has a new design that makes it easier to read and interpret. We hope you will find this a valuable tool for assessing and planning your teaching.

Content of the Continuum

Across the seven continua included in this volume, several principles are important to consider:

❑ *Children learn by talking.* Talking represents the child's thinking. We engage children in conversation that is grounded in a variety of texts—those that children read, hear read aloud, or write—and that expands their ability to comprehend ideas and use language to share their thinking.

❑ *Children need to process a large amount of written language.* A dynamic language and literacy curriculum provides many daily opportunities for children to read books of their choice independently, to read more challenging instructional material with teacher guidance, and to hear teacher-selected and grade-appropriate texts read aloud.

❑ *The ability to read and comprehend texts is expanded through talking and writing.* Children need to acquire a wide range of ways to write about their reading and also to talk about texts with their teacher and other children.

❑ *Learning deepens when children engage in reading, talking, and writing about texts across many different instructional contexts.* Each mode of communication provides a new way to process the ideas learned from oral and written texts and from each other.

This continuum provides a way to look for specific evidence of learning from prekindergarten through grade 2, and across seven curricular areas. To create it, we examined a wide range of research on language and literacy learning, and we asked teachers and researchers for feedback. We also examined the curriculum standards of many states. Some guiding principles were:

❑ Learning does not occur in stages but is a continually evolving process.

❑ The same concepts are acquired and then elaborated over time.

❑ Many complex literacy understandings take years to develop.

❑ Children learn by applying what they know to the reading and writing of increasingly complex texts.

❑ Learning does not automatically happen; most children need expert teaching to develop high levels of reading and writing expertise.

❑ Learning is different but interrelated across different kinds of language and literacy activities; one kind of learning enhances and reinforces others.

In this volume, we include seven different learning continua (see Figure I–1). Each of these continua focuses on a different aspect of our language and literacy instructional framework (Fountas and Pinnell 1996, 2001b); and each contributes substantially, in different but complementary ways, to children's development of reading, writing, and language processes. Each of the continua is described in more detail in a separate introduction, but we briefly introduce them here.

Figure I–1   The Continuum of Literacy Learning

Curriculum Component	Brief Definition	Description of the Continuum
Interactive Read-Aloud and Literature Discussion	Children engage in deep discussion with one another about a text that they have heard read aloud or one that they have read independently.	• Year by year, grades PreK-2 • Genres appropriate to grades PreK-2 • Specific behaviors and understandings that are evidence of thinking within, beyond, and about the text
Shared and Performance Reading	Children read together or take roles in reading a shared text. They reflect the meaning of the text with their voices.	• Year by year, grades PreK-2 • Genres appropriate to grades PreK-2 • Specific behaviors and understandings that are evidence of thinking within, beyond, and about the text
Writing About Reading	Children extend their understanding of a text through a variety of writing genres and sometimes with illustrations.	• Year by year, grades PreK-2 • Genres/forms for writing about reading appropriate to grades PreK-2 • Specific evidence in the writing that reflects thinking within, beyond, and about the text
Writing	Children compose and write their own examples of a variety of genres, written for varying purposes and audiences.	• Year by year, grades PreK-2 • Genres/forms for writing appropriate to grades PreK-2 • Aspects of craft, conventions, and process that are evident in children's writing, grades PreK-2
Oral, Visual, and Technological Communication	Children present their ideas through oral discussion and presentation or through the use of technology.	• Year by year, grades PreK-2 • Specific behaviors and understandings related to listening and speaking, presentation, and technology
Phonics, Spelling, and Word Study	Children learn about the relationships of letters to sounds as well as the structure of words to help them in reading and spelling.	• Year by year, grades PreK-2 • Specific behaviors and understandings related to nine areas of understanding related to letters, sounds, and words, and how they work in reading and spelling
Guided Reading	Children read a teacher-selected text in a small group; the teacher provides explicit teaching and support for reading increasingly challenging texts.	• Level by level, Pre-A to N • Genres appropriate to grades PreK-2 • Specific behaviors and understandings that are evidence of thinking within, beyond, and about the text • Specific suggestions for word work (drawn from the phonics and word analysis continuum)

Reading Process: Systems of Strategic Actions

Four of the continua specifically address reading: interactive read-aloud and literature discussion, shared and performance reading, guided reading, and writing about reading. Here we focus on strategic actions for thinking:

- ❑ *Within the text* (literal understanding achieved through solving words, monitoring and correcting, searching for and using information, summarizing, maintaining fluency, and adjusting for purposes and genre of text)

- ❑ *Beyond the text* (making predictions, making connections with personal experience, content knowledge and other texts, inferring what is implied but not stated, and synthesizing new information)

- ❑ *About the text* to (analyzing or critiquing the text)

In *Interactive read-aloud and literature discussion,* often children have an opportunity to extend their understandings through talk. In interactive read-aloud you have the opportunity to engage children with texts that are usually more complex than they can read for themselves. You can take strategic moments to stop for quick discussion during the reading and continue talking after the end. Children's talk provides evidence of their thinking.

Shared and performance reading offer an authentic reason for reading aloud. As they read in unison or read parts in readers' theater, children need to read in phrases, notice punctuation and dialogue, and think about the meaning of the text. All of these actions provide evidence that they are understanding the text and processing it effectively. On these familiar texts, you have the opportunity to support and extend children's understandings.

Guided reading offers small-group support and explicit teaching to help children take on more challenging texts. As they read texts that are organized along a gradient of difficulty, children expand their systems of strategic actions by meeting the demands of increasingly complex texts. They provide evidence of their thinking through oral reading, talk, and extension through writing. The Guided Reading continuum is related to text reading levels rather than grade levels because we envision continuous progress along these levels. In the introduction to the Guided Reading continuum, you will find a chart indicating a range of levels that approximately correlates with goals for each grade level.

In addition to specific evidence of thinking within, beyond, and about a text, each of these three continua lists genres of texts that are appropriate for use at each grade level or text level.

Writing about reading, which often includes drawing, is another way for children to extend their understanding and provide evidence of thinking. Writing about reading may be used in connection with interactive read-aloud and literature discussion or guided reading.

As you work with the continua related to reading, you will see a gradual increase in the complexity of the kinds of thinking that readers do. Most of the principles of learning cannot be pinpointed at one point in time or even one year. You will usually see the same kind of principle (behavior or understanding) repeated across grades or across levels of text; each time, remember that the learner is applying the principle in a more complex way to read harder texts.

Oral and Written Communication

Writing is a way of experimenting with and deepening understanding of genres children have read. Although writing about reading is an excellent approach to help children extend their thinking and support discussion, it does not take the place of specific instruction devoted to helping children develop as writers. Through the writing workshop, teachers help young writers continually expand their learning of the craft, conventions, and process of writing to communicate meaning to an audience. The Writing continuum in this book lists specific understandings for each grade level related to craft, conventions, and process. It also suggests genres for children to write at each grade level.

Oral, visual, and technological communication are integral to all literacy processes; you'll see their presence in all other continua. This continuum singles out particular behaviors and understandings for intentional instruction.

Word Study

Finally, we include a continuum for phonics, spelling, and word study. This grade-by-grade continuum is drawn from the longer continuum published in *Phonics Lessons: Letters, Words, and How They Work* (Pinnell and Fountas, Heinemann, 2003). For each grade, you will find specific principles related to the nine areas of learning: (1) early literacy concepts; (2) phonological awareness; (3) letter knowledge; (4) letter-sound relationships; (5) spelling patterns; (6) high-frequency words; (7) word meaning; (8) word structure; and (9) word-solving actions. Here you will find specific understandings related to spelling, which interface with the section on conventions provided in the Writing continuum.

Some Cautions

In preparing these continua we considered the typical range of children that can be found in prekindergarten through grade 2 classrooms. We also consulted teachers about their expectations and vision as to appropriate instruction at each grade level. We examined the district and state standards. We need to have a vision of expected levels of learning because it helps in making effective instructional decisions; and even more importantly, it helps us to identify children who need intervention.

At the same time, we would not want to apply these expectations in an inflexible way. We need to recognize that children vary widely in their progress—sometimes moving quickly and sometimes getting bogged down. They may make faster progress in one area than another. The continua should help you intervene in more precise ways to help children. But it is also important to remember that learners may not necessarily meet *every* expectation at all points in time. Nor should any one of the understandings and behaviors included in this document be used as criteria for promotion to the next grade. Educators can look thoughtfully across the full range of grade-level expectations as they make decisions about individual children.

It is also important to recognize that just because grade-level expectations exist, not all teaching will be pitched at that level. Through assessment, you may learn that your class only partially matches the behaviors and understandings on the continuum. Almost all teachers find that they need to consult the material at lower and higher levels (one reason that the Guided Reading continuum is not graded).

Ways to Use the Continuum

We see many different uses for this continuum, including the following.

Foundation for Teaching

As you think about, plan for, and reflect on the effectiveness of providing individual, small-group, and whole-group instruction, you may consult different areas of the continuum. For example, if you are working with children in guided reading at a particular level, use the lists of behaviors and understandings to plan introductions, guide observations and interactions with individuals, and shape teaching points. The word work section of the same continuum will give you specific suggestions for principles to explore at the end of the guided reading lessons. You can plan specific teaching moves as you examine the section on interactive read-aloud and literature discussion. The interactive read-aloud as well as the writing and word study continua will be useful in planning explicit minilessons. When you and your colleagues teach for the same behaviors and understandings, your students will benefit from the coherence.

Guide for Curriculum Planning

The continuum can also be used by a grade-level team or school staff to plan the language and literacy curriculum. It offers a starting point for thinking very specifically about goals and expectations. Your team may adapt the continuum to meet your own goals and district expectations.

Linking Assessment to Instruction

Sometimes assessment is administered and the results recorded, but then the process stops. Teachers are unsure what to do with the data or where to go next in their teaching. This continuum can be used as a bridge between assessment data and the specific teaching that children need. With assessment, you learn what children know; the continuum will help you think about what they need to know next.

Evaluation and Grading

The continuum can also serve as a guide for evaluating student progress over time. You can evaluate whether children are meeting grade-level standards. Remember that no student would be expected to demonstrate every single competency to be considered on grade level. *Grade level* is always a term that encompasses a range of levels of understanding at any given time.

Reporting to Parents

We would not recommend that you show parents such an overwhelming document as this continuum. It would get in the way of good conversation. However, you can use the continuum as a resource for the kind of specific information you need to provide to parents, but in easy-to-understand language.

Guide to Intervention

Many children will need extra support in order to achieve the school's goals for learning. Assessment and observation will help you identify the specific areas in which children need help. Use the continuum to find the specific understandings that can guide intervention.

Organization of the Continuum

Seven continua are included in this document. They are arranged in the following way.

Grade-by-Grade

Within each grade, you will find the continua for: (1) interactive read-aloud and literature discussion; (2) shared and performance reading; (3) writing about reading; (4) writing; (5) oral, visual, and technological communication; and (6) phonics, spelling, and word study. These six continua are presented at each grade level, prekindergarten through grade 2. You can turn to the tabbed section for your grade level and find all six. If you have many children working below grade level, you can consult the next lower grade continuum in the area of interest; if you have children working above grade level, you can consult the continuum for the grade above for ideas.

Level-by-Level

The Guided Reading continuum is organized according to Fountas and Pinnell text gradient levels A to N (see Figure I–2). These levels typically correlate to grades K, 1, and 2, but children may vary along them in their instructional levels. It is important for all K–2 children to receive guided reading instruction at a level that allows them to process texts successfully with teacher support. If you have students performing beyond Level N, you will want to refer to the continuum document for grades 3–8, *The Continuum of Literacy Learning Grades 3–8,* (Pinnell and Fountas, Heinemann, 2011, 2008).

Additional Resources

Finally, you will find a glossary of terms at the end of the book that will assist you in interpreting the continuum. For additional information on instruction, consult the texts in the references section, also found at the end of this book.

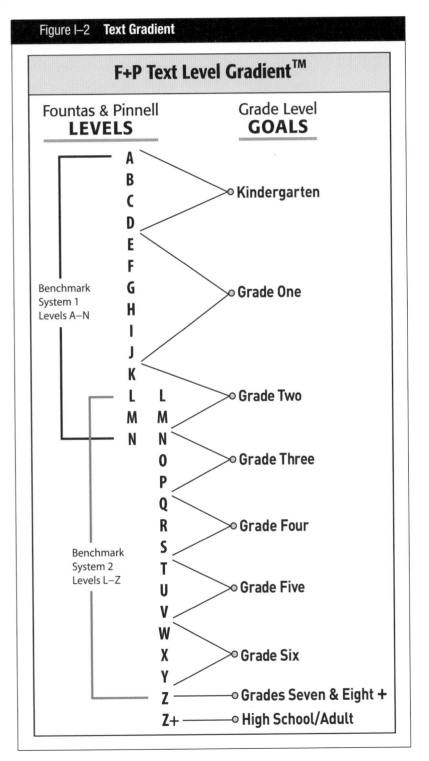

Figure I–2 **Text Gradient**

F+P Text Level Gradient™

Fountas & Pinnell **LEVELS**

Grade Level **GOALS**

Benchmark System 1 Levels A–N

Benchmark System 2 Levels L–Z

A
B
C — Kindergarten
D
E
F
G — Grade One
H
I
J
K
L — Grade Two
M
N — Grade Three
O
P
Q
R — Grade Four
S
T
U — Grade Five
V
W
X — Grade Six
Y
Z — Grades Seven & Eight +
Z+ — High School/Adult

Interactive Read-Aloud and Literature Discussion Continuum

In creating curriculum goals for an interactive read-aloud, you will want to consider text selection and opportunities for new learning. At all grade levels, children need to listen to age-appropriate texts in a variety of genres and increasingly complex texts within those genres. Story problems, characters, content, and topics should be matched to the particular age group, with consideration of children's background, experience, and interests. You will also want to consider a variety of text formats and types of texts.

Beyond text selection, it is important to think about how to support readers' thinking within, beyond, and about a text. Before, during, and after listening to a text read-aloud, you will want to notice evidence of children's literal understanding. Did they pick up important information? Could they follow the plot? Could they remember important details? In addition, you want children to think beyond the text, making predictions and important connections. Look for evidence that they can notice and incorporate new information into their own understandings, as well as make inferences based on the available information. Finally, you want children to form opinions about their reading and develop their own reading preferences. Look for evidence that they can think analytically about texts, noticing the writer's craft and style. It is also important for them to think critically about the quality, content, and accuracy of texts.

When children are actively listening to and discussing a text, all of the strategic actions for comprehending are in operation. In an interactive read-aloud, the listener is freed from decoding and is supported by the oral reader's fluency, phrasing, and stress—all elements of what we sometimes call *expression*. The scene is set for a high level of comprehending or thinking together through a text.

Interactive Read-Aloud and Literature Discussion

From prekindergarten through eighth grade, literature study and discussion are a part of shared reading and interactive read-aloud (see Fountas and Pinnell 2001, 2006). Children may discuss the book as a whole class but they will also need to be engaged in more intimate routines like a "turn and talk" (focused on any aspect of text) for a minute or two a few times within the larger discussion. These types of routines provide opportunities for individuals to engage in more talk than would otherwise be possible in a whole-group discussion. Inserting such routines into your interactive read-aloud will make whole-group discussions more lively and give all children the opportunity for active participation. After children have spent some time talking in pairs, triads, or small circles, they will become skilled in small-group discussion. After children have had a great deal of experience using the routines, you may decide they are ready for a more extended discussion with their peers—literature discussion or book club. You can find extensive information about these instructional approaches in *Teaching for Comprehending and Fluency: Thinking, Talking, and Writing About Reading, K–8* (Fountas and Pinnell, Heinemann 2006).

Interactive read-aloud and literature discussion abound with *text talk*—shared talk in which children examine ideas and think about narrative, expository, or poetic texts. Every engagement gives children opportunities for thinking about texts in new ways. The more they have a chance to do it, the better they get at text talk. As children work together in groups, they develop a backlog of shared meanings that increasingly deepens their talk.

Interactive read-aloud and literature discussion are placed together in this continuum because in both settings we seek age-appropriate, grade-appropriate reading materials that have the potential to extend children's thinking and their ability to talk about texts. For prekindergarten and grade 1 students, most literature discussion will take place during interactive read-aloud. But as students gain more experience through turn-and-talk routines, they can begin to prepare for and engage in small group discussions. For small-group literature discussion, children usually choose from several texts that you have preselected. If they can read the selection independently, they read at home or during the reading workshop. If they cannot read the text easily on their own, make an audio recording of it available. Sometimes, you will engage children in book clubs based on texts that you have read aloud to the entire class. Thus, in selecting and using books for interactive read-aloud and literature discussion, you do not need to consider a specific level, but you will want to think about the text characteristics as well as texts that are age- and grade-appropriate.

Framework for the Continuum of Learning

The continuum that follows is a guide for setting goals and creating instructional plans for interactive read-aloud and literature discussion. This continuum provides grade-by-grade information that includes:

❑ characteristics of texts (descriptions of ten text factors to keep in mind when selecting and reading aloud texts)

❑ curriculum goals (descriptions of behaviors and understandings to notice and support to help readers think within, beyond, and about the text you have selected)

Characteristics of Texts for Interactive Read-Aloud and Literature Discussion

Ten text factors are important to consider when selecting texts for any kind of reading instruction. When selecting texts for interactive read-aloud, we consider the high level of support we provide to children to help them process and think about the text. You must ensure that the vocabulary in the text is understandable to listeners. You don't need to worry about word-solving difficulty since you will be doing the decoding. Descriptions of all ten text factors, in terms of interactive read-aloud, can be seen in Figure I–3.

Curriculum Goals

We have stated curriculum goals in terms of behaviors and understandings to notice and support at each level. These systems of strategic actions are further divided into evidence that the reader is thinking *within, beyond,* and *about* the text.

- *Within the Text.* To effectively and efficiently process a text and derive the literal meaning, readers must solve the words and monitor and self-correct their reading. In interactive read-aloud, readers are relieved of the task of decoding and they hear fluent, phrased reading; but they must self-monitor their own understanding, remember information in summary form, and adjust their thinking to the understanding of different fiction and nonfiction genres.

- *Beyond the Text.* Readers make predictions and connections to previous knowledge and their own lives. They also make connections between and among texts. They bring background knowledge to the reading of a text, synthesize new information by incorporating it into their own understandings, and think about what the writer has not stated but implied. Readers may infer the feelings and motivations of characters in fiction texts or the implications of the writer's statements in nonfiction. Interactive read-aloud provides many opportunities to support children's thinking beyond the literal meaning. By engaging children in discussion before and after reading, you can demonstrate how to think beyond the text and help them expand their own ability to do so. You can also stop at selected intervals while reading aloud to discuss text elements that prompt expanded thinking.

- *About the Text.* Readers think analytically about the text as an object, noticing and appreciating elements of the writer's craft, such as use of language, characterization, organization, and structure. Reading like a writer helps children notice aspects of craft and more fully enjoy a text, sometimes revisiting it. Readers also think critically about texts, evaluating the quality and considering the writer's accuracy or objectivity. Interactive read-aloud time is ideal time for demonstrating the kind of sophisticated thinking that effective readers do. It provides the opportunity for children to engage in analytic thinking about texts. In addition, the books you read aloud become a collection of shared texts that can be turned to again and again to notice more about craft.

Figure I–3 Ten Text Factors for Interactive Read-Aloud and Literature Discussion

Genre	We have listed a variety of types of texts that are appropriate at each grade level. For the most part, you will want to use the full range of genres at every grade level, but be selective about the particular examples you choose.
Text Structure	The structure of a text refers to the way it is organized. Fiction texts are generally organized in a narrative structure, with a problem and a sequence of events that leads to the resolution of the problem. Interactive read-aloud is a context in which listeners can internalize plot structure and learn how stories work. Nonfiction texts may also be narrative; biographies, for example, usually tell the stories like fiction texts do. But most informational texts are organized categorically by subtopic with underlying structures such as description; temporal sequence; comparison and contrast; cause and effect; and problem and solution. Often these structures are used in combination. Interactive read-aloud and literature discussion provide a setting within which you can teach children to recognize and understand these structures.
Content	The subject matter of the text should be accessible and interesting to listeners. Over time, the sophistication and complexity of content can be increased. Although direct experiences are always necessary for learning, children can acquire a great deal of content knowledge from hearing written language read aloud. Content is helpful to listeners when they already have some prior knowledge to bring to understanding new information.
Themes and Ideas	The major ideas of the books you choose to read aloud should be appropriate for all children's age and background experience. Interactive read-aloud is an ideal way to stretch children's knowledge, but they must be able to make connections to their existing knowledge. They can extend their own understanding of the themes and ideas as they discuss them with others.
Language and Literary Features	The way the writer uses language creates the literary quality of a text. It is important to select texts that children can understand in terms of language and literary features. Interactive read-aloud and literature discussion provide opportunities to expand your children's ability to process literary language, including dialogue and figurative language. Other literary features include the development of elements such as setting, plot, and characters.
Sentence Complexity	The structure of sentences—their length, word order, and the number of embedded phrases and clauses-is another key factor. Through the primary, elementary, and intermediate grades, children can generally understand sentences that are more complex than those they can read. Interactive read-aloud provides a way to help them gradually internalize more complex sentence structures. Discussion with others will help children unpack complex sentences and understand them better.
Vocabulary	Vocabulary refers to the words that an individual knows and understands in both oral and written language. The words that the writer has selected may present a challenge to readers. Written text usually includes many words that are not in our everyday oral vocabulary; we constantly expand vocabulary by reading or hearing written language read aloud. Through interactive read-aloud and literature discussion, children can greatly expand their vocabulary.
Words	When selecting books for children to read for themselves, we always consider the challenges the words present: length, number of syllables, inflectional endings, and general ease of solving. In interactive read-aloud, however, the teacher solves the words, so this will not be a factor in text selection. Also, remember that for literature discussion, children may use audio recordings of texts that they are not yet ready to read independently. Attention to vocabulary will take into account word complexity.
Illustrations	Illustrations (or other forms of art) provide a great deal of information to readers and listeners. A high-quality picture book is a coherent form of literary art. Think of a picture book as a short story that has beautiful illustrations. Picture books are appropriate for a wide range of ages and all genres. For children of all ages, illustrations increase engagement and enjoyment. Illustrations for younger children provide a great deal of information; for older children they help create mood. Informational texts (and increasingly some fiction texts) also include graphics in the form of maps, diagrams, and drawings. These graphics may provide information that is additional to the body of the text. Some graphics may be large enough for children to see and discuss during interactive read-aloud, but children may attend to them during small-group discussion.
Book and Print Features	When selecting books for interactive read-aloud, you may also want to consider the physical aspects of the text, such as length, size, and layout. Book and print features also include tools like the table of contents, glossary, pronunciation guide, indexes, sidebars, and headings. All of these features may be pointed out and discussed during interactive read-aloud or literature discussion.

Using the Continuum

The continuum does not reference specific texts, topics, or content areas. You should apply the continuum's goals in connection with your district or state requirements. You can use this guide to set overall curriculum goals for grades PreK–2 or you can refer to it as you plan for interactive read-aloud.

We use the term *intentional conversation* to describe the instructional moves you can make during the conversation surrounding books in interactive read-aloud or in small-group literature discussion. Your first goals when reading aloud to your children and engaging them in small-group discussions are to engage their interest, to make the occasion enjoyable, and to guide them in active conversation. Interactive read-aloud and literature discussion give children opportunities to share their own ideas, to express their own meanings, and to contribute to deeper understanding of the text. Conversation must be genuine. You are always keeping in mind your curriculum goals; that is what makes the conversation intentional.

Without being heavy handed or stifling children's comments, you can guide the conversation so that children are constantly expanding their thinking. During the interactive read-aloud and literature discussion, the teacher:

- ❑ keeps in mind the systems of strategic actions that readers must use
- ❑ knows the text deeply and understands its demands and the opportunities it provides for learning
- ❑ provides conversational leads to focus children's attention
- ❑ models and demonstrates behaviors that help children achieve better understanding
- ❑ asks children to share their thinking in a focused way
- ❑ prompts children to listen to and respond to one another rather than always being the center of the conversation
- ❑ keeps the conversation grounded in the text
- ❑ turns the conversation back to children, asking for deeper thinking
- ❑ requires children to be accountable for their comments, asking for more than opinion and asking for evidence from the text or personal experience
- ❑ gives feedback to children on what they are learning and the kinds of thinking they are doing
- ❑ asks children to self-evaluate their conversation about the text.

You will find that interactive read-aloud and literature discussion provide rich opportunities for every student to expand background knowledge, experience age-appropriate and grade-appropriate text, and learn a variety of ways to think deeply about an engaging text.

Shared and Performance Reading Continuum

Shared reading and performance reading have many of the same goals as interactive read-aloud, but they go beyond active listening and discussion. Children actually participate in the reading in some way. We define shared reading and performance reading as instructional contexts that involve reading aloud for the pleasure of oneself and others. All forms of performed reading involve:

- ❑ processing print in continuous text
- ❑ working in a group (usually)
- ❑ using the voice to interpret the meaning of a text
- ❑ often reading in unison with others, although there may be parts or solos
- ❑ opportunities to learn more about the reading process.

In *Teaching for Comprehending and Fluency: Thinking, Talking, and Writing About Reading, K–8* (Fountas and Pinnell, Heinemann 2006), we described three contexts for shared and performance reading.

1. *Shared reading* usually refers to children's reading from a common enlarged text, either a large-print book, a chart, or a projected text. Children may have their own copies. The teacher leads the group, pointing to words or phrases. Reading is usually in unison, although there are adaptations, such as groups alternating lines or individuals reading some lines.

2. *Choral reading* usually refers to any group of people reading from a common text, which may be printed on a chart, projected on a screen, or provided as individual copies. The text is usually longer and/or more complex than one used for shared reading. The emphasis is on interpreting the text with the voice. Some reading is in unison by the whole group or subgroups, and there may be solos or duets.

3. *Readers' theater* usually refers to the enactment of a text in which readers assume individual or group roles. Readers' theater is similar to traditional play production, but the text is generally not memorized and props are rarely used. The emphasis is on vocal interpretation. Usually individuals read parts although groups may read some roles. Readers' theater scripts are usually constructed from all kinds of texts, not from original plays.

In selecting and using books and other written texts for shared and performance reading, you need to consider some of the same kinds of factors that you would for guided and independent reading; after all, children do need to be able to read and understand them. However, since you will be providing a high level of support and children will be reading texts many times, it is not necessary to use the A–Z levels (see Guided Reading continuum in this book, pages 127–185). Instead, you will want to consider features such as interesting language, rhyme and rhythm, language play, poetic language, appeal to children, and other aspects of texts that make them a good basis for performance.

Characteristics of Texts for Shared and Performance Reading

In thinking about texts for shared and performance reading, we again consider the ten text factors. As with interactive read-alouds, you must consider whether the vocabulary in the text is understandable to listeners, but word solving is a relatively minor consideration. Children can easily pronounce and appreciate words like *fantabulous* or *humongous* in humorous poems or words like *somber* or *ponderous* from reader's theater once they are taught the meaning of the words. Descriptions of all ten text characteristics, in terms of shared and performance reading, follow in Figure I–4.

Curriculum Goals

We have stated curriculum goals in terms of behaviors and understandings to notice and support at each level. These are further divided into evidence that the reader is thinking *within*, *beyond*, or *about* the text.

- *Within the Text.* To effectively and efficiently process a text and derive the literal meaning, readers must solve the words and monitor and self-correct their reading. During shared and performance reading, children need to follow what the text is saying, picking up important information that will help them reflect that meaning in their voices. They must self-monitor their own understanding, remember information in summary form, and sometimes adjust their reading to reflect the genre. One of the major benefits of shared and performance reading is that children are producing a fluent, phrased, and expressive oral reading of a text or version of a text. This instructional setting provides a great deal of practice and an authentic reason to read aloud (not simply to let the teacher check on you).

- *Beyond the Text.* Readers make predictions and connections based on previous knowledge and their own lives. They also make connections between and among texts. They bring background knowledge to the reading of a text, synthesize new information by incorporating it into their own understandings, and think about what the writer has not stated but implied. Readers may infer the feelings and motivations of characters in fiction texts or the implications of the writer's statements in nonfiction. To reflect interpretation with their voices, readers must actively seek meaning and even consider alternative meanings for a text. Shared reading, choral reading, and readers' theater all provide many opportunities for thinking beyond the text. To read with a character's voice, for example, you need to think deeply about how that character feels.

- *About the Text.* Readers think analytically about the text as an object, noticing and appreciating elements of the writer's craft, such as use of language,

Figure I–4   Ten Text Characteristics for Shared and Performance Reading

Genre	We have listed a variety of types of texts that are appropriate at each grade level. We include poetry, songs, and chants. For the most part, you will want to use the full range of genres at every grade level, but be selective about the particular examples you choose. Use both fiction and nonfiction texts for shared and performance reading. Often, a narrative text is turned into a play or poetic text to create readers' theater scripts.
Text Structure	The structure of a text refers to the way it is organized. Fiction texts are generally organized in a narrative structure, with a problem and a sequence of events that leads to the resolution of the problem. Younger children generally read short texts that have humor or rhyme. Traditional tales are an excellent resource. When longer texts are turned into plays or readers' theater scripts, they are generally shortened: children present a particular moment in time, perform the essence of the plot, or show the main character's feelings or point of view. Nonfiction texts may also be narrative; biographies, for example, are relatively easy to turn into readers' theater scripts. But most informational texts are organized categorically by subtopic with underlying structures such as description; temporal sequence; comparison and contrast; cause and effect; and problem and solution. Often these structures are used in combination. Through shared or performance reading, your students can highlight some of the underlying structures and they will enjoy turning some content-area learning (for example, a text on environmental pollution or a period of history) into readers' theater.
Content	The subject matter of the text should be accessible and interesting to listeners. Content is helpful to listeners when they already have some prior knowledge to bring to understanding new information. Through shared and performance reading, particularly of biography, children can think deeply about many different topics.
Themes and Ideas	The major ideas of the material you choose for shared and performance reading should be appropriate for all children's age and experience. Children can extend their understanding of the themes and ideas as they discuss how texts should be read or performed.
Language and Literary Features	The way the writer uses language creates the literary quality of a text. It is important to select texts that children can understand in terms of language and literary features. Shared reading and performance reading provide an ideal setting in which to "try on" different interpretations of a text through changes in the voice.
Sentence Complexity	The structure of the sentences—their length and the number of embedded phrases and clauses—is another key factor. Through the primary and elementary grades, children can generally understand sentences that are more complex than those they can read independently. Practicing sentences for performance helps children internalize various sentence structures.
Vocabulary	Vocabulary refers to the words that an individual knows and understands in both oral and written language. Working with a text in shared or performance reading, children have the opportunity to meet new words many times and thus expand their vocabularies. It is important that children understand the text used in shared and performance reading; they will not enjoy the activity if they do not understand the words.
Words	You will be offering high support for word solving, and children will be reading selections several times, so words are not a major factor in choosing texts. You will want to select texts with words that children understand and can pronounce with your help. Shared and performance reading offer an excellent context within which children can learn more about how words work. As repeated readings make a text familiar, children will gradually add to the core of high-frequency words they know. They will also begin to notice beginnings, endings, and other parts of words and make connections between words.
Illustrations	Many texts used as a basis for shared and performance reading are full of illustrations that help children interpret them. Along with the teacher support inherent in shared and performance reading, illustrations enable young children to read higher-level big books together. For older children, too, performance reading may be based on picture books (fiction and nonfiction) that have illustrations contributing to the mood. Sometimes, children may perform their reading in conjunction with a slide show of some important illustrations. For some texts, however, illustrations may not be a factor. Graphics in informational texts, for example, would be unusual to include in shared and performance reading.
Book and Print Features	When younger children are engaged in shared reading of enlarged texts (books and poems), print features such as length, layout, clarity of font, and number of lines on a page affect their ability to participate. In general, children can read more complex texts in shared reading than they can in guided or independent reading, but you will not want to overload them. Even older readers might find it difficult to read a long and complex poem in unison from an overhead transparency. For readers' theater, you may want to retype sections of a text so children can highlight their parts. We address book and print features for shared reading in prekindergarten through grade 2. After that, book and print features are not so important. In addition, readers' tools like the table of contents, glossary, pronunciation guide, indexes, sidebars, and headings are not considered here since it would be unlikely for them to be included in shared and performance reading.

characterization, organization, and structure. Reading like a writer helps children notice aspects of craft and more fully enjoy a text, sometimes prompting them to revisit it. Readers also think critically about texts, evaluating the quality and considering the writer's accuracy or objectivity. Texts are selected and created for shared and performance reading based on the quality of the writing. When children perform parts of a text or a readers' theater script made from a text, they have the opportunity to get to know the language. It is an opportunity to internalize and sometimes even memorize some high-quality language. Shared and performance reading enable you to build a large repertoire of shared texts that can be revisited often to notice more about the writer's craft.

Using the Continuum

This continuum does not reference specific texts, topics, or content areas. You should apply the continuum's goals in connection with your district or state requirements. You can use this guide to set overall curriculum goals for grades PreK-2, or you can refer to it as you plan for and assess teaching shared and performance reading.

Writing About Reading Continuum

Written responses to what they have read provide evidence of children's thinking. When we examine writing in response to reading, we can make hypotheses about how well readers have understood a text. But there are more reasons to make writing an integral part of your reading instruction. Through writing—and drawing as well—readers can express and expand their thinking and improve their ability to reflect on a text. They can also communicate their thinking about texts to a variety of audiences for a variety of purposes. By examining effective examples of writing about reading, children learn the characteristics of each form and can "try it out" for themselves. The models serve as "mentor texts" that children can refer to as they use different forms of writing to reflect on reading.

Young children can learn how to write about texts through shared or interactive writing:

- In *shared writing*, the teacher and children compose a text together. The teacher is the scribe. Often, especially with younger children, the teacher works on a chart displayed on an easel. Children participate in the composition of the text, word by word, and reread it many times. Sometimes the teacher asks children to say the word slowly as they think about how a word is spelled. At other times, the teacher (with student input) writes a word quickly on the chart. The text becomes a model, example, or reference for student writing and discussion. (See McCarrier, Fountas, and Pinnell 2000.)

- *Interactive writing*, an approach for use with young children, is identical to and proceeds in the same way as shared writing, with one exception: Occasionally the teacher, while making teaching points that help children attend to various features of letters and words, will invite a student to come up to the easel and contribute a letter, a word, or part of a word. (See McCarrier, Fountas, and Pinnell 2000.)

After older children are confident with a form of writing through the analysis of effective examples, whole- or small-group discussion can support their independent writing about reading. Discussion reminds writers of key characteristics of the text and the author's craft.

In this continuum, we describe many different forms of writing about reading in four categories: functional writing, narrative writing, informational writing, and poetic writing. The goal is for children to read many examples in each category, identify the specific characteristics, and have opportunities to apply their understandings in independent writing.

Functional Writing

Functional writing is undertaken for communication or to "get a job done." During a literacy block, a great deal of functional writing takes place around reading.

Children make notes to themselves about written texts that they can use as a basis for an oral discussion or presentation or to support writing of more extended pieces. Or they may write notes or letters to others to communicate their thinking. A key tool for learning in grades 2 through 8 is the reader's notebook, in which children reflect on their reading in various forms, including dialogue letters that are answered by the teacher.

Second graders can begin with a simple blank notebook. You provide minilessons to help them understand the various kinds of functional writing they can place in the notebook. (See Fountas and Pinnell 2001 and 2006.) Some examples of functional writing about reading are:

- ❑ notes and sketches—words, phrases, or sketches on sticky notes or in a notebook
- ❑ "short-writes"—a few sentences or paragraphs produced quickly in a notebook or a large sticky note that is then placed in a notebook
- ❑ graphic organizers—words, phrases, sketches, or sentences
- ❑ letters—letters written to other readers or to the author or illustrator of a book
- ❑ diary entries—an entry or series of entries in a journal or diary from the perspective of a biographical subject or character.

Narrative Writing

Narrative writing tells a story. Children's narrative writing about reading might re-tell some or all of a plot or recount significant events in the life of a biographical subject. Or children might tell about an experience of their own that is similar to the one in a text or has a similar theme. Some examples of narrative writing about reading are:

- ❑ summary—a few sentences that tell the most important information in a text
- ❑ cartoon/storyboarding—a succession of graphics or stick figures that present a story or information.

Informational Writing

Informational writing organizes facts into a coherent whole. To compose an informational piece, the writer organizes data into categories and may use underlying structures such as description; comparison and contrast; cause and effect; time sequence; and problem and solution. Some examples of informational writing about reading are:

- ❑ author study—a piece of writing that provides information about an author and his or her craft
- ❑ illustrator study—a piece of writing that provides information on an illustrator

- ❑ interview (with an author or expert)—a series of questions and responses designed to provide information about an author or expert on a topic
- ❑ "how-to" book—an explanation of how something is made or done
- ❑ "all-about" book—factual information presented in an organized way.

Poetic Writing

Poetic writing entails carefully selecting and arranging words to convey meaning in ways that evoke feelings and sensory images. Poetry condenses meaning into short language groupings. It lends itself to repeated readings and to being read aloud for the pleasure of listening to the language. Poetic writing about reading includes poetry written in response to a prose text or to reflect or respond to a poem. Poetic writing may be used for choral reading.

Using the Writing About Reading Continuum

All the genres and forms for writing about reading will give you evidence of how children are thinking and will help them become more reflective about their reading. The continuum is organized by grade. First, we list the genres and forms that are appropriate for children to be writing at the grade level. Then we specify behaviors and understandings to teach, notice, and support as children think within, beyond, and about a text. (Notice that you can find evidence in both illustrations and writing.) Remember that genres and forms are demonstrated and co-constructed through the use of interactive and shared writing *before* children are expected to produce them independently as assignments. After experiencing the genres or forms several times with group support, children will be able to produce them on their own. Gradually, they will build up a repertoire of ways of writing about reading that they can select from according to their purpose.

Writing Continuum

The classroom, from prekindergarten through middle school, is a place where writers grow. They learn by engaging in the writing process with the expert help of the teacher and with the support of their peers. Writing is multifaceted in that it orchestrates thinking, language, and mechanics. The writing process can be described as a series of steps (getting an idea, drafting, revising, editing, and publishing), but it is in fact a recursive process in which all these things may happen almost simultaneously.

Writing is a basic tool for learning as well as for communicating with others. In our schools, children are expected to write in every subject area. We want them to become individuals who can use many types of writing for a wide range of purposes and audiences throughout their lives. Elsewhere we have written that "the writing terrain spreads out in many directions, real and imaginary, and encompasses in-depth intellectual investigations of biology, geology, history, anthropology, and other fields" (Fountas and Pinnell 2001b, 423).

We want to help children develop a basic knowledge of the writing process and know how to vary the process for different genres and purposes. Preschoolers can "make books" by telling a story through drawings even before they can read or write! Even young children can produce simple publications; as they write year after year, they engage in the same basic process but at more sophisticated levels. Their range becomes broader and their publications more complex.

Demonstration Almost every genre listed in the continuum is first demonstrated in a read-aloud or with examples of *shared, interactive,* or *modeled writing.* Young children will have a shared or group experience in all genres they are eventually expected to produce independently. Even young children can have this important experience through shared, interactive, or modeled writing:

- ❏ In *shared writing,* the teacher and children compose a text together. The teacher is the scribe. Often, especially with very young children, the teacher works on a chart displayed on an easel. Children contribute each word of the composition and reread it many times. Sometimes the teacher asks the children to say the word slowly as they think how a word is spelled. At other times the teacher (with child input) writes the composition on the chart more quickly. The text becomes a model, example, or reference for student writing and discussion.

- ❏ *Interactive writing* is identical to and proceeds in the same way as shared writing, with one exception: occasionally the teacher, while making teaching points that help children attend to various features of letters and words, will invite a child to come up to the easel and contribute a letter, word, or part of a word.

- ❏ *Modeled writing* may be used at every grade level. Here, the teacher demonstrates the process of writing in a particular genre, sometimes thinking aloud to reveal what is going on in her mind. The teacher may have prepared the piece of writing prior to class but talks through the process with the children.

Mentor Texts: A major component in learning to write in a particular genre is to study mentor texts—works of children's literature, fiction and nonfiction, that you have read and discussed—and we have built the study of mentor texts into every appropriate Selecting Purpose and Genre section. Writers learn from other writers. If children experience several books by an author and illustrator, they soon learn what is special about a particular book by that author. They start to notice topics, characteristics of illustrations, types of stories, and language. They may record or remember words and language in order to borrow it. As they grow more sophisticated, they understand that writers use other writers as examples and learn from them. They notice what writers do to make their writing effective and begin to use mentor texts as models when planning, revising, and publishing writing. They notice purpose, topic, and genre choice and begin to make those choices for themselves. Children may even participate in formal study of authors to learn about their craft—how they portray characters, use dialogue, and organize information. Graphics and illustrations offer many examples to young writers relative to illustrating their work clearly. Very sophisticated readers and writers are still learning from mentor texts as they seek examples of the treatment of themes or ideas, create dialogue and show character development, and prepare persuasive or critical pieces. Through the process of taking on all of the understandings listed in this continuum, children realize that published authors can be their mentors.

English Language Learners: Additional complexity is introduced into the process of becoming a writer if the child is an English language learner. The expectations for each grade level of the continuum are the same for children whose first language is English and for those who are learning English as a second language. The expectations for *instruction,* however, are different. English language learners will need a greater level of support as they expand their control of oral English and, alongside it, written English. Start where children are, but give them rich opportunities to hear written language read aloud and to talk about concepts and ideas before they are expected to write about them. Interactive writing is an effective tool for helping English language learners begin to compose and construct written text. By composing text collaboratively, with the teacher as scribe to guide the structure and control conventions, children can create their own exemplar texts. Interactive writing offers group support and strong models. As children reread the interactive writing, they internalize conventional English syntactic patterns, relevant vocabulary, and the features of the genre. In individual conferences, teachers can help English language learners rehearse what they want to write and help them expand their ideas. Also include frequent experiences with shared and performance reading, which involves children in re-reading and thinking about the meaning of familiar texts.

This Writing continuum is presented in a one-year span, the goals ideally to be achieved by the end of the grade. Since learning to write can be conceptualized as a spiral, you will see many of the same goals repeated across the grades. However, children will be working toward these goals in increasingly sophisticated ways.

In this continuum, we describe writing in four major areas: purpose and genre; craft; conventions; and process. These four areas of learning apply to all children, kindergarten through grade 8.

Purpose and Genre

When writers write, they may have a purpose in mind and select the genre accordingly. You may want to tell a story that will communicate a larger meaning; you may want to inform or entertain; you may want to persuade people to take action on an issue that is important to you. It is important to recognize that effective writers do not write in a genre just to practice it. They choose the genre that will best convey the meaning they intend. Of course, teachers introduce new genres to children so that they can learn to write in those genres, but the ultimate goal is to establish a repertoire of genres from which they can choose. It is important to establish the desire to write in a genre by making it interesting and enjoyable. For instructional purposes, we have described traditional genres within each purpose category, even as we recognize that virtually any genre might be used to support a given purpose—an informational friendly letter, for example, or a functional poem.

In the overall PreK–8 continuum, we categorize writing genres under four purposes: narrative; informational; poetic; and functional. For grades 6–8, we have added a fifth category, hybrids. Hybrid texts combine genres to support any chosen purpose. For each genre within these categories, we have two important sets of information: Understanding the Genre, which reflects key understandings particular to the genre (what children need to *know* about the genre); and Writing in the Genre, which refers to the way the student demonstrates understanding by taking on the various kinds of writing within the genre (what children *do* with the genre). Also for each genre, we list sample forms of writing that can, among others, be part of the writing curriculum.

Narrative Genres

A narrative is a story with a beginning, a series of events, and an ending. Narratives may be fiction or nonfiction, and they usually tell about important or exciting events from a character's (or subject's) life. A narrative can be very simple or highly complex. This continuum encompasses three kinds of narratives: memoir, short fiction, and biography. For each type of text, we describe important understandings and identify specific goals related to writing in that genre.

Memoir. Memoir includes personal narrative. We want children to learn the craft and conventions of memoir by writing about their own lives. Very young children begin by sketching, telling, and writing simple stories about their families, friends, and pets. It is important for children to understand from the beginning that they are writing about what they know. In doing so, they will learn to observe their worlds closely, looking for examples that will be true to life. Children develop the ability to write fiction by telling these stories from experience.

Throughout the grades, children continue to write memoir. They learn to write about small moments that capture strong feelings or significant experiences. They begin to understand the more formal notion of memoir as a brief, often intense memory of an event or person. A memoir has an element of reflection and teaches the reader a larger meaning.

Short fiction. Children can think of fiction as a short story about an event in the life of a main character that gets across a point. We want them to learn that good fiction reveals something about life, connects with readers, and communicates the deeper meanings of a theme. Short fiction can be realistic fiction or fantasy, contemporary or historical. Younger children may write very simple stories about people or animals; they may retell their own version of an animal fantasy. As they grow more sophisticated, children will undertake such aspects of fiction as characterization and plot development.

Biography. Biography is nonfiction but it is usually presented as a narrative. We want children to learn that biography is a true story about a person. Younger writers can tell simple stories about family members or friends; older writers can produce fully documented biographical sketches or profiles of role models or public figures, contemporary or historical. In all cases, the biographer selects a subject for stated reasons and selects events and tells the story in a way that shows readers the writer's perspective. Writers use craft to make the biography interesting. It may be fictionalized for interest and readability, but the writer must disclose anything that is not documented.

Informational Genres

Informational texts include literary nonfiction, expository nonfiction, and essays.

Literary nonfiction. Not all nonfiction writing takes the form of reports or text-books! Especially in recent years we have seen the publication of highly engaging and literary short and longer nonfiction. We want children to learn from these mentor texts how to produce interesting, literary nonfiction that focuses on a topic or one aspect of a topic. They learn how to use resources to be sure they have accurate information and how to sustain focus. They also learn that they need to make the writing interesting to readers and help readers learn about the topic in new ways.

Expository nonfiction. Throughout our schooling and beyond, the ability to write a feature article or a report is useful and necessary. Children learn that a feature article focuses on one aspect of a topic and that a report includes several aspects of a topic. In both kinds of texts, the writer makes statements and backs them up with facts, examples, and other evidence. The writer may seek to persuade readers to take a particular view or take action. (We do not teach this genre to younger writers because of the sophistication it requires.)

Essay. An essay is a highly sophisticated, short literary composition in which the author clearly states a point of view. The essay may be analytical, critical, or persuasive. The ability to compose an essay is based on many years not only of writing but also of engaging in critical thinking. Essays are appropriate in the upper elementary grades and middle school.

Poetic Genres

Young writers need to learn to understand poetry as a special genre for communicating meaning and describing feelings and sensory images. There are many different forms of poetry: traditional rhymes, songs, and verses; free verse; lyric poetry; narrative poetry; limericks; cinquains; concrete poetry; haiku; "found" poetry; list poems; and formula poems. Once children have a well-established understanding of free verse, you can introduce them to a variety of other forms through mentor texts. Before writing poetry, children need to hear poems read aloud and read poems aloud themselves. This exposure gives children the feel of poetry and lets them gradually internalize the forms it can take. They learn to observe the world closely and to experiment with words and phrases so that they begin to produce poetic language.

Functional Genres

As adults, we use a large range of functional texts every day, ranging from very simple communications to sophisticated letters. The genres that follow are categorized as functional.

Friendly letters. Notes, cards, invitations, email, and friendly letters are written communications that require the writer to provide particular kinds of information and to write in a tone and form that is appropriate.

Formal letters. Business letters and editorials are formal documents written with a particular purpose. They get right to the point, exclude extraneous details, and have required parts.

Lists and procedures. Lists are planning tools that help people accomplish daily tasks; they are also the building blocks of more complicated texts, such as poems and informational pieces. Procedures, like how-to texts and directions, require student writers to think through and clearly explain the steps in a process.

Test writing. Test writing is required in academia. Children must learn that some writing is for the expressed purpose of showing someone else how much you know. They need to analyze a test for the expectations and write to the point.

Writing about reading. Writing about reading, too, is required in school to reflect children's thinking within, beyond, and about a text they have read. Almost any genre or form can be used to respond to a text. We have provided a complete separate continuum for this important area of literacy.

Hybrids

Hybrid texts, those that combine more than one genre into a coherent whole, serve any purpose the writer chooses. They may engage, inform, persuade, or serve a functional purpose. We have included these at the upper levels only. At their simplest—embedding a friendly letter into an ongoing narrative, for example— they may be manageable for the fluent middle-grade writer. More complex forms —parallel explanation and narrative, for example—require deft perspective and style changes that can only be managed by advanced writers.

The previous section describes the product of writing—what young writers are expected to produce as an outcome. Getting to that product is an educational process and requires attention to skills and strategies in the next three sections: craft, conventions, and writing process.

Craft

All the previous genres involve crafting an effective piece of writing that is clearly organized and contains well-developed ideas. The writer must use language appropriate for the genre, to include the specific words selected. We want younger children to consider word choice carefully so that the piece conveys precise meaning. Older children will have larger vocabularies, but they can also use tools like a thesaurus. Above all, the writing must have *voice*—it must reveal the person behind the writing. That means the writing takes on characteristics that reveal the writer's unique style. Younger children can write with voice if they are expressing feelings or telling about events that are important to them. Voice develops throughout a writer's career, and it is revealed in the way the writer uses every aspect of craft—sentence structure, word choice, language, and punctuation.

The craft section of the continuum states goals for each area. These goals apply in general to all genres, though some goals are more relevant to some genres than they are to others. We include the following:

Organization. This section addresses the way the writer arranges the information or structures the narrative. It includes the structure of the whole text—beginnings and endings, and the arrangement of ideas.

Idea development. Idea development focuses on the way the writer presents and supports the main ideas and themes of the text.

Language use. This section describes goals for the way the writer uses sentences, phrases, and expressions to describe events, actions, or information.

Word choice. Word choice refers to the particular words the writer selects to convey meaning.

Voice. Voice is the individual's unique style as a writer.

Conventions

Knowing and observing the conventions of writing make it possible to communicate ideas clearly. Substance must be there and so must craft, but without correct spelling, conventional grammar, and punctuation, it will be difficult to get people to value the writing. Of course, great writers often violate some of these conventions, especially in fiction, but they do so for an artistic purpose. The first eight years of school is the time to establish a firm grasp of the conventions of writing, including:

Text layout. Young children must learn the basics of writing words left to right across the page with spaces between them. But even sophisticated writers must develop the ability to use layout in a way that contributes to and enhances meaning.

Grammar. The grammar of written language is more formal than spoken language. There are rules for how sentences are put together, how parts of speech are used, how verb tense is made consistent, and how paragraphs are formed.

Capitalization. The appropriate use of capital letters makes texts more readable and signals proper nouns and specialized functions (titles, for example).

Punctuation. Punctuation adds meaning to the text, makes it more readable, and signals to the reader the writer's intentions in terms of using meaningful phrases.

Spelling. Conventional spelling is critical to the presentation of a piece of writing, both in appearance and meaning.

Handwriting and word processing. The writer's handwriting must be legible. Effective handwriting also increases writing fluency and ease, so the writer can give more attention to the message. For the same reasons, it is important for children to develop rapid, efficient keyboarding skills.

Learning these conventions is a challenging and complex task, one accomplished over many years. We do not want children to devote so much time and energy to conventions that they become fearful writers or do not develop voice. We do want conventions to be an important part of the editing process.

Writing Process

Children learn to write by writing—by engaging in all of the component processes many times. The writing process is recursive; the components take place roughly in order, but at any point in the process the writer can and will use any or all of the components. In this continuum, we describe four key phases in the process: rehearsing and planning, drafting and revising, editing and proofreading, and publishing. In addition, we've included two overarching categories that pervade the entire process: sketching and drawing, and viewing self as a writer.

Rehearsing and Planning

Rehearsing and planning involves gathering information, trying out ideas, and thinking about some critical aspects of the text, such as purpose and audience, before beginning to write. Of course, a writer will often stop during drafting and gather more information or rethink the purpose after discussing it with others. This area includes curriculum goals for:

Purpose. Writers have a clear purpose for writing the text, and this purpose influences genre selection and organization.

Audience. Writers think of the audience, which may be known or unknown. It is important even for younger children to think of the audience as all readers of the text—not just the teacher.

Oral language. Writers can generate ideas and try out their ideas through conversation with others.

Gathering seeds. An important writer's tool is a notebook in which they can collect ideas, experiment, sketch, diagram, and freewrite. Writers use notebooks as a resource for ideas, formats, and techniques.

Content, topic, theme. Writers carefully select the content or topic of the piece with interest, purpose, and theme in mind.

Inquiry and research. In preparation for writing informational texts and biography, writers will often spend an extended time gathering information. This is also true when an individual is writing historical fiction or developing a plot in an unfamiliar setting.

Genre/form. With audience in mind, as well as content or purpose, writers select the genre for the piece and the particular form of the genre.

Drafting and Revising

A writer may produce an initial draft and then revise it to make it more effective, but most writers revise while drafting and sometimes also draft more material after revising. There are several ways to draft and revise a text, and all of these may be used any time during the process. Children use them throughout the grades:

Producing a draft. Writers write an initial draft, getting ideas down quickly.

Rereading. Writers reread to remember what has been written, to assess clarity, and to revise.

Adding information. Writers add ideas, details, words, phrases, sentences, paragraphs, or dialogue to a piece of writing to make it more effective.

Deleting information. Writers delete redundancy, unimportant information, and extraneous details to make the piece clearer.

Reorganizing information. Writers move information around to make the piece more logical or more interesting.

Changing text. Writers identify vague parts and provide specificity, work on transitions, or changes words, phrases, and sentences.

Using tools and techniques. Writers acquire a repertoire of tools and techniques for drafting and revising a text.

Understanding the process. Writers actively work on drafting and revising and use other writers as mentors and peer reviewers.

Editing and Proofreading

Once the content and organization are in place, children may wish to polish selected drafts to prepare them for publication. The editing and proofreading phase focuses on the form of the composition.

Editing for conventions. Over the years, as children acquire knowledge of the conventions, we can expect them to use that knowledge in editing their writing.

Using tools. Children also need to learn the tools that will help them in editing—for example, the dictionary, a thesaurus, and computer technology.

Understanding the process. Children learn when, how, and why to elicit editing help.

Publishing

Writers may produce many final drafts that are shared with their peers, but sometimes they also publish pieces. These pieces will have received a final edit and will include all of the elements of a published work, including a cover with all the necessary information, typed and laid-out text, and graphics as appropriate. For some children, publishing means reading a piece to peers to celebrate the writing. Taking this final step is important for young writers because it gives them a sense of accomplishment and gives them an opportunity to share their talent with a wider audience. Over time, as students build up many published pieces, they can reflect on their own development as writers.

Sketching and Drawing

Whether used to capture ideas, store quick images to aid recall, visually arrange ideas to clarify structure or information in a draft, or enhance the effectiveness of a published work, sketching and drawing support the entire writing process. Goals in this section apply to all phases of the writing process.

Viewing Self as Writer

Finally, we need to think of our children as lifelong writers. Developing as a writer means more than producing piece after piece and gradually improving. We want our children to make writing a part of their lives—to see themselves as writers who are constantly observing the world and gathering ideas and information for their writing. They need to become independent, self-motivated writers, consciously entering into their own learning and development and in the process, expanding the ability to know themselves and their world. Most of all, they need to be able to seek out mentors so they can continue to expand their understandings of the possibilities of this craft. In the last section of the continuum, we list goals in this area.

Oral, Visual, and Technological Communication Continuum

Language is a child's first and most powerful learning tool. Within all of the instructional contexts that are part of a comprehensive language and literacy curriculum, learning is mediated by oral language. There are numerous references to oral language in every continuum presented in this book. Children reveal their thinking about texts through discussion with others. Their talk is a prelude to writing. They learn how words work through listening to, talking about, and working with them. By listening to texts read aloud, they internalize language that they will use as they talk and write. They learn language by using it for a variety of purposes. So, in a sense, oral communication is not only an integral part of every component of the curriculum but a building block toward future communication. We need to intentionally develop the kind of oral language skills that children need to take them into the future. We have created this continuum to focus on the broader area of *communication* beyond the printed word. We cannot now know exactly the kinds of communication skills that will be important in 2020 and beyond, but we can equip our children with the foundational competencies in listening, speaking, and technology that will allow them to take advantage of new opportunities for communication. In this continuum, we examine critical curriculum goals in three areas: listening and speaking, presentation, and technology.

Listening and Speaking

Children learn by listening and responding to others. Interaction is key to gaining a deeper understanding of texts. Children need the kind of interactive skills that make good conversation possible; they also need to develop the ability to sustain a deeper and more extended discussion of academic content. This area includes:

❑ *Listening and Understanding.* Children spend a good deal of time in school listening to explanations and directions. They learn by active listening, so it is important that they develop a habit of listening with attention and remembering details. Also, it is important that they listen actively to texts read aloud. Through listening during daily interactive read-alouds, children have the opportunity to internalize the syntactic patterns of written language, to learn how texts work, and to expand vocabulary. You will find specific information related to vocabulary development in the Phonics, Spelling, and Word Study continuum (see Word Meaning); however, listening is an important part of the process.

❑ *Social Interaction.* Social interaction is basic to success on the job as well as a happy personal life. Through conversation, people bond with each other and get things done. In the elementary and middle school, children develop their ability to interact with others in positive ways. They learn the social conventions that make conversation work.

❑ *Extended Discussion.* In content areas, social interaction extends to deeper discussion. Discussion is central to learning in all areas, but it is critical to the development of reading comprehension. Through extended discussion, children expand their understanding of texts they have read or heard read aloud. They develop the ability to remember the necessary details of texts and to think beyond and about them. Extended discussion requires knowledge and skill. Children need to be able to sustain a thread of discussion and to listen and respond to others. They need to learn such conventions as getting a turn in the discussion or taking the role of leader. Even young children can begin to learn how to sustain a text discussion and their ability only grows across the years.

❑ *Content.* It also matters what children talk about. Their ideas must be substantive. They need to be able to explain and describe their thinking, make predictions and inferences, and back up their talk with evidence from texts. Through daily discussion over the years, they learn the art of argument.

Growing competence in listening, social interaction, extended discussion, and content will help children use language as a tool for learning across the curriculum.

Presentation

The ability to speak effectively to a group—small or large—is an enormous advantage. Many children are afraid of speaking to a group, largely because of inexperience or even a bad experience. We see performance as a basic skill that needs to be developed across the years. Even young children can talk to the class about their own lives or their writing; they can even prepare illustrations to help them. As children move into the upper elementary grades, they have many tools to help them, such as PowerPoint™ and other presentation tools that enable them to combine media, for example. We describe a continuum of learning in six areas related to presentation: voice, conventions, organization, word choice, ideas and content, and media.

❑ *Voice.* Here, *voice* refers to the speaker's personal style. We have all watched gifted speakers who captivate their audience. While we are not expecting every student to become a public speaker, we do hope that each individual can develop ways of speaking that capture the interest and attention of those listening. Speakers learn how to begin in a way that engages the audience and to use voice modulation and gesture in interesting ways.

❑ *Conventions.* Certain conventions are basic to making effective presentations. For example, the speaker needs to enunciate words clearly, talk at an appropriate volume, and use an effective pace—not too slow and not too fast. Looking directly at the audience and making eye contact is also helpful. With practice, these conventions can become automatic, freeing the speaker to concentrate on the ideas he is expressing.

❑ *Organization.* An effective presentation is well planned and organized. The speaker can organize information in various ways—comparison and contrast or cause and effect, for example. Effective presentations are concise and clear rather than unfocused and random. The speaker needs to keep the audience in mind when planning the organizational structure of a particular presentation.

❑ *Word Choice.* Effective speakers choose their words carefully both to make an impact on the audience and to communicate meaning clearly. Speakers often need to use specific words related to the content area they are covering, and they may need to define these words for the audience. Speakers can also use more literary language to increase listeners' interest. Speakers choose their words with the audience in mind; more formal language may be needed in a professional presentation than in an everyday conversation or a discussion.

❑ *Ideas and Content.* The substance of a presentation is important. Technique is wasted if the ideas and content are not substantive. Effective speakers demonstrate their understanding through the information they have chosen to present. They know how to establish an argument, use persuasive strategies, provide examples, and cite relevant evidence.

❑ *Media.* Media can be overused, but in general presentations are enhanced by the use of visual displays. For young children, this may mean pictures, drawings, or posters. As their presentations grow more sophisticated, children can make use of a wide array of electronic resources to create multimedia presentations. Speakers may even need to think of presentation in new ways; for example, the creation of interactive, nonlinear websites that members of the audience can explore individually is a kind of extended presentation.

Technology

Learning to use technology to communicate is an absolute necessity in today's society. From basic computer functions to the more complex tasks of comprehending and creating digital texts, often it seems that students are much more sophisticated than their teachers in this area of literacy learning. Yet, we need to give careful attention to what students know and are able to do as they utilize their technological skills in the interest of becoming more literate.

❑ *Computer Literacy.* At a functional level, students need to understand how and why to use a computer and other digital devices to create documents, find information, and communicate with others. We want them to be comfortable with electronic conversations and learning groups, to use rapid and efficient keyboarding for word processing, to create websites and multimedia presentations, and to use the Internet as a tool for gathering information. When used properly, spelling and grammar checkers, cutting and pasting, and access to digital images have made creating well-written and well-designed final drafts easier than ever. At the same time, it is important that even our youngest students begin to understand that using technology and the Internet requires both a different set of literacy skills as well as particular attention to their own ethical and responsible behavior.

❑ *Online Reading and Information Literacy.* In addition to traditional forms of text, nonprint media from radio, television, and the Internet have become primary sources for learning about the world. Providing opportunities for students to understand, explore, and document the use of these various media has become a critical part of a literacy curriculum. When they are online, texts have the ability to change constantly, both in terms of content and design, and this requires that students develop new comprehension strategies. From basic web searching and documentation in the early grades to more sophisticated database research, citation management, and integration of multiple sources of information at the upper grades, reading online texts and developing information literacy skills have both become key components of our students' overall literacy development.

❑ *Composing and Publishing Digital Texts.* As our concept of writing broadens to include the processes of composing images, websites, presentations, and audio and visual media, students now have a number of ways to communicate their messages to a wider variety of audiences. Students can integrate what they have learned about how to comprehend online texts in order to develop their own texts. Moreover, electronic tools such as digital cameras, graphic editors, and presentation software all have the potential to enhance students' communication. At the same time, students need to be aware of how to manage and cite their sources, as well as how to incorporate materials, especially copyrighted materials, from these sources in an appropriate and ethical manner.

Today, digital communication has become a core component of our students' literacy learning. We need our students to be as effective in comprehending and creating oral, visual, and technological media as they are with comprehending and creating traditional print texts. In turn, they can rely on multiple forms of media to read and write about their individual and professional interests, as well as to be informed, engaged, and thoughtful citizens.

Phonics, Spelling, and Word Study Continuum

This continuum of learning for phonics, spelling, and word study is derived from lessons we have previously published (Fountas and Pinnell, Heinemann 2003, Fountas and Pinnell, Heinemann 2004). These lessons are based on a detailed continuum specifying principles that learners develop over time. In this book, we present these same understandings in two different ways: as a grade-by-grade continuum and as word work in guided reading. All of the principles are based on the nine areas of learning that we have previously described and summarize here.

Grade-by-Grade Continuum

The grade-by-grade Phonics, Spelling, and Word Study continuum presents a general guide to the kinds of understandings children will need to acquire by the end of each grade. These understandings are related to the texts that they are expected to read at the appropriate levels. In presenting this grade-by-grade continuum, we are not suggesting that children should be held back because they do not know specific details about letters, sounds, and words. Instead, we are suggesting that specific teaching will be needed to support learners. The continuum can support instruction and extra services.

Word Work for Guided Reading

The Guided Reading continuum contains additional information about phonics, spelling, and word study. Here we have selected principles that have good potential for the word work teachers include within guided reading at a particular text level. At the end of a guided reading lesson, consider including a few minutes of work with letters or words to help readers develop fluency and flexibility in taking words apart. You may demonstrate a principle on chart paper or a white board. Children may write on individual white boards or use magnetic letters to make words and take them apart. The principles in guided reading are stated in terms of the actions teachers may take, but remember they are selected from a larger set. Evaluate them against assessment of your own children and visit the grade-by-grade learning continuum for more goals.

Nine Areas of Learning

Each grade level lists principles over which children will have developed control by the end of the school year. Across grades PreK through 8, the principles are organized into nine broad categories of learning. These are related to the levels of text that children are expected to read upon completing that grade. (They are also related to writing in that children use letter-sound relationships, spelling patterns, and word structure as they spell words while writing meaningful messages. You will find much evidence of learning about phonics as you examine their writing.) The nine areas of learning follow.

Early Literacy Concepts

Even before they can read, children begin to develop some awareness of how written language works. For example, early understandings about literacy include knowing that:

- ❑ print and pictures are different but are connected
- ❑ you read the print, not the pictures
- ❑ you turn pages to read and look at the left page first
- ❑ you read left to right and then go back to the left to start a new line
- ❑ words are groups of letters with a space on either side
- ❑ there is a difference between a word and a letter
- ❑ there are uppercase (or capital) and lowercase letters
- ❑ a letter is always the same and you look at the parts to identify it
- ❑ the first word in a sentence is on the left and the last word is before the ending punctuation mark
- ❑ the first letter in a word is on the left and the last letter is right before the space (or ending punctuation).

More of the understandings above are stated in the PreK–2 continuum.

Many children enter kindergarten with good knowledge of early literacy concepts. If they do not, explicit and systematic instruction can help them become oriented quickly. While most of these early literacy concepts are not considered phonics, they are basic to the child's understanding of print and should be mastered early.

Phonological Awareness

A key to becoming literate is the ability to hear the sounds in words. Hearing individual sounds allows the learner to connect sounds to letters. Children respond to the sounds of language in a very natural way. They love rhyme, repetition, and rhythm. Young children naturally enjoy and remember nursery rhymes and songs because of the way they sound. This general response to the sounds of language is called *phonological awareness*. As children become more aware of language, they notice sounds in a more detailed way. *Phonemic awareness* involves recognizing the *individual* sounds in words and, eventually, being able to identify, isolate, and manipulate them. Children with phonemic awareness have an advantage in that being able to hear the sounds allows them to connect sounds with letters.

Letter Knowledge

Letter knowledge refers to what children need to know about the graphic characters in our alphabet—how the letters look, how to distinguish one from another, how to detect them within continuous text, and how to use them in words. A finite set of twenty-six letters, a capital and a lowercase form of each, is used to indicate all the sounds of the English language (approximately forty-four phonemes). The sounds in the language change as dialect, articulation, and other speech factors vary, but all must be connected to letters. Children will also encounter alternative forms of some letters (*a* and *a* for example) and will eventually learn to recognize letters in cursive writing. Children need to learn the names and purposes of letters, as well as their distinguishing features (the small differences that help you separate a *d* from an *a*, for example). When children can identify letters, they can associate them with sounds, and the alphabetic principle is mastered.

Letter-Sound Relationships

The sounds of oral language are related in both simple and complex ways to the twenty-six letters of the alphabet. Learning the connections between letters and sounds is basic to understanding written language. Children tend to learn the regular connections between letters and sounds (*b* for the first sound in *bat*) first. But they must also learn that often letters appear together—for example, it is efficient to think of the two sounds at the beginning of *black* together. Sometimes a single sound like /*ch*/ is represented by two letters; sometimes a group of letters represents one sound, as in *eigh* for /*a*/. Children learn to look for and recognize these letter combinations as units, which makes their word solving more efficient.

Spelling Patterns

Efficient word solvers look for and find patterns in the way words are constructed. Knowing spelling patterns helps children notice and use larger parts of words, thus making word solving faster and easier. Patterns are also helpful to children in writing words because they can quickly produce the patterns rather than work laboriously with individual sounds and letters. One way to look at word patterns is to examine the way simple words and syllables are put together. In this consonant-vowel-consonant (CVC) pattern, the vowel is usually a short (terse) sound, as in *tap.* In the consonant-vowel-consonant-silent *e* (CVCe) pattern, the vowel usually has a long (lax) sound. You will not be using this technical language with children, but they can learn to compare words with these patterns.

Phonograms are spelling patterns that represent the sounds of *rimes* (the last parts of words or syllables within words). They are sometimes called *word families.* Some examples of rimes are *-at, -am,* and *-ot.* When you add the *onset* (first part of the word or syllable) to a phonogram like *-ot,* you can make *pot, plot,* or *slot.* A word like *ransom* has two onsets (*r-*and *s-*) and two rimes (*-an* and *-om*). You will not need to teach every phonogram as a separate item. Once children understand that there are patterns, know many examples, and learn how to look for patterns, they will quickly discover more for themselves.

High-Frequency Words

Knowing a core of high-frequency words is a valuable resource for children as they build their reading and writing processing systems. We can also call these *high-utility* words because they appear often and can sometimes be used to help in solving other words. Automatically recognizing high-frequency words allows children to concentrate on understanding and on solving new words. In general, children first learn simple words and in the process develop efficient systems for learning more words; the process accelerates. Children continuously add to the core of high-frequency words they know. Lessons devoted to high-frequency words can develop automaticity and help children look more carefully at the features of words.

Word Meaning and Vocabulary

The term *vocabulary* refers to the words one knows in oral or written language. For comprehension and coherence, children need to know the meaning of the words in the texts they read and write. It is important for them to expand their listening, speaking, reading, and writing vocabularies constantly and to develop a more complex understanding of words they already know (for example, words may have multiple meanings or be used figuratively). Expanding vocabulary means developing categories of words: labels, concept words, synonyms, antonyms, and homonyms. The meaning of a word often varies with the context; accuracy in spelling frequently requires knowing the meaning if you want to write the word. Comprehending words and pronouncing them accurately are also related to knowing word meanings. Knowing many synonyms and antonyms will help children build more powerful systems for connecting and categorizing words.

Word Structure

Words are built according to rules. Looking at the structure of words will help children learn how words are related to one another and how they can be changed by adding letters, letter clusters, and larger word parts. Readers who can break down words into syllables and notice categories of word parts can also apply word-solving strategies efficiently.

An *affix* is a letter or letters added before a word (in which case it's called a *prefix*) or after a word (in which case it's called a *suffix*) to change its function and meaning. A *base word* is a complete word; a *root word* is the part that may have Greek or Latin origins (such as *phon* in *telephone*). It will not be necessary for young children to make these distinctions when they are beginning to learn about simple affixes, but noticing these word parts will help children read and understand words as well as spell them correctly. Word parts that are added to base words signal meaning. For example, they may signal relationships (*tall, taller, tallest*) or time (*work, worked; carry, carried*). Principles related to word structure include understanding the meaning and structure of compound words, contractions, plurals, and possessives.

Word-Solving Actions

Word solving is related to all of the categories of learning previously described, but we have created an additional category devoted specifically to word solving that focuses on the strategic moves readers and writers make when they use their knowledge of the language system while reading and writing continuous text. These strategies are "in-the-head" actions that are invisible, although we can often infer them from overt behaviors. The principles listed in this section represent readers' and writers' ability to use all of the information in the continuum.

The Phonics, Spelling, and Word Study Continuum and Reading

Word solving is basic to the complex act of reading. When readers can employ a flexible range of strategies for solving words rapidly and efficiently, attention is freed for comprehension. Word solving is fundamental to fluent, phrased reading.

We place the behaviors and understandings included in the Phonics, Spelling, and Word Study continuum mainly in the "thinking within the text" category in the twelve systems for strategic actions. At the bottom line, readers must read the words at a high level of accuracy in order to do the kind of thinking necessary to understand the literal meaning of a text. In addition, the continuum focuses on word meanings, or vocabulary. Vocabulary development is an important factor in understanding the meaning of a text and has long been recognized as playing an important role in reading comprehension.

You can use the grade-by-grade Phonics, Spelling, and Word Study continuum as an overall map when you plan your school year. It is useful for planning phonics and vocabulary minilessons, which will support student's word solving in reading, as well as for planning spelling lessons, which will support children's writing. For a detailed description of competency lessons for teaching and specific assessments, see the three volumes: *Phonics Lessons, Grades K, 1, and 2: Letters, Words and How They Work* (Pinnell and Fountas, Heinemann, 2003). In addition, this continuum will serve as a good resource in teaching word study strategies during shared and guided reading lessons.

Guided Reading Continuum

The following level-by-level continuum contains detailed descriptions of ways readers are expected to think *within, beyond,* and *about* the texts they are processing. We have produced the A–Z continuum to assist teachers who are using a gradient of texts to teach guided reading lessons or other small-group lessons. You will see the gradient again in Figure I–5. For approximate expectations for each grade level, also see Figure I–5. Your school board or district may want to adjust the goals, but we view these as reasonable expectations.

It may also be helpful as you confer with individual children during independent reading. We include levels A-N here as appropriate to most children in kindergarten to grade 2. If you need higher levels, please refer to *The Continuum of Literacy Learning, Grades 3–8.*

Guided reading is a highly effective form of small-group instruction. Based on assessment, the teacher brings together a group of readers who are similar enough in their reading development that they can be taught together. They read independently at about the same level and can take on a new text selected by the teacher

Figure I–5 F&P Text Level Gradient™ and Instructional Level Expectations for Reading

FOUNTAS & PINNELL LEVELS

Benchmark System 1, Levels A–N: A, B, C, D, E, F, G, H, I, J, K, L, M, N

Benchmark System 2, Levels L–Z: L, M, N, O, P, Q, R, S, T, U, V, W, X, Y, Z, Z+

GRADE LEVEL GOALS

- Kindergarten (Levels A–D)
- Grade One (Levels E–H)
- Grade Two (Levels L–M)
- Grade Three (Levels N–O)
- Grade Four (Levels P–R)
- Grade Five (Levels S–U)
- Grade Six (Levels V–X)
- Grades Seven & Eight + (Level Z)
- High School/Adult (Level Z+)

	Beginning of Year (Aug.–Sept.)	1st Interval of Year (Nov.–Dec.)	2nd Interval of Year (Feb.–Mar.)	End of Year (May–June)
Grade K		C+	D+	E+
		B	C	D
		A	B	C
				Below C
Grade 1	E+	G+	I+	K+
	D / E	F	H	J
	C	E	G	I
	Below C	Below E	Below G	Below I
Grade 2	K+	L+	M+	N+
	J / K	K	L	M
	I	J	K	L
	Below I	Below J	Below K	Below L
Grade 3	N+	O+	P+	Q+
	M / N	N	O	P
	L	M	N	O
	Below L	Below M	Below N	Below O
Grade 4	Q+	R+	S+	T+
	P / Q	Q	R	S
	O	P	Q	R
	Below O	Below P	Below Q	Below R
Grade 5	T+	U+	V+	W+
	S / T	T	U	V
	R	S	T	U
	Below R	Below S	Below T	Below U
Grade 6	W+	X+	Y+	Z
	V / W	W	X	Y
	U	V	W	X
	Below U	Below V	Below W	Below X
Grade 7	Z	Z	Z+	Z+
	Y / Z	Y	Z	Z
	X	X	Y	Y
	Below X	Below X	Below Y	Below Y
Grade 8	Z+	Z+	Z+	Z+
	Z	Z	Z	Z
	Y	Y	Y	Y
	Below Y	Below Y	Below Y	Below Y

KEY

- Exceeds Expectations
- Meets Expectations
- Approaches Expectations: Needs Short-Term Intervention
- Does Not Meet Expectations: Needs Intensive Intervention

The Instructional Level Expectations for Reading chart is intended to provide general guidelines for grade level goals, which should be adjusted based on school/district requirements and professional teacher judgement.

that is just a little more challenging. The teacher supports the reading in a way that enables children to read a more challenging text with effective processing, thus expanding their reading powers. The framework of a guided reading lesson is detailed in Figure I–6.

General Aspects of the Continuum

As you use the continuum, there are several important points to keep in mind.

1. The cognitive actions that readers employ while processing print are essentially the same across levels. Readers are simply applying them to successively more demanding levels of text. Beginning readers are sorting out the complex concepts related to using print (left-to-right directionality, voice-print match, the relationships between spoken and written language), so their processing is slower and their overt behaviors show us how they are working on print. They are reading texts with familiar topics and very simple, natural language, yet even these texts demand that they understand story lines, think about characters, and engage in more complex thinking such as making predictions.

For higher-level readers, much of the processing is unconscious. These readers automatically and effortlessly solve large numbers of words, tracking print across complex sentences that they process without explicit attention to the in-the-head actions that are happening. While reading, they focus on the meaning of the text and engage in complex thinking processes (for example, inferring what the writer is implying but not saying, critically examining the ideas in the text, or noticing aspects of the writer's craft). Yet at times, higher-level readers will need to closely examine a word to solve it or reread it to tease out the meaning of especially complex sentence structures.

All readers are simultaneously employing a wide range of systems of strategic actions while processing print. The twelve systems of strategic actions include:

- ❑ *Solving the words using a flexible range of strategies.* Early readers are just beginning to acquire ways of looking at words, and they work with a few signposts and word features (simple letter-sound relationships and word parts). High-level readers employ a broad and flexible range of word-solving strategies that are largely unconscious, freeing attention for deep thinking.

- ❑ *Self-monitoring their reading for accuracy and understanding and self-correcting when necessary.* Beginning readers will overtly display evidence of monitoring and self-correcting while higher-level readers keep this evidence "underground"; but readers are always monitoring, or checking on themselves as they read.

- ❑ *Searching for and using information.* Beginning readers will overtly search for information in the letters and words, the pictures, or the sentence structure; they also use their own background knowledge.

Figure I–6   Structure of a Guided Reading Lesson

Element	Potential Teaching Moves to Support Reading with Comprehension and Fluency
Introduction to the Text	• Activate and/or provide needed background knowledge. • Invite children to share thinking. • Enable children to hear and sometimes say new language structures. • Have children say and sometimes locate specific words in the text. • Help children make connections to present knowledge of texts, content, and experiences. • Reveal the structure of the text. • Use new vocabulary words in conversation to reveal meaning. • Prompt children to make predictions based on the information revealed so far. • Draw attention to the writer's craft to support analysis. • Draw attention to accuracy or authenticity of the text-writer's credentials, references, or presentation of evidence as appropriate. • Draw attention to illustrations—pictures, charts, graphs, maps, cutaways—and the information they present.
Reading the Text	• Demonstrate, prompt for, or reinforce the effective use of systems of strategic actions (including word solving, searching for and using information, maintaining fluency, detecting and correcting errors, summarizing, and adjusting reading). • Prompt for fluency and phrasing.
Discussing the Meaning	• Gather evidence of comprehension by observing what children say about the text. • Invite children to pose questions and clarify their understanding. • Help children learn to discuss the meaning of the text together. • Extend children's expression of understandings through questioning, summarizing, restating, and adding to their comments.

Teaching for Processing Strategies	• Revisit the text to demonstrate or reinforce any aspect of reading, including all systems of strategic actions:
	  • Solving words • Predicting
	  • Monitoring and checking • Making connections
	  • Searching for and using information • Synthesizing
	  • Summarizing (remembering information) • Inferring
	  • Maintaining fluency • Analyzing
	  • Adjusting reading (purpose and genre) • Critiquing
	• Provide explicit demonstrations of strategic actions using any part of the text that has just been read.

Word Work (optional)	• Teach any aspect of word analysis–letter-sound relationships, using analogy, or breaking words apart. • Have children manipulate words using magnetic letters or use white boards or pencil and paper to make or take apart words.
Extending the Meaning (optional)	• Use writing, drawing, or extended talk to explore any aspect of understanding the text.

❑ *Remembering information in summary form.* Summarizing implies the selection and reorganization of important information. Readers constantly summarize information as they read a text, thus forming prior knowledge with which to understand the rest of the text; they also remember this summary information long after reading.

❑ *Sustaining fluent, phrased reading.* At early levels (A, B, C), readers will be working to match one spoken word to one written word and will usually be pointing crisply at each word to assist the eye and voice in this process; however, even at level C, when dialogue is first presented, they will begin to make their reading sound like talking. As the finger is withdrawn and the eyes take over the process at subsequent levels, children will read increasingly complex texts with appropriate rate, word stress, phrasing, and pausing in a smoothly operating system. In and of itself, fluency is not a stage or level of reading. Readers apply strategies in an integrated way to achieve fluent reading at every level after the early behaviors are in place. Fluency is an important aspect of effective reading.

❑ *Adjusting reading in order to process a variety of texts.* At all levels, readers may slow down to problem solve words or complex language and resume a normal pace, although at higher levels this process is mostly unobservable. Readers make adjustments as they search for information; they may reread, search graphics or illustrations, go back to specific references in the text, or use specific readers' tools. At all levels, readers also adjust expectations and ways of reading according to purpose, genre, and previous reading experiences. At early levels, readers have only beginning experiences to draw on, but at more advanced levels, they have rich resources in terms of the knowledge of genre (see Fountas and Pinnell 2006, 159 ff).

❑ *Making predictions.* At all levels, readers constantly make and confirm or disconfirm predictions. Usually, these predictions are implicit rather than voiced, and they add not only to understanding but also to enjoyment of a text. All readers predict based on the information in the text and their own background knowledge, with more advanced readers bringing a rich foundation of knowledge, including how many varieties of texts work.

❑ *Making connections.* At all levels, readers use their prior knowledge as well as their personal experiences and knowledge of other texts to interpret a text. As they expand their reading experience, they have more information to help them understand every text. At the most advanced levels, readers are required to understand mature and complex ideas and themes that are in most cases beyond their personal experience; yet they can empathize with the human condition, drawing from previous reading.

❑ *Synthesizing new information.* At all levels, readers gain new information from the texts they read, although readers who are just beginning to construct a reading process are processing texts on very familiar topics. As they move through successive levels of text, readers encounter much new information, which they incorporate into their own background knowledge.

❑ *Reading "between the lines" to infer what is not explicitly stated in the text.* To some degree, all texts require inference. At very simple levels, readers may infer characters' feelings (surprised, happy, sad) or traits (lazy, greedy). But at high levels, readers need to infer constantly to understand both fiction and nonfiction texts.

❑ *Thinking analytically about a text to notice how it is constructed or how the writer has crafted language.* Thinking analytically about a text means reflecting on it, holding it up for examination, and drawing some conclusions about it. Readers at early levels may comment that the text was funny or exciting; they do not, however, engage in a great deal of analysis, which could be artificial and detract from enjoying the text. More advanced readers will notice more about how the writer (and illustrator when appropriate) has organized the text and crafted the language.

❑ *Thinking critically about a text.* Thinking critically about a text involves complex ways of evaluating it. Beginning readers may simply say what they like or dislike about a text, sometimes being specific about why; but increasingly advanced readers engage in higher-level thinking as they evaluate the quality or authenticity of a text, and this kind of analysis often enhances enjoyment.

2. *Readers are always meeting greater demands at every level because the texts are increasingly challenging.* The categories for these demands may be similar, but the specific challenges are constantly increasing. For example, at many of the lower levels of text, readers are challenged to use phonogram patterns (or consonant clusters and vowel patterns) to solve one-syllable words. At upper levels, they are challenged to use these same patterns in multisyllable words. In addition, starting after level E, readers must use word endings as they take apart words. Word endings change words and add meaning. At lower levels, readers are attending to endings such as *-s, -ed,* and *-ing,* but as words become increasingly complex at successive levels, they will encounter endings such as *-ment, -ent, -ant, -ible,* and *-able.*

At all levels, readers must identify characters and follow plots; but at lower levels, characters are one-dimensional and plots are a simple series of events. Across the levels, however, readers encounter multiple characters that are highly complex and change over time. Plots have more episodes; subplots are full of complexity.

3. *Readers' knowledge of genres expands over time but also grows in depth within genres.* For some texts at very low levels, it is difficult to determine genre. For example, a simple repetitive text may focus on a single topic, such as fruit, with a child presenting an example of a different type of fruit on each page. The pages could be in just about any order, except that there is often some kind of conclusion at the end. Such a text is organized in a structure that is characteristic of nonfiction, which helps beginning readers understand information presented in categories, but it is technically fiction because the narrator is not real. At this level, however, it is not important for children to read pure genre categories, but simply to experience and learn about a variety of ways to organize texts.

Moving across the levels of the gradient, however, examples of genres become more precise and varied. At early levels, children read examples of fiction (usually realistic fiction, traditional literature, and simple fantasy) and simple informational texts on single topics. Across the levels, nonfiction texts become more and more complex, offering information on a variety of topics, as well as a range of underlying structures for presentation (description; comparison and contrast; cause and effect; temporal sequence; and problem and solution). These underlying structures appear at all levels after the very beginning ones, but they are combined in increasingly complex ways.

4. *At each level, the content load of texts becomes heavier, requiring an increased amount of background knowledge.* Content knowledge is a key factor in understanding texts; it includes vocabulary and concepts. Beginning texts are necessarily structured to take advantage of familiar content that most young children know; yet, even some very simple texts may require knowledge of some labels (for example, *zoo animals*) that may be unfamiliar to the children you teach. Success at successive levels will depend not only on study in the content areas but on wide reading of texts that expand the individual's vocabulary and content knowledge.

5. At each level, the themes and ideas are more mature, requiring readers to consider perspectives and understand cultures beyond their own. Children can connect simple themes and ideas to their own lives, but even at beginning levels they find that their experiences are stretched by realistic stories, simple fantasy, and traditional tales. At levels of increasing complexity, readers are challenged to understand and empathize with characters (and the subjects of biography) who lived in past times or in distant places and who have very different experiences and perspectives from the readers' own. At higher levels, fantasy requires that readers understand completely imaginary worlds. As they meet greater demands across the levels, they must depend on previous reading, as well as on discussions of the themes and ideas.

6. *The specific descriptions of thinking within, beyond, and about text do not change dramatically from level to level.* As you look at the continuum of text features along the gradient A to Z, you will see only small changes level to level. The gradient represents a gradual increase in the demands of text. Similarly, the expectations for readers' thinking change gradually over time as children develop from kindergarten through grade 8. If you look at the demands across two or three levels you will notice only a few changes in expectations. But if you contrast levels like the following, you will find some very clear differences.

□ Level A with Level D

□ Level E with Level H

□ Level I with Level N

The continuum represents progress over time, and if you examine the expectations in the ranges suggested, you get a picture of the remarkable growth our children make from prekindergarten through grade 8, or for primary grades, level A through N.

Using the Continuum

The Guided Reading continuum for PreK–grade 2 is organized by level, A to N. Each level has several sections.

Section 1: Characteristics of Readers

The first section of this continuum provides a brief description of what you may find to be generally true of readers at the particular level. For a much more detailed description, see our *Leveled Books, K–8: Matching Texts to Readers for Effective Teaching* (Fountas and Pinnell, Heinemann, 2006). Remember that all readers are individuals and that individuals vary widely. It is impossible to create a description that is true of all readers for whom a level is appropriate for independent reading or instruction. In fact, it is inappropriate to refer to any individual as "a level ___ reader"! We level *books,* not *readers.* But it is helpful to keep in mind the general expectations of readers at a level so that books may be well selected and appropriate support may be given to individuals and groups.

Section 2: Selecting Texts for Guided Reading Lessons

This section provides detailed descriptions of texts characteristic for each level A–N. It is organized into ten categories as shown in Figure I–7.

Studying the text characteristics of books at a given level will provide a good inventory of the challenges readers will meet across that level. Remember that there are a great variety of texts within each level, and that these characteristics apply to what is *generally true* for texts at the level. For the individual text, some factors may be more important than others in making demands on the readers. Examining these texts factors relative to the books you select for guided reading will help in planning introductions that help readers meet the demands of more challenging texts and process them effectively.

Figure I–7	**Ten Text Characteristics for Guided Reading**
Genre/Form	*Genre* is the type of text and refers to a system by which fiction and nonfiction texts are classified. *Form* is the format in which a genre may be presented. Forms and genres have characteristic features.
Text Structure	*Structure* is the way the text is organized and presented. The structure of most fiction and biographical texts is *narrative*, arranged primarily in chronological sequence. Factual texts are organized categorically or topically and may have sections with headings. Writers of factual texts use several underlying structural patterns to provide information to readers. The most important are *description; chronological sequence; comparison and contrast; cause and effect;* and *problem and solution*. The presence of these structures, especially in combination, can increase the challenge for readers.
Content	*Content* refers to the subject matter of the text—the concepts that are important to understand. In fiction, content may be related to the setting or to the kinds of problems characters have. In factual texts, content refers to the topic of focus. Content is considered in relation to the prior experience of readers.
Themes and Ideas	These are the big ideas that are communicated by the writer. Ideas may be concrete and accessible or complex and abstract. A text may have multiple themes or a main theme and several supporting themes.
Language and Literary Features	Written language is qualitatively different from spoken language. Fiction writers use dialogue, figurative language, and other kinds of literary structures such as character, setting, and plot. Factual writers use description and technical language. In hybrid texts you may find a wide range of literary language
Sentence Complexity	Meaning is mapped onto the syntax of language. Texts with simpler, more natural sentences are easier to process. Sentences with embedded and conjoined clauses make a text more difficult.
Vocabulary	Vocabulary refers to words and their meanings. The more known vocabulary words in a text, the easier it will be. The individual's *reading and writing vocabularies* refer to words that she understands and can also read or write.
Words	This category refers to recognizing and solving the printed words in the text. The challenge in a text partly depends on the number and the difficulty of the words that the reader must solve by recognizing them or decoding them. Having a great many of the same high-frequency words makes a text more accessible to readers.
Illustrations	Drawings, paintings, or photographs accompany the text and add meaning and enjoyment. In factual texts, illustrations also include graphics that provide a great deal of information that readers must integrate with the text. Illustrations are an integral part of a high-quality text. Increasingly, fiction texts are including a range of graphics.
Book and Print Features	*Book and print features* are the physical aspects of the text—what readers cope with in terms of length, size, and layout. Book and print features also include tools like the table of contents, glossary, pronunciation guides, indexes, and sidebars.

Section 3: Demands of the Text—Ways of Thinking

The heart of the Guided Reading continuum is a description of the expectations for thinking on the part of readers at the level. The descriptions are organized into three larger categories and twelve subcategories, as shown in Figure I–8. As you work with readers at each level, examine the specific descriptions within categories.

- ❑ *Planning introductions to texts.* Examine the categories to determine what might be challenging for readers. Frame the introduction to help them engage in particular thinking processes.

- ❑ *Guiding interactions with individual readers.* Observe reading behaviors and converse with children to determine what they are noticing and thinking about. Draw

Figure I–8 Systems of Strategic Actions

Ways of Thinking	Systems of Strategic Actions for Processing Written Texts	
Thinking Within the Text	Solving Words	Using a range of strategies to take words apart and understand what words mean while reading continuous text
	Monitoring and Correcting	Checking on whether reading sounds right, looks right, and makes sense
	Searching for and Using Information	Searching for and using all kinds of information in a text
	Summarizing	Putting together and carrying important information while reading and disregarding irrelevant information
	Maintaining Fluency	Integrating sources of information in a smoothly operating process that results in expressive, phrased reading
	Adjusting	Reading in different ways as appropriate to purpose for reading and type of text
Thinking Beyond the Text	Predicting	Thinking about what will follow while reading continuous text
	Making Connections • personal • world • text	Searching for and using connections to knowledge that readers have gained through their personal experiences, learning about the world, and reading other texts
	Synthesizing	Putting together information from the text and from the reader's own background knowledge in order to create new understandings
	Inferring	Going beyond the literal meaning of a text to think about what is not there but is implied by the writer
Thinking About the Text	Analyzing	Examining elements of a text to know more about how it is constructed
	Critiquing	Evaluating a text based on the reader's personal, world, or text knowledge

their attention to what they need to know through demonstrating, prompting, or reinforcing actions. (See *Prompting Guide 1* and *2*, Fountas and Pinnell, Heinemann.)

- ❑ *Discussing the meaning of a text after reading the whole text or a part of it.* Invite readers to comment on various aspects of the text and to build on one another's points. Refer to the continuum as you think about the evidence of understanding they are demonstrating through conversation. Guide the discussion when appropriate to help them engage in new ways of thinking.

- ❑ *Making specific teaching points after reading.* Demonstrate effective ways of operating on a text in a way that will help readers learn how to do something as readers that they can apply to other texts.

- ❑ *Planning ways to extend the meaning of the text.* Plan writing, drawing, or deeper discussion that will support children in engaging in deeper ways of thinking about texts. (See the Writing About Reading continuum for examples.)

Section 4: Planning Word Work for Guided Reading

In Thinking within the Text section at each level, a separate section provides suggestions for phonics and word work. Guided reading is intended to be used as one component of an integrated literacy framework that includes specific lessons on phonics, spelling, and word study. The details of that curriculum—for lessons and independent activities—are presented in the Phonics, Spelling, and Word Study continuum and expanded in *Phonics Lessons and Word Study Lessons, K–3* (Pinnell and Fountas, 2003, 2004). These lessons are systematic, sequenced, and multilevel in the activities used to help children apply principles, usually as whole-class activities. The goals embedded in guided reading apply the principles during text reading where phonics and word study instruction is most effective.

As they read texts, individuals are always applying phonics principles, and across the gradient they do so on more and more complex words. Word solving includes not only decoding but deriving the meaning of words, as indicated in the Solving Words category in the second column of Figure I–8. In addition, an important component of a guided reading lesson is some brief but focused attention to words and how they work. This quick word work should address children's needs in visual processing. The goal is to build their fluency and flexibility in taking words apart. In this section, you will find a list of suggestions to help you select word study activities that will enable you to tailor instruction on words to the specific demands of the level of text. Make principles related to word solving visible to children through the following types of activities:

- ❑ Have children match or sort picture cards to illustrate letter-sound relationships.

- ❑ Have students match or sort letters.

- ❏ Demonstrate the principle using a white board (or chalkboard) that all children can see. Invite them to read the examples that you present. Change, take away, or add word parts to build flexibility and speed.

- ❏ Demonstrate the principle using magnetic letters on a vertical board. Magnetic letters are particularly helpful when demonstrating how to take words apart or change words to make new ones.

- ❏ Have children make words, change words, and take apart words using magnetic letters.

- ❏ Have children use individual small white boards (or chalkboards) to write and change words to demonstrate the principles. (Each student can have a small eraser or an old sock on one hand so that changes can be made quickly.)

- ❏ Give children individual word cards for instant word recognition.

- ❏ Ask children to sort word cards into categories to illustrate a principle.

- ❏ Have children match word cards to illustrate a principle.

- ❏ Make word webs to illustrate the connections and relationships between words.

As you plan, conduct, and reflect on guided reading lessons at the various levels, move to the appropriate level and note what your children already know and do well and what they need to be able to do so that your introduction, interactions, and teaching points can be more specific to their needs at any given point in time.

PRE-KINDERGARTEN

The goals in this section apply to the early learning of three- and four-year olds and provide a strong foundation for language and literacy learning. For a more detailed description of the prekindergarten program, see Literacy and Language in Prekindergarten: Continuum to Guide Teaching *(Pinnell and Fountas, Heinemann, 2011).*

Interactive Read-Aloud and Literature Discussion

❑ **Selecting Texts:** *Characteristics of Texts for Reading Aloud and Discussion*

GENRES/FORMS

Genres
- Short poems, nursery rhymes, and songs
- Language and word play
- Traditional folktales
- Animal fantasy
- Realistic fiction
- Memoir
- Factual texts (simple and straightforward ABC books, label books, concept books, counting books, very simple informational books)

Forms
- Oral stories
- Picture books
- Wordless picture books
- Informational picture books
- Books with texture, padding, pop-ups, unusual features that promote interaction

TEXT STRUCTURE

- Informational texts that present a clear and simple sequence—one idea on each page spread
- Informational texts with simple description—one concept on each page spread
- Informational texts and stories with repeating patterns
- Many traditional tales with particular structures (cumulative tales, circular stories, and the use of "threes")
- Stories with simple narrative structure—beginning, series of episodes, and an ending
- Many books with repetition of episodes and refrains
- Texts with rhyme and rhythm

CONTENT

- Language and word play (rhymes, nonsense, alliteration, and alphabet)
- Everyday actions familiar to young children (playing, making things, eating, getting dressed, bathing, cooking, shopping)
- Familiar topics (home, toys, pets, animals, food, playground, park, friends and family)
- A few topics related to the neighborhood or surrounding area (farm, zoo, park, woods, traffic, etc.)
- Themes and content that reflect a full range of cultures

THEMES AND IDEAS

- Humor that is easy to grasp (silly characters, obvious jokes, funny situations)
- Obvious themes (friendship, family relationships, first responsibilities, growing, behavior)

LANGUAGE AND LITERARY FEATURES

- Simple plots
- Easy to understand problems and solutions
- Memorable characters that are straightforward and uncomplicated
- Characters that change for obvious reasons (learn lessons, learn new things)
- Characters' actions that have clear consequences (reward for trying, etc.)
- Predictable character traits (sly, brave, silly)
- Stories with multiple characters, each easy to understand and predictable
- Some figurative language that will be familiar to most children
- Rhyme, rhythm, repetition
- Simple dialogue easily attributed to characters
- Some repetitive dialogue

SENTENCE COMPLEXITY

- Simple sentences, although more complex than children generally use in oral language
- Sentences that are easy for children to follow

VOCABULARY

- Many words that are in children's oral vocabulary
- Some memorable words that children can take on as language play
- Labels for familiar objects, animals, and activities

ILLUSTRATIONS

- Large, clear, colorful illustrations in a variety of media
- Illustrations that add meaning to a story or informational text and offer high support for comprehension
- Very simple illustrations for informational texts—sometimes with labels
- Illustrations that sometimes move or have texture

BOOK AND PRINT FEATURES

- Some books with large print that children can see during read-aloud (labels, onomatopoeic words, simple phrases or sentences)
- Some special features in the illustrations and print that engage interest and make texts interactive (pop-up books, lift-the-flap books, see-through holes, sound effects)
- Title, author, and illustrator on cover and title page

Interactive Read-Aloud and Literature Discussion

❏ **Selecting Goals:** *Behaviors and Understandings to Notice, Teach, and Support*

Thinking *Within* the Text

- Notice and acquire understanding of new words from read-aloud context
- Use new words in discussion of a text
- Follow the events of a simple plot and remember them enough to discuss or reenact a story
- Understand simple problems and talk about them
- Talk about interesting information learned from a text
- Pick up important information while listening and use it in discussion
- Notice and use important information from the pictures
- Retell a story using the pictures after hearing several times
- Ask questions to clarify or deepen understanding of a text
- After hearing a story several times, join in on refrains or repeated sentences, phrases, and words
- Tell stories in response to pictures
- Play with words or language orally (for example, nonsense words or refrains from texts read aloud)
- Show awareness of a topic (content from a text) and make related comments or pose related questions)
- Mimic the teacher's expression and word stress when reenacting a text or joining in
- Use hand and body movements showing understanding that the pictures and words of a text convey meaning
- Turn pages front to back when looking at a picture book

Thinking *About* the Text

- Understand when texts are based on established sequences such as numbers, days of the week, or seasons
- Understand the meaning of some aspects of text structure (beginning, end, next)
- Understand that an author wrote the book
- Understand that an illustrator created the pictures in the book (or a photographer took photographs)
- Recognize that one author or illustrator might create several books
- Begin to form opinions about books and say why
- Share thinking about a story or topic
- Talk about how texts are similar and how they are different
- Understand that there can be different versions of the same story
- Identify favorite books and tell why
- Use specific vocabulary to talk about texts: *author, illustrator, cover, title, page, problem, beginning, ending*

Thinking *Beyond* the Text

- Use background knowledge to understand settings, story problems, and characters
- Use background knowledge to understand the content of a text
- Acquire new content from listening to stories and informational texts
- Predict what will happen next in a story
- Talk about what a character is like, how a character feels, or what a character might do (inference)
- Make connections between new texts and those heard before
- Identify and repeat specific language that characters use in stories
- Make connections between texts and their own lives
- Interpret meaning from illustrations
- Understand that there can be different interpretations of the illustrations
- Use details from illustrations in discussion of a story or informational text
- Give reasons (either text-based or personal experience) to support thinking
- Discuss motivations of characters
- Discuss the problems in a story
- Discuss new information learned

Shared and Performance Reading

❑ **Selecting Texts:** *Characteristics of Texts for Sharing and Performing*

GENRES/FORMS

Genres

- Simple fantasy, most with talking animals or magic creatures
- Factual texts–ABC books, label books, concept books, counting books, very simple informational books
- Short poems, nursery rhymes, and songs
- Language and word play (including finger rhymes, hand rhymes, body movements)
- Traditional folktales
- Memoir
- Realistic fiction

Forms

- Enlarged poems, rhymes, and songs
- Enlarged picture story books and informational texts
- Texts produced through interactive and shared writing–lists, directions, sequences of actions, stories, poems, descriptions, dialogue from stories

TEXT STRUCTURE

- Stories with simple plot structure (beginning, middle, ending)
- Stories with repeating patterns
- Many books with repetition of episodes and refrains
- Informational texts with very simple statements of description, simple chronological sequence, or simple naming
- Simple traditional tales that are familiar to many children

CONTENT

- Stories with simple, easy-to-understand problems–beginning, events, and ending
- Language and word play–rhymes, alliteration
- ABC books, concepts such as colors, shapes, counting
- Familiar topics–animals, pets, families, food, neighborhood, friends, growing, weather such as rain or snow
- Informational texts about one simple, familiar topic
- Topics that may be in settings different from children's own but that have universal appeal

THEMES AND IDEAS

- Obvious humor–silly situations and nonsense
- Familiar themes for children such as play, families, homes, and preschool

LANGUAGE AND LITERARY FEATURES

- Simple stories with beginning, middle (events of a plot), and ending
- Many texts with rhyme, rhythm, and repetition
- Some memorable characters
- Simple, understandable dialogue that is easily attributed to characters
- Characters' actions that have clear consequences (reward for trying, etc.)
- Predictable plots and stories
- Simple humor that appeals to young children

SENTENCE COMPLEXITY

- Short, simple sentences that are easy for children to understand and remember (consider ELL)
- Sentences with a limited number of adjectives, adverbs, and clauses

VOCABULARY

- A few content words (labels) related to concepts that children can understand
- Texts that contain mostly words that are in children's oral vocabularies
- A few words that are new to children but easy to understand in context
- Some words of high interest and novelty that will be memorable (for example, *huffed and puffed; roared; bam!*)

WORDS

- Simple plurals using *–s* or *–es*
- Some complex plurals that are in children's oral vocabulary (*children, sheep*)
- Some words with endings that are in children's oral vocabulary (*running, painting*) or that are easy to understand
- Words that have the same ending (rime–*it, bit, sit*)
- Many very simple high-frequency words that may over time become familiar enough to be visual signposts
- Alliterative sequences

ILLUSTRATIONS

- Bright, clear, colorful illustrations in a variety of media
- Details that add interest rather than overwhelm or distract
- Illustrations that provide high support for comprehending and language
- Poems or pieces of shared writing that have only small labels to cue language

BOOK AND PRINT FEATURES

- All texts on charts or in enlarged texts
- Print in a font big enough for the whole group (or a small group) to see clearly
- Clear spaces between words and between lines
- Limited number of lines on a page (usually 1 or 2 unless they are reading a well known short poem or song)
- Simple punctuation (period, comma, question mark, exclamation mark, quotation marks)
- Title, author, and illustrator on cover and title page for books
- Page numbers
- Layout that supports phrasing by presenting word groups
- Words in bold or varying type sizes

Shared and Performance Reading

❑ **Selecting Goals:** *Behaviors and Understandings to Notice, Teach, and Support*

Thinking *Within* the Text

- Notice and use information from pictures to understand and remember text
- Follow the teacher's pointer in a coordinated way while reading text with group support
- Begin to notice aspects of print to help in tracking it during shared reading
- Understand the meaning of new words after reading them in a text and talking about them
- Engage in shared reading with fluency and expression
- Use expression in response to questions and exclamation marks
- Begin to recognize some simple punctuation
- Notice some letters in print
- Connect some letters in print with their names or with words they know
- Using phrasing, pausing, and word stress with the teacher's support
- Remember and use repeating language patterns
- Mimic the teacher's expression
- Talk about characters, problems, and events in a story
- Discuss how to read a text with the teacher and other children

Thinking *Beyond* the Text

- Make predictions as to what will happen in a story
- Anticipate exciting places or the ending of a story in discussion with the teacher
- Anticipate exciting places or the ending of a story by remembering it
- Express personal connections with the content of texts, characters, or events in a story
- Notice and talk about texts that are alike in some way
- Infer feelings of characters in stories

Thinking *About* the Text

- Recognize and talk about the beginning and the ending of a story
- Understand that a book was written by a person and begin to use the term "author"
- Understand that a picture book was illustrated by a person and begin to use the term "illustrator"
- Talk about whether or not they liked a book and say why
- Talk about favorite parts of a story
- Recognize the same tale (traditional story) in different books
- Notice when a text is funny and say why
- Notice when the writer/illustrator has used special features of print such as very large print
- Notice and follow texts that are organized around a special feature such as numbers, days of the week, ABCs
- Notice when the writer has made the text rhyme

Writing About Reading

❑ **Selecting Genres and Forms:** *Most writing for preschool children is generated through very simple shared or interactive writing, and the genres and forms are likewise demonstrated through very simple interactive or shared writing. Often, teachers label pictures or children's drawings as a demonstration of writing. Preschool children's independent writing largely consists of drawing or painting accompanied by the use of whatever they have noticed about writing. They may write their names (or parts of them); they may use letter-like forms mixed with some known letters. They may use the letters they know over and over again in strings. It is helpful for teachers to invite children to talk about their drawings (stories or just labels). Teachers may write a simple sentence or two that the child dictates. Some children can remember and "read" this sentence.*

FUNCTIONAL WRITING

- Drawings or paintings that reflect the subject of an informational book or something in a story
- Dictated labels or short sentences describing a drawing
- Lists of all kinds (things we like, things we are going to do, ingredients for cooking)
- Notes, messages, and simple letters
- Labels for photographs
- Directions showing a simple sentence

INFORMATIONAL WRITING

- Drawings with labels showing information (what we learned) from a book
- Simple sentence telling an interesting fact (what we learned) from a book

NARRATIVE WRITING

- Drawings showing sequence of events in a story
- Speech bubbles showing dialogue (a word, phrase, or simple sentence)
- Simple sentence summarizing or telling the end of a story

A prekindergartener's writing about her brother

Writing About Reading

❑ **Selecting Goals:** *Behaviors and Understandings to Notice, Teach, and Support*

Thinking *Within* the Text

- Use drawing (or other art media) to represent characters and actions from a story
- Use drawing (or other art media) to represent information from a book
- Label drawings (dictated, temporary spelling, or letter-like forms)
- Reenact or retell stories that have been heard
- Use some vocabulary from stories
- Reread (shared) to remember something from a story
- Find important details in illustrations
- Discuss the meaning of illustrations
- Use names of authors and illustrators

Thinking *Beyond* the Text

- Draw to show how a character feels
- Label drawings to show what a character might be saying
- Dictate or use interactive writing to predict what might happen in a story
- Use interactive writing and drawing to show the events of a story in sequence (story map)
- Draw and sometimes label or dictate sentences about something in their lives prompted by characters or events in a story

Thinking *About* the Text

- Use some letter-like forms, letters, or temporary spellings to create texts that have some of the characteristics of published texts (cover, title, author, illustrations)
- Use interactive writing or temporary spellings to represent a funny or exciting part of a story.
- Notice and remember some interesting language from a text, sometimes using it to dictate stories or talk about drawings.

Writing

❑ **Selecting Purpose and Genre:** *Most writing for preschool children is generated through dictated writing or very simple shared or interactive writing. The teacher may guide children to tell about their own experiences or to retell something from a story. Sometimes teachers label pictures or children's drawings as a demonstration of writing. Preschool children's independent writing consists largely of drawing or painting accompanied by the use of whatever they have noticed about writing. They may write their names (or parts of them); they may use non-letter-like or letter-like forms mixed with some known letters. They may use the letters they know over and over in strings. Even if children are only pretending to write, we can tell a great deal about their growing knowledge of and interest in written language by observing how they use the space or create forms on the page. From their attempts we can observe that they are beginning to distinguish between pictures and print. You may want to invite children to talk about their drawings (stories or just labels). If the child requests it, you may write a simple sentence or two that the child dictates, but it is important not to write on the child's paper. If the child wants it, write on stick-on notes. Most children can remember and "read" their own sentences even if you cannot.*

NARRATIVE: *(To tell a story)*

MEMOIR *(personal narrative, autobiography)*

Understanding the Genre

- Understand that you can talk, draw, and write about things that have happened to you
- Understand that when you talk about or write about something from your own life, you often use the words *I* or *we*
- Understand that you need to tell a story in the order in which things happened so your readers will understand them
- Understand that stories you tell should be interesting to your listeners or readers

Writing in the Genre

- Draw a picture and tell a story about it
- Draw a sequence of related pictures and tell about them
- Draw pictures in a simple book, sometimes including approximated writing, and tell a story in sequence about them
- Tell, draw, or approximate writing about stories they have heard or read
- Tell, draw, or approximate writing to tell about personal experiences
- Use some words orally that indicate passage of time (*then, again, after*)
- Talk about one's feelings while telling a story of an experience
- With teacher help, begin to use some features of narrative texts (drawings matching text, titles, page numbers, speech bubbles)

INFORMATIONAL: *(To explain or give facts about a topic)*

LITERARY NONFICTION

Understanding the Genre

- Understand that you can write to tell what you know about something
- Understand that a writer (and illustrator) wants to tell others information
- Begin to notice how the writers of nonfiction texts show facts (labeling, making clear drawings, showing pictures)

Writing in the Genre

- Make a drawing of an object or process and approximate writing or talking about it
- Make a series of drawings showing an object or process and approximate writing or talking about it
- Use a short book with related ideas to talk or approximate writing about a topic
- Show awareness of audience when drawing and approximating writing
- Begin to use (with teacher help) some features of informational text (page numbers, titles, labeled drawings)

Writing

❑ **Selecting Purpose and Genre:** *(cont.)*

POETIC: *(To express feelings, sensory images, ideas, or stories)*

POETRY *(free verse, rhyme)*

Understanding the Genre

- Understand that a writer (or illustrator) can represent a song or rhyme
- Understand poetry (as well as songs and rhymes) as a pleasurable way to talk about feelings, tell stories, or tell how something looks or feels
- Notice interesting words (words for sounds, figurative words, unusual words) when reading poetry in a shared way
- Notice rhyming words when reading poetry in a shared way
- Begin to notice how space and lines are used in poems, songs, and rhymes
- Understand that a poem can be serious or funny

Writing in the Genre

- Actively participate in shared writing of a poem, song, or rhyme
- Illustrate poems with drawings
- Begin to intentionally use space in a way that represents poetry
- Talk about how something looks, smells, tastes, feels, or sounds
- Notice and enjoy rhyme and humor

FUNCTIONAL: *(To perform a practical task)*

LABELS

Understanding the Genre

- Understand that a writer or illustrator can add labels to help readers understand drawings
- Understand that labels provide important information

Writing in the Genre

- Begin to label drawings in approximated writing
- Participate actively in suggesting labels during shared writing
- Create friendly letters in approximated form (notes, cards, invitations, email)

FRIENDLY LETTERS

Understanding the Genre

- Understand that people use writing to communicate with each other
- Understand the different kinds of written communication people use (notes, letters, email)
- Understand that written communication can be used for different purposes (information, invitations, "thank you" letters)
- Understand that people include their names (and recipients' names) in written communications
- Understand that invitations must include specific information

Writing in the Genre

- Participate actively in writing notes, letters, invitations, etc., through shared and interactive writing
- Use shared or approximated writing to write to a known audience
- Actively participate in suggesting information to include in writing during shared/interactive writing
- Add illustrations to written messages

LISTS AND PROCEDURES *(how-to)*

Understanding the Genre

- Understand the purpose of a list
- Understand that the form of a list is usually one item under another and it may be numbered
- Understand that captions can be written under pictures to give people more information
- Understand that a list of directions can help in knowing how to do something
- Understand that pictures will help readers understand information or how to do something

Writing in the Genre

- Actively participate in group writing of lists to help remember how to do something
- Suggest items for lists
- Actively participate in suggesting the order of items in a list
- Add drawings to lists
- Make a list for an authentic purpose

WRITING ABOUT READING *(all genres)*

(See the Writing About Reading continuum, on pages 58–59.)

Writing

❏ Behaviors and Understandings to Notice, Teach, and Support

CRAFT

ORGANIZATION

Text Structure

- Express ideas related to a topic or a thematic study so that someone else can write them (dictation)
- Actively participate in shared or interactive writing around a topic or theme
- Tell stories for dictation that have a beginning, middle, and end
- Use approximated writing and pictures to make short books that tell a story or have information about a topic or theme
- Begin to write the title and author's name on the cover of a story

Beginnings, Endings, Titles

- Suggest titles for pieces of shared or interactive writing
- Suggest beginnings and endings for pieces of shared or interactive writing
- Use approximated writing to write either titles or endings of pieces of writing

Presentation of Ideas

- Tell about experiences or topics in a way that can be written by the teacher
- Present ideas in logical sequence
- Provide some supportive ideas for bigger ideas in talking about a topic or theme
- Suggest logically related ideas in group story or topic writing

IDEA DEVELOPMENT

- Provide details that support main topics or ideas during shared/interactive writing
- Explain points in dictated or shared/interactive writing

LANGUAGE USE

- Understand that what you think you can say, and what you say you can write
- When talking about or retelling stories for dictation or shared/interactive writing, show evidence of awareness of the language of books

WORD CHOICE

- Show awareness of new words encountered in interactive read-aloud or conversation
- Use new words when talking about drawings
- Use new words when telling stories or talking about an informational topic

VOICE

- Begin to develop interesting ways of talking about personal experiences
- Begin to tell stories from a particular perspective
- Share thoughts about a theme or topic
- Add ideas and opinions about a theme or topic
- Participate actively in shared/interactive writing about what is known or remembered from a text

CONVENTIONS

TEXT LAYOUT

- Begin to understand that print is laid out in certain ways and the lines and spaces are important
- Begin to understand that print is placed from top to bottom on a page
- Separate print (or approximated print) from pictures
- Begin to write words, letters, or approximated letters in clusters to show the look of words
- Show awareness of layout and use of space when copying print
- Show awareness of left-to-right directionality during shared/interactive writing
- Identify spaces between words in a piece of shared/interactive writing

GRAMMAR

Sentence Structure (note that English Language Learners may need more time and support)

- Use simple but conventional sentence structure when suggesting ideas for interactive/shared writing
- Dictate simple but conventional sentences

Parts of Speech (note that English Language Learners may need more time and support)

- Use nouns and verbs in agreement most of the time when suggesting ideas for shared/interactive writing or producing language for dictation
- Use prepositional phrases when suggesting ideas for shared/interactive writing or producing language for dictation
- Use modifiers (*red* dress; ran *fast*)

Tense

- Use past tense in describing past events when suggesting ideas for shared/interactive writing or producing language for dictation
- Use present tense to describe something (*I like. . .*)
- Begin to use future tense (*I'm going to go . . .*)

CAPITALIZATION

- Understand that there are upper- and lowercase versions of letters
- Locate capital letters at the beginning of a sentence during shared/interactive writing or in a piece of dictated writing
- Write names with a capital letter at the beginning
- Show awareness of the first place of capital letters in words

Writing

❑ Behaviors and Understandings to Notice, Teach, and Support *(cont.)*

PUNCTUATION

- Understand that there are punctuation marks in print
- Understand that punctuation marks are different from letters
- Understand that punctuation marks are related to the way text is read
- Sometimes use punctuation marks in approximated writing

SPELLING

- Write in scribbles or random strings
- Mix in some letter-like symbols when writing in scribbles
- Write name conventionally (all capital letters or capital letter and lowercase)
- Use known letters from name to make repeated patterns on a page
- Understand that your name is a word
- Begin to be aware that a word is always spelled the same

HANDWRITING/WORD-PROCESSING

- Hold pencil or marker with satisfactory grip
- Hold pencil or marker efficiently to begin to approximate writing or write a few letters
- Begin to understand that writers make decisions about where to start
- Begin to understand that writers make decisions about the placement of pictures and print
- Write with a preferred hand
- Locate letters on a keyboard and understand how to press them to make them appear on a screen
- Use simple programs on the computer with adult help

WRITING PROCESS

REHEARSING/PLANNING

Purpose

- Draw and write for a specific purpose
- Plan drawing and writing for different purposes
- Begin to adjust drawing and dictated messages according to the purpose
- Choose paper for writing
- Choose topics to draw and write about (both as individuals and in groups)
- Write (or approximate writing) for a variety of purposes in particular environments (for example, restaurants, house, shops, doctor's office)
- Actively contribute to shared/interactive writing around a topic or theme
- Write name on drawing and writing

Audience

- Become aware of the people who will read the writing and what they will want to know
- Include important information that the audience needs to know

Oral Language

- Generate and expand ideas through talk with peers and the teacher
- Look for ideas and topics in personal experiences, shared through talk
- Use storytelling to generate and rehearse language (that may be written later)
- Tell stories in chronological order
- Retell stories in chronological order

Writing

❑ Behaviors and Understandings to Notice, Teach, and Support *(cont.)*

Gathering Seeds/Resources/Experimenting with Writing

- Talk about ideas for writing and drawing
- Understand how writers get their ideas (telling about things that have happened or about what they know)
- Record information in drawing and approximated writing
- Use drawings as a source for ideas for writing

Content, Topic, Theme

- Understand a group of ideas related to an area of study or inquiry
- Observe objects in the environment (people, animals, etc.) as a source for group or individual writing
- Select topics or information for drawing and writing

Inquiry/Research

- Use drawings to tell a series of ideas learned through inquiry about a topic
- Use drawings to add information or revise thinking
- Ask questions about a topic
- Remember important information about a topic and contribute ideas to shared/interactive writing
- Remember important labels for drawings and dictate or write them approximately

DRAFTING/REVISING

Understanding the Process

- Understand the role of a conference with the teacher to help in drawing and writing
- Understand that writers can share their writing with others
- Understand that writers can add to their drawings or approximated writings
- Actively participate in adding to or changing interactive/shared writing
- Understand that writers can create drawings or write like other writers and illustrators

Producing a Draft

- Talk about, draw, and approximate writing to produce a piece
- Draw and approximate writing about a continuous message on a simple topic

Rereading

- Share drawing and writing with others
- Talk about, approximate the reading of, or read a message or story to the teacher
- Look carefully at drawings to see if details should be added

A prekindergartener's story about visiting her grandma

Writing

❏ Behaviors and Understandings to Notice, Teach, and Support *(cont.)*

Adding Information
- Add details to drawings
- Add additional details in dictated or approximated writing to expand on a topic
- Add speech balloons to pictures to use dialogue

Deleting Information
- Delete or cover parts of drawings that do not fit

Reorganizing Information
- Understand that writers can change the way their writing is organized
- Give suggestions for moving sentences from one part to another to make the writing more interesting in group writing
- Give suggestions for adding words or sentences to provide more information in group writing
- Reorder drawings by cutting them apart and laying them out as pages

Changing Text
- Cross out to change a text
- Understand that writers can change text or drawings to make them clearer or more interesting to readers
- Participate in group decisions about changing text

Using Tools and Techniques
- Learn to use sticky notes to add information to drawings or writing
- Add pages to a book or booklet
- Cross out letters or words that are not needed

EDITING AND PROOFREADING

Understanding the Process
- Understand that writers try to make their writing and drawings interesting and informative
- Understand that making letters clearly and using space makes writing easier to read

Editing for Conventions
- Understand that the teacher is pointing out something in group writing that needs to be changed
- Notice as the teacher points out correct letter formation in group writing

Using Tools
- (Not applicable)

PUBLISHING
- Create illustrations for a piece of group writing (shared/interactive)
- Share completed writing and drawing by talking about it to the class

SKETCHING AND DRAWING
- Use drawing as a way to plan for writing
- Use drawing and other art media to represent ideas and information
- Add or remove details to drawings to revise

VIEWING SELF AS A WRITER
- Take on approximated writing independently
- Demonstrate confidence in attempts at drawing and writing
- Have ideas in mind to tell, write, draw about
- Select favorite drawings and writings from a collection
- Produce a quantity of drawing and approximated writing within the time available (for example, one per day)
- Keep working independently rather than waiting for the teacher to help
- Make attempts to solve problems
- Try out techniques that they see others using

I got ice cream and it fell down

Then we went home

Oral, Visual, and Technological Communication

❏ **Selecting Goals:** *Behaviors and Understandings to Notice, Teach, and Support*

LISTENING AND SPEAKING

LISTENING AND UNDERSTANDING

- Listen with attention to texts that are read aloud
- Listen with attention and understanding to simple and clear directions
- Remember and follow directions that may have more than more than two steps
- Look at the person who is talking
- Listen actively to others as they read or talk
- Learn new words related to topics of inquiry in the classroom
- Show interest in words
- Show interest in listening to and talking about stories, poems, or informational texts
- Compare personal knowledge and experiences with what is heard
- Act out sentences in rhymes or stories

SOCIAL INTERACTION

- Speak in an audible voice
- Speak at appropriate volume for indoors
- Adjust volume as appropriate for different contexts
- Use polite terms such as *please* and *thank you*
- Engage in conversation during imaginary play
- Enter a conversation appropriately
- Sustain a conversation with others (teacher, family, peers)
- Engage in the turn-taking of conversation
- Engage in dramatic play
- Act out stories either with or without props

EXTENDED DISCUSSION

- Understand and use words related to familiar common experiences and topics (pets, body parts, food, clothes, transportation, classroom objects, home, family, and neighborhood)
- Follow the topic and add to the discussion
- Respond to and build on the statements of others
- Form clear questions to get information
- Participate actively in whole-class discussion or with a partner or in a small group
- Use some specific vocabulary (book, page, title, cover, author, illustrator)
- Learn new words related to topics of inquiry in the classroom
- Show interest in words and word play
- Act out stories with or without props
- Engage in dramatic play

CONTENT

- Begin to verbalize reasons for problems, events, and actions
- Begin to discuss the concept of cause and effect
- Express opinions and explain reasoning (*because . . .*)
- Predict future events in a story
- Talk about what is already known about a topic
- Describe people and places in a story
- Report what is known or learned about an informational text
- Share knowledge of story structure by describing story parts or elements such as characters
- Talk about how people, places, or events are alike and different
- Talk about one's own feelings and those of others
- Recognize that others have feelings different from one's own
- Ask questions (demonstrate curiosity)

Oral, Visual, and Technological Communication

❏ **Selecting Goals:** *Behaviors and Understandings to Notice, Teach, and Support (cont.)*

PRESENTATION

VOICE

- Speak about a topic with enthusiasm
- Talk smoothly with little hesitation
- Tell stories in an interesting way
- Talk with confidence

CONVENTIONS

- Speak at appropriate volume to be heard, but not too loud
- Look at the audience (or other person) while talking
- Speak at an appropriate rate to be understood
- Enunciate words clearly

ORGANIZATION

- Have a topic or response in mind before starting to speak
- Tell personal experiences in a logical sequence
- Show awareness of the audience when speaking
- Present information or ideas in an understandable way
- Speak to one topic and stay on topic

WORD CHOICE

- Understand and use words related to familiar experiences and topics such as pets, body parts, food, clothes, transportation, classroom objects, home and family, neighborhood
- Use some language from stories when retelling them
- Use some words that describe (adjectives and adverbs)

IDEAS AND CONTENT

- Recite songs and short poems
- Tell stories from personal experiences
- Retell stories from texts

TECHNOLOGY

COMPUTER LITERACY

- Recognize the computer as a source of information and entertainment
- Find buttons and icons on the computer screen to use simple programs
- Know how to use the mouse and basic keyboard functions
- Begin to understand the computer as a way to communicate

ONLINE READING AND INFORMATION LITERACY

- Search for information with adult help
- Use simple websites with adult help

Phonics, Spelling, and Word Study

❏ **Selecting Goals:** *Behaviors and Understandings to Notice, Teach, and Support*

EARLY LITERACY CONCEPTS

- Notice and talk about photographs, pictures, drawings, and familiar written words (names, *Mom*)
- Note print in the environment and look for its meaning
- Understand that print conveys meaning
- Distinguish between print and pictures
- Use print in a variety of ways–labels, signs, stories, books
- Follow the print during shared reading (as cued by the pointer)
- Read a known text in unison with others
- Hold and handle books correctly (turning pages front to back, etc.)
- Understand the variety of purposes of print in reading
- Understand that a book has a title, author, and illustrator
- Understand that books are sources of information
- Recognize one's name
- Use letters in one's name to represent it or communicate other messages
- Understand the concept of *word*
- Use left-to-right directionality and return to the left in shared reading of print and in group writing
- Understand the concept of *first* and *last* in written language

PHONOLOGICAL AWARENESS

WORDS

- Hear word boundaries
- Understand that words are made up of sounds

RHYMING WORDS

- Hear and say rhyming words
- Hear and connect rhyming words

SYLLABLES

- Clap the syllables of words with teacher help

ONSETS AND RIMES

- Say the onsets and rimes of words with teacher help

PHONEMES [PA]

- Be aware that words have sounds in them
- Play with the sounds of language
- Enjoy stories and poems that illustrate play with the sounds of language
- Recognize words that stand for sounds (*bang, pop*)

LETTER KNOWLEDGE

IDENTIFYING LETTERS

- Notice that letters have different shapes
- Understand the concept of a letter
- Match letters that are alike by looking at their shapes
- Connect particular letters to their lives (names, names of family, environmental print)
- Distinguish letter forms by noticing particular parts (sticks, tails, dots, slants, circles, curves, tunnels, crosses)
- Categorize and connect letters by features (sticks, tails, dots, slants, circles, curves, tunnels, crosses)
- Produce some letter names

RECOGNIZING LETTERS IN WORDS AND SENTENCES

- Understand that words are made up of letters
- Locate some known letters in print

FORMING LETTERS

- Use writing tools
- Use drawings to represent meaning
- Produce approximated writing
- Use approximated writing functionally (labels, lists, signs, names)
- Begin to use efficient and consistent motions to form letters

Phonics, Spelling, and Word Study

❏ Selecting Goals: *Behaviors and Understandings to Notice, Teach, and Support (cont.)*

LETTER/SOUND RELATIONSHIPS

- Understand that there is a relationship between letters and the sounds in words
- Say words slowly as part of shared/interactive writing

WORD MEANING

- Notice and use new and interesting words heard in texts read aloud and in conversation
- Notice new and interesting words in poems and other shared reading texts
- Use new words in conversation, in writing dictated to the teacher, and in shared/interactive writing
- Know the meaning of some concept words—simple colors, number words, shapes, days of the week, months of the year, holidays
- Learn the meaning of some words related to inquiry in the classroom

SPELLING PATTERNS

- Recognize that there are patterns in words that you can hear and say

HIGH-FREQUENCY WORDS

- Understand that you look at the letters in a word to read it
- Recognize own name
- Recognize a few high-frequency words after experience in shared reading and interactive writing

WORD STRUCTURE

SYLLABLES

- Understand that words can have more than one part that you can hear
- Clap words to show awareness of syllables

WORD-SOLVING ACTIONS

- Recognize and locate own name
- Recognize and locate a few high-frequency words
- Make connections between own name and other words (same letters)
- Use own name and other known words as a resource in approximated writing

KINDERGARTEN

Interactive Read-Aloud and Literature Discussion

❑ **Selecting Texts:** *Characteristics of Texts for Reading Aloud and Discussion*

GENRES/FORMS

Genres
- Short poems, nursery rhymes, and songs
- Poems
- Traditional folktales
- Animal fantasy
- Memoir
- Realistic fiction
- Factual texts (ABC books, label books, concept books, counting books, simple informational books)

Forms
- Oral stories
- Picture books
- Wordless picture books
- Informational picture books

TEXT STRUCTURE

- Informational texts that present a clear and simple sequence
- Informational texts with simple description on each page—sometimes repeating patterns
- Many traditional tales with particular structures (cumulative tales, circular stories, and use of "three's")
- Simple structure with beginning, series of episodes, and an ending
- Many books with repetition of episodes and refrains
- Stories with repeating patterns

CONTENT

- Language and word play (rhymes, nonsense, alliteration, alphabet)
- Everyday events (eating, playing, shopping)
- Familiar topics (animals, pets, families, food, plants, school, friends, growing, senses, neighborhood, weather and seasons, health)
- A few topics beyond children's immediate experiences (such as the farm)
- Themes and content that reflect a full range of cultures

THEMES AND IDEAS

- Humor that is easy to grasp (silly characters, situations, games)
- Obvious themes (sharing, being friends, belonging, working, growing, responsibility, behavior)

LANGUAGE AND LITERARY FEATURES

- Simple plots with clear problems and resolutions
- Memorable characters
- Characters that change for reasons that are clear within the text (learn lessons from mistakes)
- Memorable characters, many in folktales, that have predictable characteristics (sly foxes)
- Stories with multiple characters
- Some figurative language that is easy to understand
- Rhyme, rhythm, repetition
- Simple dialogue easily attributed to characters
- Memorable language or dialogue that is repeated

SENTENCE COMPLEXITY

- Sentences that are more complex than children would use in oral conversation
- Sentences that are complex but also easy for children to follow
- A few sentences that are long and many embedded phrases and clauses

VOCABULARY

- Some words of high interest that will be memorable to children
- Many words that are in children's speaking vocabulary
- A few new content words related to concepts that are easy to explain

ILLUSTRATIONS

- Large, clear colorful illustrations in a variety of medias
- Very simple graphics (maps, labeled drawings)
- Illustrations that offer high support for comprehension

BOOK AND PRINT FEATURES

- Some books with large print for children to see during read-aloud
- Some special features in the illustrations and print that engage interest and make texts interactive (pop-up books, lift-the-flap books, see-through holes, sound effects)
- Title, author, and illustrator on cover and title page

Interactive Read-Aloud and Literature Discussion

❑ **Selecting Goals:** *Behaviors and Understandings to Notice, Teach, and Support*

Thinking *Within* the Text

- Acquire understanding of new words from context
- Use new words in discussion of a text
- Acquire new vocabulary from listening and use in discussion
- Follow the events of a plot and remember them after reading
- Talk about interesting information in a text or illustrations
- Pick up important information and remember it to use in discussion
- Tell a summary of the text after reading
- Understand the meaning of the words during reading
- Talk about characters, settings, problems, and events in a story
- Notice and ask questions when meaning is lost or understanding is interrupted
- Notice and derive information from pictures
- Mimic the teacher's intonation and stress when joining in on refrains or repetitive text
- Notice and respond to stress and tone of voice while listening and afterward

Thinking *Beyond* the Text

- Bring background knowledge to understanding characters and their problems
- Bring background knowledge to understanding the content of a text
- Predict what will happen next
- Make connections between texts and their own life experiences
- Make connections between new texts and those heard before
- Make predictions about what a character is likely to do
- Infer characters' intentions or feelings
- Interpret the illustrations
- Use details from illustrations to support points made in discussion
- Recognize interesting new information and add it to their understandings
- Give reasons to support thinking

Thinking *About* the Text

- Notice and understand texts that are based on established sequences such as numbers, days of the week, months, seasons
- Recognize and identify some aspects of text structure, such as beginning and ending
- Understand that an author wrote the book
- Understand that an artist illustrated the book
- Notice words that the writer has used to make the story or content interesting
- Recognize some authors by the style of their illustrations, their topics, or the characters they use
- Have some favorite writers or illustrators
- Have opinions about texts and state the basis for opinions (tell why)
- Notice how texts are different from each other (such as fiction versus nonfiction)
- Check information in the text against own experiences
- Compare different versions of the same story, rhyme, or traditional tale
- Use specific vocabulary to talk about texts: *author, illustrator, cover, wordless picture book, informational book, picture book, character, problem*

Shared and Performance Reading

❑ **Selecting Texts:** *Characteristics of Texts for Sharing and Performing*

GENRES/FORMS

Genres
- Simple fantasy, most with talking animals
- Factual texts—ABC books, label books, concept books, counting books, very simple informational books
- Short poems, nursery rhymes, and songs
- Traditional folktales
- Memoir
- Realistic fiction

Forms
- Texts produced through interactive writing—lists, letters, stories, poems, description
- Enlarged poems
- Enlarged picture books

TEXT STRUCTURE
- Stories with simple and predictable repeating patterns
- Many books with repetition of episodes and refrains
- Informational texts with simple description on each page—sometimes repeating patterns
- Informational texts that present a clear and simple sequence
- Simple structure with beginning, series of episodes, and an ending
- Many traditional tales with particular structures (cumulative tales, circular stories, use of "three's")

CONTENT
- Nonsensical situations and characters
- Language and word play—rhymes, alliteration, alphabet
- Familiar topics—animals, pets, families, food, plants, school, friends, growing, senses, neighborhood, weather and seasons, health
- A few topics beyond children's immediate experience; for example, farm, fire station, trains

THEMES AND IDEAS
- Obvious humor—silly situations, and language play
- Familiar themes such as work, solving problems, playing tricks, friends, family

LANGUAGE AND LITERARY FEATURES
- Some figurative language that is easy to understand
- Simple but complete stories with beginning, middle, end
- Many texts with rhyme and rhythm
- Some memorable characters
- Simple dialogue easily attributed to characters
- Characters' actions that have clear consequences (rewarding good and punishing naughtiness)
- Predictable plots and stories

SENTENCE COMPLEXITY
- Sentences that are more complex than children would use in oral conversation (consider ELL in this)
- Sentences that are easy for children to follow—no tricky sentence structures that children find hard to repeat (consider ELL children in this)

VOCABULARY
- A few new content words related to concepts children are learning that are easy to explain
- Many words that are in children's speaking vocabulary
- Some words of high interest that will be memorable to children

WORDS
- Simple plurals using –s or –es
- Some words with endings, for example, -ed, -ing
- Some complex plurals that are in children's oral vocabulary such as *children, sheep*
- Words that have the same rime (ending part such as –it, bit, sit) at the end
- Many high-frequency words that will help children to build a beginning repertoire and over time may become visual signposts
- Alliterative sequences

ILLUSTRATIONS
- Some poems and pieces from interactive writing that have no pictures
- Illustrations that offer high support for comprehending
- Large, clear, colorful illustrations in a variety of media

BOOK AND PRINT FEATURES
- All texts on charts or in big books
- Enlarged print that the entire group of children can see
- Some words in bold to assist in stress
- From 1 or 2 lines of print per page at the beginning of the year to about 6 lines at the end of the year
- Simple punctuation (period, comma, question mark, exclamation mark, quotation marks)
- Title, author, and illustrator on cover and title page for books
- Ample space between words and between lines
- Layout that supports phrasing by presenting word groups
- Page numbers

Shared and Performance Reading

❑ **Selecting Goals:** *Behaviors and Understandings to Notice, Teach, and Support*

Thinking *Within* the Text

- Follow the teacher's pointer in a coordinated way while reading
- Acquire understanding of new words from context
- Understand the meaning of the words during reading
- Recognize a few high-frequency words as signposts in continuous texts
- Remember and use repeating language patterns when rereading
- Notice and use spaces to define word boundaries
- Track print left to right, return to left, and top to bottom with the assistance of the teacher's pointer
- Read the punctuation (period, question mark, exclamation point)
- Notice and ask questions when meaning is lost or understanding is interrupted
- Notice information in pictures
- Talk about characters, problems, and events in a story
- Remember and talk about interesting information in a text
- Follow the events of a story and remember them after reading in summary form
- Read along with others on familiar texts
- Mimic the teacher's expression
- Reflect meaning with the voice through pause, stress, and phrasing
- Recognize and use simple punctuation (reflecting it in the voice while reading)
- Discuss how to read a text with the teacher and other children

Thinking *Beyond* the Text

- Make predictions as to what will happen next
- Show interpretation of character's intentions or feelings in the voice while reading (infer)
- Show anticipation in the voice when reading
- Express personal connections through discussion
- Make connections between texts that they have read or heard before

- Use background knowledge and experience to contribute to text interpretation
- Use details from illustrations to support points made in discussion

Thinking *About* the Text

- Recognize and identify some aspects of text structure, such as beginning and ending
- Understand that a person wrote the book
- Understand that a person illustrated the book
- Have opinions about texts
- Notice how the writer has used language or words to make a text interesting or funny
- Recognize when texts are realistic, fantasy, or true informational texts
- Compare different versions of the same story, rhyme, or traditional tale
- Notice and understand texts that are based on established sequences such as numbers, days of the week, months, seasons
- Notice how layout of pictures or print affects the way you read it—for example, larger font or bold
- Check information in the text against their own experiences

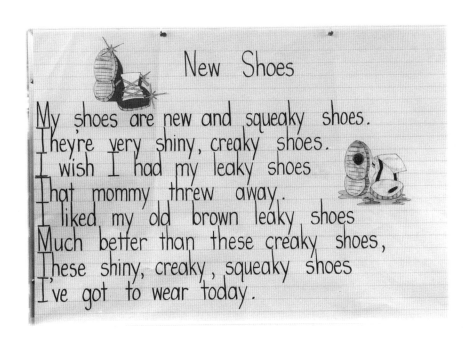

New Shoes

My shoes are new and squeaky shoes.
They're very shiny, creaky shoes.
I wish I had my leaky shoes
That mommy threw away.
I liked my old brown leaky shoes
Much better than these creaky shoes,
These shiny, creaky, squeaky shoes
I've got to wear today.

Writing About Reading

❑ **Selecting Genres and Forms:** *Genres and forms for writing about reading are demonstrated through interactive, shared, or modeled writing, often with close attention to mentor texts. Children learn how to respond to reading in different forms and for a variety of purposes and audiences. After they learn about the forms in a supported experience, they use them independently as they respond to books they read. At the beginning of kindergarten, children's writing about reading may be mostly drawings, letter-like forms, and a few known words; but by the end of the year they will be producing many readable messages.*

FUNCTIONAL WRITING

- Sketches or drawings that reflect content of a text
- Selected interesting words from a text (written or illustrated)
- Short sentences responding to a text (for example, stating a prediction, an opinion, or an interesting aspect of the text)
- Lists to support memory (characters, events in a story)
- Notes to other classes or individuals in the school (about text or based on them)
- Labels for photographs or any kind of drawing
- Directions that show a simple sequence of actions based on a text

NARRATIVE WRITING

- Drawings showing the sequence of events in a text (sometimes with speech bubbles to show dialogue)
- Simple statements summarizing a text

- Simple statements telling the sequence of events
- Innovations on known texts (for example, new endings or similar plots with different characters) showing the sequence of events in a text (sometimes with speech bubbles to show dialogue)

INFORMATIONAL WRITING

- List of facts from a text
- Short sentences and/or drawings reporting some interesting information from a text
- A few simple sentences with information about an author or illustrator

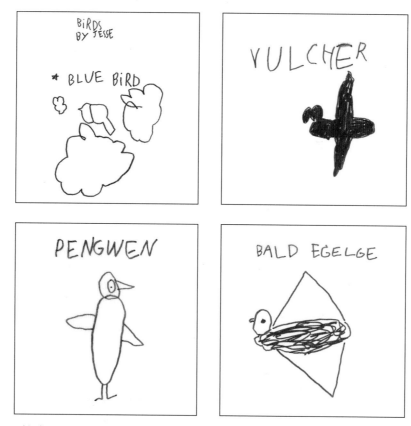

A kindergartener writes about his study of birds

Writing About Reading

❏ **Selecting Goals:** *Behaviors and Understandings to Notice, Teach, and Support*

Thinking *Within* the Text

- Record interesting information about events or characters from a text
- Illustrate a text by drawing (for example, characters or events)
- Write or draw about interesting facts
- Notice and sometimes use new words from a text
- Reread to remember what has been written
- Notice and use some details from texts in group or independent writing
- Compose notes, lists, letters, or statements based on a text in a group or independently
- Tell important information from writing
- Reread to assure meaningfulness, language structure, and appropriate word use
- Use the names of authors and illustrators

Thinking *About* the Text

- Create texts that have some of the characteristics of published texts (cover, title, author, illustrator, illustrations, beginning, ending, events in a sequence, about the author page)
- Sometimes borrow the style or some words or expressions from a writer
- Express opinions about facts or information learned
- Recognize and use some aspects of text structure (for example, beginning and ending or a pattern)
- Differentiate between stories and informational texts
- Notice and sometimes use interesting language from a text

Thinking *Beyond* the Text

- Predict what will happen next in a text or what a character will do
- Express opinions about stories or poems
- Express opinions about characters or about their feelings or motives
- Infer how a character feels
- Reflect what a character is really like
- Compose innovations on very familiar texts
- Write or draw about something in the reader's own life when prompted by a text

Writing

❑ **Selecting Purpose and Genre:** *At the beginning of the year, most writing for kindergarteners consists of shared or interactive writing and their own approximated attempts. Quickly they learn to use everything they know—their names, a few known words, and known letters—to generate their own pieces of writing. They use drawing extensively to express their ideas and support their thinking. By the end of the year, we can observe them using space to define words, writing left to right and top to bottom on pages, matching print with drawings in a meaningful way, spelling many words conventionally, and composing messages and stories. Conversation with teachers and peers supports the process.*

NARRATIVE: *(To tell a story)*

MEMOIR *(personal narrative, autobiography)*

Understanding the Genre

- Understand how to craft personal narratives and memoirs from mentor texts
- Understand that a story from your life is usually written in first person (using I)
- Understand that writers tell stories from their own lives
- Understand that the writer can look back or think about the memory or experience and share thoughts and feelings about it
- Understand that a story should be one that is important to the writer

Writing in the Genre

- Think of topics, events, or experiences from own life that are interesting to write about
- Write an engaging beginning and a satisfying ending to stories
- Understand that a story can be a "small moment" (description of a brief but memorable experience)
- Provide some descriptive details to make the story more interesting
- Use dialogue as appropriate to add to the meaning of the story
- Use simple words that show the passage of time (then, after)
- Explain one's thoughts and feelings about an experience or event
- Develop voice as a writer through telling own stories or memories from own life
- Usually write in first person to achieve a strong voice
- Tell a story across several pages in order to develop the story or idea
- Tell events in order that they occurred in personal narratives

INFORMATIONAL: *(To explain or give facts about a topic)*

LITERARY NONFICTION

Understanding the Genre

- Understand how to write literary nonfiction from mentor texts
- Understand literary nonfiction as writing that engages and entertains readers but teaches them about a topic

Writing in the Genre

- Write books or short pieces that are enjoyable to read and at the same time give information to readers about a topic
- Use features (for example, page numbers, title, labeled pictures, table of contents, or others) to guide the reader

- Think about the audience when writing on a topic
- Select interesting information to include in a piece of writing

POETIC: *(To express feelings, sensory images, ideas, or stories)*

POETRY *(free verse, rhyme)*

Understanding the Genre

- Understand that a writer can use familiar poems as mentor texts
- Understand poetry as a way to communicate in sensory images about everyday life
- Understand poetry as a unique way to communicate about and describe thoughts and feelings
- Understand the way print and space work in poems and use this knowledge when writing poems
- Understand that poems can be created from other kinds of text
- Notice specific words when reading poetry
- Understand that there are different kinds of poems
- Understand that poems do not have to rhyme
- Notice language that "sounds like" a poem (rhythmic, descriptive, or sensory language)

Writing in the Genre

- Closely observe the world (animals, objects, people) to get ideas for poems
- Approximate the use of line breaks and white space when writing poems
- Place words on the page to look like a poem
- Write poetic like language to convey feelings or images
- Use language to describe how something looks, smells, tastes, feels, or sounds

Writing

❑ **Selecting Purpose and Genre** *(cont.)*

FUNCTIONAL: *(To perform a practical task)*

LABELS

Understanding the Genre
- Understand that a writer or illustrator can add labels to help readers
- Understand that labels can add important information

Writing in the Genre
- Write labels for objects in the classroom
- Add words to pictures
- Create labels for illustrations that accompany written pieces
- Make label books as one type of book

FRIENDLY LETTERS *(notes, cards, invitations, email)*

Understanding the Genre
- Understand how to learn about writing notes, cards, and invitations by noticing the characteristics of examples
- Understand that the receiver and sender must be clearly shown
- Understand notes, cards, invitations, and email as written communication among people
- Understand that invitations must include specific information
- Understand that the form of written communication is related to the purpose

Writing in the Genre
- Write notes, cards, invitations, and emails to others
- Write to a known audience or a specific reader
- Write with the specific purpose in mind
- Include important information in the communication
- Write with a friendly tone (conversational language)

LISTS AND PROCEDURES *(how-to)*

Understanding the Genre
- Understand that the form of a list is usually one item under another and it may be numbered
- Understand that captions can be written under pictures to give readers more information
- Understand procedural writing (how-to) as a list of sequential directions for how to do something with lists of what is needed
- Understand that pictures can accompany the writing to help readers understand the information
- Understand lists are a functional way to organize information

Writing in the Genre
- Use lists to plan activities or support memory
- Place items in the list that are appropriate for its purpose or category
- Make lists in the appropriate form with one item under another
- Use drawing in the process of drafting, revising, or publishing procedural writing
- Write captions under pictures

WRITING ABOUT READING (ALL GENRES)

(See the Writing About Reading continuum, pages 76–77.)

Writing

❏ **Selecting Goals:** *Behaviors and Understandings to Notice, Teach, and Support*

CRAFT

ORGANIZATION

Text Structure

- Create a picture book as one form of writing
- Include facts and details in informational writing
- Put together the related details on a topic in a text
- Put the facts or information in order
- Write stories that have a beginning, a series of things happening, and an ending
- Write a title and the author's name on the cover of a story or book
- Write an author page at the beginning or end of a book that gives information about the author (picture, writing)
- Dedicate a story to someone and write dedication on the cover, on the title page or copyright page, or on a page of its own
- Create a picture book as a form of writing

Beginnings, Endings, Titles

- Use a variety of beginnings through drawing and/or writing to engage the reader
- Use endings that are interesting or leave the reader satisfied
- Select an appropriate title for a poem, story, or informational book

Presentation of Ideas

- Tell about experiences or topics the way one would talk about them to others
- Tell one part, idea, or group of ideas on each page of a book
- Present ideas in logical sequence
- Introduce ideas followed by supportive details and examples
- Use time appropriately as an organizing tool

IDEA DEVELOPMENT

- Communicate clearly the main points intended for readers to understand
- Provide supportive description or details to explain the important ideas

LANGUAGE USE

- Understand that the writer is using language to communicate meaning
- Show evidence of using language from books that have been read aloud

WORD CHOICE

- Learn new words or phrases from reading and try them out in writing
- Use vocabulary appropriate for the topic

VOICE

- Write with a unique perspective
- Write in the way one would speak about an experience, event, or topic
- State information in a unique or surprising way
- Share one's thoughts and feelings about a topic
- Write about what is known and remembered

CONVENTIONS

TEXT LAYOUT

- Use spaces between words to help readers understand the writing
- Place words in lines, starting left to right, top to bottom
- Place titles and headings in the appropriate place on a page
- Understand that layout of print and illustrations are important in conveying the meaning of a text
- Understand that the print and pictures can be placed in a variety of places on the page within a book

GRAMMAR

Sentence Structure

- Use conventional sentence structure (noun + verb)

Parts of Speech

- Use noun and verb agreement (*I can*)
- Use prepositional phrases (*to the bus, on the bus*)
- Use modifiers (*red dress; ran fast*)

Tense

- Write in past tense (*I went home yesterday.*)
- Write in present tense (*I like . . .*)
- Write in future tense (*I'm going to go . . .*)

Writing

❏ **Selecting Goals:** *Behaviors and Understandings to Notice, Teach, and Support (cont.)*

CAPITALIZATION

- Demonstrate knowledge of the use of upper-and lowercase letters of the alphabet
- Use capital letters in the beginning position in a few familiar, known proper nouns
- Show awareness of the first place position of capital letters in words
- Use a capital letter for the first word of a sentence
- Capitalize *I*
- Use uppercase letters in titles

PUNCTUATION

- Notice the use of punctuation marks in books and try them out in own writing
- Use periods, exclamation points, and question marks as ending marks
- Read one's writing aloud and think where punctuation would go

SPELLING

- Spell twenty-five or more high-frequency words conventionally
- Use a few simple phonogram patterns to generate words (cat, fat)
- Attempt unknown words through sound analysis
- Say words slowly to hear a sound and write a letter that represents it
- Write some words with consonant letters appropriate for sounds in words (beginning and ending)
- Write a letter for easy-to-hear vowel sounds
- Understand that letters represent sounds
- Construct phonetic spellings that are mostly readable
- Use conventional symbols to write words
- Use simple resources to check spelling (word walls)

HANDWRITING/WORD-PROCESSING

- Write letters in groups to form words
- Leave appropriate space between words
- Hold pencil or pen with satisfactory grip
- Write left to right in lines
- Return to the left margin to start a new line
- Use a preferred hand consistently for writing
- Write letters and words that can be easily read
- Form upper-and lowercase letters efficiently in manuscript print
- Form upper-and lowercase letters proportionately in manuscript print
- Access and use simple programs on the computer (easy word-processing, games)
- Locate letter keys on a computer keyboard to type simple messages

WRITING PROCESS

REHEARSING/PLANNING

Purpose

- Write for a specific purpose
- Think about the purpose for writing each text
- Think about how the purpose affects the kind of writing
- Choose type of text to fit the purpose (for example, poem, factual book, alphabet book, photo book, label book, story with pictures)
- Choose paper to match desired organization and the genre
- Write to inform or entertain readers
- Write name and date on writing
- Tell whether a piece of writing is a story or an informational text

Audience

- Think about the people who will read the writing and what they will want to know
- Include information that the readers will need to understand the text

Oral Language

- Generate and expand ideas through talk with peers and teacher
- Look for ideas and topics in personal experiences, shared through talk
- Use storytelling to generate and rehearse language (that may be written later)
- Tell stories in chronological order
- Retell stories in chronological order

Gathering Seeds/Resources/Experimenting with Writing

- Make lists or ideas for writing
- Understand that writers gather information for their writing
- Record information in words or drawings
- Use drawings to share or remember thinking

Content, Topic, Theme

- Observe carefully (objects, animals, people, places, actions) before writing about them
- Select own topics for informational writing
- Select information or facts that will support the topic
- Select topics for story or poem writing

Inquiry/Research

- Use drawings to tell about a topic or tell a story
- Ask questions and gather information on a topic
- Remember important information about a topic in order to write about it
- Participate actively in experiences and remember details that contribute to writing and drawing
- Remember important labels for drawings

Writing

❑ **Selecting Goals:** *Behaviors and Understandings to Notice, Teach, and Support (cont.)*

DRAFTING/REVISING

Understanding the Process
- Understand the role of the writing conference in helping writers
- Understand that writers can get help from other writers
- Understand that writers can change writing in response to peer or teacher feedback
- Understand that writers can learn how to write from other writers

Producing a Draft
- Use words and drawings to compose and revise writing
- Write a continuous message on a simple topic

Rereading
- Reread writing each day (and during writing on the same day) before continuing to write
- Reread stories to be sure the meaning is clear
- Reread the text to be sure there are no missing words or information
- Review drawings to revise by adding (or deleting) information

Adding Information
- Add words, phrases, or sentences to make the writing more interesting or exciting for readers
- Add words, phrases, or sentences to provide more information to readers
- Add dialogue to provide information or provide narration (in quotes or speech balloons)
- Add details to drawings to give more information to the reader

Deleting Information
- Delete words or sentences that do not make sense
- Delete pages when information is not needed

Reorganizing Information
- Move sentences from one part to another to make the sequence better
- Reorder writing by cutting apart or laying out pages
- Reorder drawings by cutting apart or laying out pages
- Reorder pages by laying them out and reassembling them

Changing Text
- Add information to make writing or drawings clear

Using Tools and Techniques
- Add letters, words, phrases, or sentences using a caret or sticky note
- Add words, phrases, or sentences using spider legs or an extra piece of paper glued, taped, or stapled to the piece
- Add pages to a book or booklet
- Remove pages from a book or booklet
- Cross out words or sentences with pencil or marker

A kindergartener's memoir about a dog he loves

Writing

❏ **Selecting Goals:** *Behaviors and Understandings to Notice, Teach, and Support (cont.)*

EDITING AND PROOFREADING

Understanding the Process
- Understand that the writer shows respect to the reader by applying what is known to correct errors
- Understand that the better the spelling and space between words, the easier it is for the reader to read it

Editing for Conventions
- Check and correct letter formation or orientation
- Edit for spelling errors by making another attempt
- Edit for spelling errors by circling words that do not look right and trying to spell them another way
- Recognize that the teacher may be the final editor who will make the edits the writer has not yet learned how to do prior to publishing

Using Tools
- Use beginning reference tools (for example, word walls or personal word collections or dictionaries)

Publishing
- Create illustrations for pieces of writing
- Share writing by reading it to the class
- Put several stories or poems together
- Select a poem, story, or informational book to publish
- Use labels and captions on drawings that are displayed

SKETCHING AND DRAWING
- Use sketches and drawing to plan, draft, revise, and publish writing
- Create drawings that are related to the written text and increase readers' understanding and enjoyment
- Use drawings to represent people, places, things, and ideas
- Add or remove details to drawings to revise

VIEWING SELF AS A WRITER
- Take on writing independently
- Take risks as a writer
- View self as writer
- Have a list of topics in mind to write about
- Think about what to work on next as a writer
- Select best pieces of writing from own collection
- Self-evaluate own writing and talk about what is good about it and what techniques were used
- Produce a quantity of writing within the time available (for example, one or two pages per day)
- Keep working independently rather than waiting for teacher instructions
- Make attempts to solve own problems
- Try out techniques other writers used

Oral, Visual, and Technological Communication

❑ **Selecting Goals:** *Behaviors and Understandings to Notice, Teach, and Support*

LISTENING AND SPEAKING

LISTENING AND UNDERSTANDING

- Listen with attention and understanding to directions
- Demonstrate the ability to remember and follow simple directions
- Listen actively to others read or talk about their writing and give feedback
- Show interest in listening to and talking about stories, poems, or informational texts
- Listen with attention and understanding to oral reading of stories, poems, and informational texts
- Compare personal knowledge with what is heard

SOCIAL INTERACTION

- Engage in imaginary play
- Enter into dramatic dialogue in play or role play contexts
- Use polite conversational conventions (please, thank you, greetings)
- Speak at an appropriate volume—not too loud but loud enough to be heard and understood by others
- Adjust volume as appropriate for different contexts
- Speak clearly enough to be understood by others in conversation
- Enter a conversation appropriately
- Engage in the turn-taking of conversation
- Sustain a conversation with a variety of audiences, including peers, teacher, and family

EXTENDED DISCUSSION

- Follow the topic and add to the discussion
- Build on the statements of others
- Engage actively in routines (for example, turn and talk)
- Form clear questions to gain information
- Participate actively in whole-class discussion or with peers as partners, or in a small group
- Use grade level-appropriate specific vocabulary when talking about texts (*title, author*)

CONTENT

- Begin to verbalize reasons for problems, events, and actions
- Explain cause-and-effect relationships
- Express opinions and explain reasoning (*because . . .*)
- Predict future events in a story
- Offer solutions and explanations for story problems
- Explain and describe people, events, places, and objects
- Describe similarities and differences among people, places, events, and objects
- Report interesting information from background experience or reading
- Ask many questions, demonstrating curiosity
- Initiate and join in on songs, rhymes, and chants
- Share knowledge of story structure by describing setting, characters, events, or ending
- Show interest in the meaning of words
- Express and reflect on feelings of self and others

PRESENTATION

VOICE

- Speak about a topic with enthusiasm
- Talk with confidence
- Tell stories in an interesting way

CONVENTIONS

- Speak at appropriate volume to be heard
- Look at the audience while talking
- Speak at an appropriate rate to be understood by the audience
- Enunciate words clearly

ORGANIZATION

- Have the topic or story in mind before starting to speak
- Show knowledge of story structure
- Tell personal experiences in a logical sequence
- Have an audience in mind before starting to speak
- Have a clear purpose
- Present ideas and information in a logical sequence

WORD CHOICE

- Use language from stories when retelling them
- Use words that describe (adjectives and adverbs)

IDEAS AND CONTENT

- Recite short poems and songs
- Tell stories and retell familiar stories
- Tell personal experiences
- Make brief oral reports that demonstrate understanding of a simple, familiar topic

MEDIA

- Use props, images, or illustrations to extend the meaning of a presentation
- Perform plays and puppet shows that involve speaking as a character

Oral, Visual, and Technological Communication

❑ **Selecting Goals:** *Behaviors and Understandings to Notice, Teach, and Support (cont.)*

TECHNOLOGY

COMPUTER LITERACY

- Find buttons and icons on the computer screen to use simple programs that require interaction (e.g., math, literacy, drawing)
- Use mouse and keyboard effectively
- Use email for conversation

ONLINE READING AND INFORMATION LITERACY

- Search for and locate approved websites and use them for entertainment or to get information

Phonics, Spelling, and Word Study

❏ Selecting Goals: *Behaviors and Understandings to Notice, Teach, and Support*

EARLY LITERACY CONCEPTS

- Distinguish between print and pictures
- Understand the purpose of print in reading and writing
- Locate the first and last letters of words in continuous text
- Recognize one's name
- Understand that one says one word for one group of letters when you read
- Understand the concept of sentence (as a group of words with ending punctuation)
- Understand the concepts of letter and word (as a single character or group of characters)
- Understand the concepts of first and last in written language
- Use left-to-right directionality of print and return to left in reading and writing
- Use one's name to learn about words and make connections to words
- Use spaces between words when writing
- Match one spoken to one written word while reading and pointing

PHONOLOGICAL AWARENESS

- Segment sentences into words
- Blend two or three phonemes in words (*d-o-g, dog*)
- Segment words into phonemes (*b-a-t*)
- Manipulate phonemes (*mat-at, and-hand*)
- Connect words by the sounds (*sat, sun*)
- Hear and recognize word boundaries
- Hear and say beginning phonemes (sounds) in words (*run/race, mom/make*) and ending (*win/fun, get/sit*)
- Hear and say syllables (*to-ma-to, can-dy, um-brel-la*)
- Hear, say, connect, and generate rhyming words (*fly, high, buy, sky*)

LETTER KNOWLEDGE

- Categorize letters by features—by slant lines (*v, w, x*) and straight lines (*p, l, b, d*); by circles (*o, b, g, p*) and no circles (*k, x, w, r*); by tunnels (*n, h*); by tails (*y, p, g*); by no tails (*r, s*); by dots/no dots; by tall/ short; by consonants/vowels
- Distinguish letter forms
- Make connections between words by recognizing letters (*bat, big, ball*), letter clusters (feat, meat, heat), and letter sequences
- Recognize and produce the names of most upper-and lowercase letters
- Identify a word that begins with the sound of each letter
- Recognize consonants and vowels
- Recognize letters that are embedded in words and in continuous text
- Recognize uppercase and lowercase letters
- Understand alphabetical order
- Understand special uses of letters (capital letters, initials)
- Use efficient and consistent motions to form letters when writing

LETTER/SOUND RELATIONSHIPS

- Recognize and use beginning consonant sounds and the letters that represent them to read and write words
- Understand that there is a relationship between sounds and letters
- Recognize simple CVC words (*cat, sun*)
- Attempt to write words by writing one letter for each sound heard

SPELLING PATTERNS

- Recognize and use a few simple phonograms with a VC pattern (easiest): (*-ad, -ag, -an, -am, -at, -ed, -en, -et, -ig, -in, -it, -og, -op, -ot, -ut*)
- Recognize that words have letter patterns that are connected to sounds (phonograms and other letter patterns)
- Recognize and use the consonant-vowel-consonant (CVC) pattern (*cab, fad, map*)

HIGH-FREQUENCY WORDS

- Write a core of twenty to twenty-five high-frequency words (*a, am, an, and, at, can, come, do, go, he, I, in, is, it, like, me, my, no, see, so, the, to, up, we, you*)
- Read a core of twenty to twenty-five high-frequency words (*a, am, an, and, at, can, come, do, go, he, I, in, is, it, like, me, my, no, see, so, the, to, up, we, you*)

WORD MEANING

CONCEPT WORDS

- Recognize and use concept words (color names, number words, days of the week, months of the year)
- Recognize the parts of compound words and discuss their meaning when obvious
- Recognize and use simple compound words (*into, myself, itself, cannot, inside, maybe, nobody*)

Phonics, Spelling, and Word Study

❑ **Selecting Goals:** *Behaviors and Understandings to Notice, Teach, and Support (cont.)*

WORD STRUCTURE

SYLLABLES

- Understand that words can have one, two, or more syllables
- Understand that you can hear syllables and demonstrate by clapping (*horse, a-way, farm-er, morn-ing, bi-cy-cle, to-geth-er, ev-er-y*)

WORD-SOLVING ACTIONS

- Recognize and locate words (names)
- Make connections between names and other words
- Use own first and last names (and same names of others) to read and write words
- Use known words to help in spelling new words
- Recognize and spell known words quickly
- Use known words to monitor reading and spelling
- Use letters and relationships to sounds to read and write words

GRADE **1**

Interactive Read-Aloud and Literature Discussion

❏ **Selecting Texts:** *Characteristics of Texts for Reading Aloud and Discussion*

GENRES/FORMS

Genres
- Short poems, nursery rhymes, and songs
- Poems
- Traditional folktales
- Animal fantasy
- Realistic fiction
- Factual texts (ABC books, label books, concept books, counting books, simple informational books)
- Memoir

Forms
- Oral stories
- Picture books
- Wordless picture books
- Informational picture books

TEXT STRUCTURE
- Informational texts that present a clear and simple sequence
- Informational texts with simple description on each page—sometimes repeating patterns
- Factual texts with clearly defined categories
- Many traditional tales with particular structures and motifs (cumulative tales, circular stories, and use of "three's")
- Simple narrative structure with beginning, series of episodes, and an ending
- Many books with repetition of episodes and refrains
- Stories with repeating patterns

CONTENT
- Everyday events (eating, playing, seasons, weather, shopping, games)
- Familiar topics (animals, pets, families, food, plants, school, friends, growing, senses, neighborhood, weather and seasons, health)
- Content beyond most students' immediate experience (historic animals, zoo animals in nature, space, the environment—ocean and desert, nutrition)
- Themes and content that reflect a full range of cultures

THEMES AND IDEAS
- Humor that is easy to grasp (play with words)
- Obvious themes (sharing, friends, belonging, working, growing, family, responsibility, behavior)
- Some themes going beyond everyday events

LANGUAGE AND LITERARY FEATURES
- Simple plots with clear problems and resolutions
- Memorable characters in realistic stories or fantasy
- Characters that change for reasons that are clear within the text (learn lessons from mistakes)
- Characters, many in folktales, that have predictable traits (sly foxes)
- Stories with multiple characters
- Some figurative language that is easy to understand
- Simple dialogue easily attributed to speakers

SENTENCE COMPLEXITY
- Sentences that are more complex than children would use in oral conversation
- A few sentences that are long with embedded phrases and clauses

VOCABULARY
- Some words of high interest that will be memorable to children
- Many words that are in children's speaking vocabulary
- A few new content words related to concepts children are learning and that are easy to explain

ILLUSTRATIONS
- Large, clear, colorful illustrations in a variety of media
- Very simple graphics (maps, labeled drawings)
- Illustrations that offer high support for comprehension

BOOK AND PRINT FEATURES
- Some books with large print for children to see during read-aloud
- Some special features in the illustrations and print that engage interest and make texts interactive (popup books, lift-the-flap books, see-through holes, sound effects)
- Title, author, and illustrator on cover and title page

Interactive Read-Aloud and Literature Discussion

❏ **Selecting Goals:** *Behaviors and Understandings to Notice, Teach, and Support*

Thinking *Within* the Text

- Follow the events of a plot with multiple events
- Follow plots that have particular patterns, such as accumulation or a circular structure
- Pick up important information and remember it to use in discussion
- Tell a summary of the text after reading
- Talk about interesting and new information in a text
- Understand the problem in a story
- Understand when and why the problem is solved
- Recognize characters and report important details after reading
- Notice and ask questions when meaning is lost or understanding is interrupted
- Notice and derive information from pictures
- Understand the words while listening to a story or factual text
- Acquire new vocabulary from listening and use in discussion
- Derive meaning of new words from context
- Know what the story is about after hearing the beginning
- Provide specific examples and evidence from the text to support thinking
- Use details from illustrations to support points made in discussion
- Mimic the teacher's intonation and stress when joining in on refrains or repetitive text
- Notice and respond to stress and tone of voice while listening and afterward

Thinking *Beyond* the Text

- Bring background knowledge to understanding characters and their problems
- Bring background knowledge to understanding the content of a text
- Make connections between texts and their own life experiences
- Predict what will happen next
- Predict what will happen after the end
- Make predictions about what a character is likely to do
- Use evidence from the text to support predictions (*I think . . . because . . .*)
- Infer characters' intentions or feelings
- Interpret the illustrations
- Discuss specific examples from the text to support or justify the ideas they are expressing
- Make connections between familiar texts and discuss similarities and differences
- Develop new concepts and ideas from listening to and discussing texts

Thinking *About* the Text

- Notice and understand texts that are based on established sequences such as numbers, days of the week, months, seasons
- Recognize and identify some aspects of text structure, such as beginning, events in sequential order, and ending
- Understand that an author wrote the book
- Understand that an artist illustrated the book
- Recognize the names of some authors and illustrators and have favorites
- Notice similarities and differences among texts that are by the same author or are on the same topic
- Discuss the characteristics of the work of some authors and illustrators
- Notice words that the writer has used to make the story or content interesting
- Name some favorite authors or illustrators and state reasons for liking them
- Have opinions about texts and state the basis for opinions (tell why)
- Notice how texts are different from each other (such as fiction versus nonfiction)
- Understand fiction as stories that are not real and nonfiction as texts that provide real information
- Understand realistic fiction as stories that could be real and fantasy as stories that could not be real
- Compare different versions of the same story, rhyme, or traditional tale
- Use specific vocabulary to talk about texts: *author, illustrator, cover, wordless picture book, picture book, character, problem, solution, informational book, nonfiction, fiction*

Shared and Performance Reading

❑ **Selecting Texts:** *Characteristics of Texts for Sharing and Performing*

GENRES/FORMS

Genres
- Simple fantasy—many with talking animals
- Factual texts—ABC books, label books, concept books, counting books, very simple informational books
- Short poems, nursery rhymes, and songs
- Traditional folktales
- Memoir
- Realistic fiction

Forms
- Easy, brief plays and readers' theater scripts (toward the middle and end of the year)
- Texts produced through interactive writing—lists, letters, stories, poems, descriptions, story retellings, directions, informational reports
- Enlarged poems
- Individual poetry anthologies
- Enlarged picture books

TEXT STRUCTURE

- Many books with repetition of episodes and refrains
- Informational texts with simple description on each page—sometimes repeating patterns
- Informational texts that present a clear and simple sequence
- Simple structure with beginning, series of episodes, and an ending
- Many traditional tales with particular structures and motifs (cumulative tales, circular stories, use of "three's")

CONTENT

- Language and word play—rhymes, nonsense, alliteration, alphabet
- Familiar topics—animals, families, food, plants, school, transportation, community, health and nutrition, differences
- Topics and ideas beyond children's immediate experience—exotic or fanciful animals and people, historic animals, zoo animals in nature, space, environment (*ocean, desert*)
- Content that verifies as well as extends students' experiences
- Stories with repeating patterns that increase in complexity across the year
- Everyday events—eating, playing, seasons, weather, shopping, games

THEMES AND IDEAS

- Obvious humor—silly situations, and language play
- Familiar themes such as sharing, friends, belonging, growing, responsibility, behavior

LANGUAGE AND LITERARY FEATURES

- Some figurative language that is easy to understand
- Simple but complete stories with beginning, middle, end
- Many texts with rhyme and rhythm
- Some memorable characters
- Simple dialogue easily attributed to characters
- Characters' actions that have clear consequences (rewarding good and punishing naughtiness)
- Predictable plots and stories

SENTENCE COMPLEXITY

- A few sentences that are long with embedded phrases and clauses
- Sentences that are more complex than children would use in oral conversation (consider ELL in this)
- Sentences that are easy for children to follow—no tricky sentence structures that children find hard to repeat (consider ELL children in this)

VOCABULARY

- New content words related to concepts children are learning that are easy to explain
- Words that guide readers in interpretation of the text
- Many words that are in children's speaking vocabulary
- Some words of high interest that will be memorable to children

WORDS

- A full range of plurals in contexts that make them easy to understand and use language syntax
- Many multisyllable words with endings—*ed, -ing*
- Words that have the same rime (ending part such as *-ing, ring, sing; -ight, fight, might*) at the end; full range of complex rimes
- Many high-frequency words that will help children to build a beginning repertoire

ILLUSTRATIONS

- Some poems and pieces from interactive writing that have no pictures
- Large, clear, colorful illustrations in a variety of media
- Illustrations that offer high support for comprehending

BOOK AND PRINT FEATURES

- Most texts on charts or in big books
- Enlarged print that the entire group of children can see
- Some words in bold to assist in using appropriate word stress
- From 2 to lines of print per page at the beginning of the year to about 10–12 lines at the end of the year
- Simple punctuation (period, comma, question mark, exclamation mark, quotation marks)
- Title at the top of poems and other pieces
- Some individual copies of plays or scripts
- Ample space between words and between lines
- Layout that supports phrasing by presenting word groups
- Variation in layout across a text
- Parts of a letter (date, salutation, body, closing, P.S.)

Shared and Performance Reading

❑ **Selecting Goals:** *Behaviors and Understandings to Notice, Teach, and Support*

Thinking *Within* the Text

- Track print left to right and top to bottom with the assistance of the teacher's pointer either pointing to words, sliding under words, or pointing to the beginning of a line (changing across the year)
- Recognize and use simple punctuation, reflecting it in the voice while reading (period, question mark, exclamation point)
- Acquire understanding of new words through repeated reading
- Understand the meaning of the words during reading
- Recognize a core of high-frequency words as signposts in continuous texts
- Participate in more complex reading with alternate parts, recognizing turn by cues from the text
- Read along with others on familiar texts, demonstrating high accuracy
- Read aloud with fluency
- Reflect meaning with the voice through pause, stress, and phrasing
- Remember and use repeating language patterns when rereading
- Notice and use spaces to define word boundaries
- Mimic the teacher's expression
- Notice and ask questions when meaning is lost or understanding is interrupted
- Notice and use information from pictures
- Talk about characters, problems and events in a story in a discussion of how to read the text

Thinking *Beyond* the Text

- Make predictions as to what will happen next in a story
- Show interpretation of character's intentions or feelings in the voice while reading
- Show anticipation in the voice when reading
- Express personal connections through discussion
- Make connections between texts that they have read, heard read, or read in unison with others
- Use background knowledge and experience to contribute to text interpretation
- Use details from illustrations to support points made in discussion
- Predict what a character will do in preparation for reading
- Infer a character's feelings or motivations in preparation for reading

Thinking *About* the Text

- Recognize and identify parts of stories, such as beginning, series of events, and endings
- Understand and discuss title, author, and illustrator
- Express opinions about the appropriateness of the ending
- Notice how the writer has used language or words to make a text interesting or funny
- Recognize when texts are realistic, fantasy, or true informational texts
- Compare different versions of the same story, rhyme, or traditional tale
- Notice and understand texts that are based on established sequences such as numbers, days of the week, seasons
- Notice how layout of pictures or print affects the way you read it—for example, larger font or bold
- Check information in the text against their own experiences

Writing About Reading

❑ **Selecting Genres and Forms:** *Genres and forms for writing about reading are demonstrated through interactive, shared, or modeled writing, often with close attention to mentor texts. Children learn how to respond to reading in different forms and for a variety of purposes and audiences. After they learn about the forms in a supported experience, they use them independently as they respond to books they read. Across the year, first graders will grow steadily in their ability to write meaningful messages in a variety of genres for writing about reading, and they will gain control of many conventions.*

FUNCTIONAL WRITING

- Sketches or drawings that reflect content of a text
- Interesting words or phrases from a text
- Short sentences responding to a text (for example, stating a prediction, an opinion, or an interesting aspect of the text)
- Lists to support memory (characters, events in a story)
- Simple charts (graphic organizers) to show comparison or sequence
- Letters to other readers or to authors and illustrators (including dialogue letters in a reader's notebook)
- Labels for photographs or any kind of drawing
- Written directions (sometimes with drawings) that show a simple sequence of actions based on a text

INFORMATIONAL WRITING

- List of facts from a text
- Short sentences and/or drawings reporting some interesting information from text
- Summaries of information learned with headings to show sections
- One or two simple sentences with information about an author or illustrator
- Representations (through writing and drawing) of a sequence of actions or directions from a text
- Labeling of drawings that represent interesting information from a text

NARRATIVE WRITING

- Simple statements telling the sequence of events
- Drawings showing the sequence of events in a text (sometimes speech bubbles to show dialogue)
- Graphic representations of stories
- Simple statements summarizing a text
- Innovations on known texts (for example, new endings or similar plots with different characters)

A first grader's writing about what she has learned about dinosaurs

Writing About Reading

❏ **Selecting Goals:** *Behaviors and Understandings to Notice, Teach, and Support*

Thinking *Within* the Text

- Write short sentences to report or summarize important details from a text
- Represent a character through drawing or writing
- Represent a sequence of events through drawing (often with labels or legends)
- Notice and sometimes use new words from a text
- Tell important information from a story
- Reread to assure accuracy of sentence structure and word use as well as meaningfulness
- Use text as a resource for words, phrases, ideas
- Remember information from a text to produce lists, simple sequence of actions, and directions
- Use the names of authors and illustrators

Thinking *Beyond* the Text

- Reflect both prior knowledge and new knowledge from the text
- Predict what will happen next in a text or what a character will do
- Infer how a character feels
- Reflect what a character is really like
- Express opinions about stories or poems
- Compose innovations on very familiar texts
- Produce innovations on a text by changing ending, series of events, the characters, or the setting
- List or write sentences and opinions about new information learned from a text
- Write or draw about something in the reader's own life when prompted by a text

Thinking *About* the Text

- Create texts that have some of the characteristics of published texts (cover, title, author, illustrator, illustrations, beginning, ending, events in a sequence, about the author page)
- Sometimes borrow the style or some language from a writer
- Express opinions about a story or poem
- Notice the way a text is organized and sometimes apply organization to writing (for example, sequence of events or established sequence such as numbers or days of the week)
- Recognize and use some aspects of text structure (for example, beginning and ending)
- Differentiate between informational and fiction texts
- Notice and sometimes use interesting language from a text
- Produce some simple graphic representations of a story (for example, story map or timeline)
- Use specific vocabulary to write about texts (*author, illustrator, cover, title character, problem, events*)

Writing

❑ **Selecting Purpose and Genre:** *Most first graders will begin the year with a repertoire of known words and some experience in drawing and writing to express their ideas. Some may be only beginning to realize the functions of print. They will benefit from rich demonstrations of writing through shared and interactive writing for a variety of purposes. First graders will also benefit from writing workshop with a daily minilesson, independent writing, individual conferring with the teacher, and sharing with peers. By the end of the year, they will demonstrate writing narratives, informational texts, a variety of functional texts, and some poetic texts. They will demonstrate the use of conventions in terms of lines, spaces, many correctly spelled words, and many good attempts at more complex words. Opportunities to draw will extend their thinking.*

NARRATIVE: *(To tell a story)*

MEMOIR *(personal narrative, autobiography)*

Understanding the Genre

- Understand how to craft personal narratives and memoirs from mentor texts
- Understand that writers tell stories from their own lives
- Understand that a story from your life is usually written in first person (using I)
- Understand that the writer can look back or think about the memory or experience and share thoughts and feelings about it
- Understand that a story should be one that is important to the writer

Writing in the Genre

- Think of topics, events, or experiences from own life that are interesting to write about
- Write an engaging beginning and a satisfying ending to stories
- Understand that a story can be a "small moment" (description of a brief, memorable experience)
- Provide some descriptive details to make the story interesting
- Use dialogue as appropriate to add to the meaning of the story
- Use simple words that show the passage of time (then, after)
- Explain one's own thoughts and feelings about a topic
- Develop voice as a writer through telling own stories or memories from own life
- Usually write in first person to achieve a strong voice
- Tell a story across several pages in order to develop the story or idea
- Tell events in order that they occurred in personal narratives

INFORMATIONAL: *(To explain or give facts about a topic)*

LITERARY NONFICTION

Understanding the Genre

- Understand how to write literary nonfiction from mentor texts
- Understand literary nonfiction as writing that engages and entertains readers but teaches them about a topic
- Understand that the writer works to get readers interested in a topic

Writing in the Genre

- Write books and short pieces of writing that are enjoyable to read and at the same time give information to readers about a topic
- Use features (for example, headings, page numbers, labeled pictures, table of contents, or others) to guide the reader
- Think about the readers (audience) and what they need to know
- Select interesting information to include in a piece of writing

POETIC: *(To express feelings, sensory images, ideas, or stories)*

POETRY *(free verse, rhyme)*

Understanding the Genre

- Understand that a writer can use familiar poems as mentor texts
- Understand poetry as a way to communicate in sensory images about everyday life
- Understand poetry as a unique way to communicate about and describe thoughts and feelings
- Understand the way print and space work in poems and use this knowledge when writing poems
- Understand that poems can be created from other kinds of texts
- Understand the importance of specific word choice in poetry
- Understand that there are different kinds of poems
- Understand that poems do not have to rhyme
- Recognize poetic language (rhythm, descriptive words that evoke senses, some rhyme)

Writing in the Genre

- Closely observe the world (animals, objects, people) to get ideas for poems
- Use line breaks and white space when writing poems
- Shape words on the page to look like a poem
- Write poems that convey feelings or images
- Use language to describe how something looks, smells, tastes, feels, or sounds
- Write poems from other kinds of texts (story, informational text)
- Sometimes borrow specific words or phrases from writing and make them into a poem

Writing

❑ **Selecting Purpose and Genre:** *(cont.)*

FUNCTIONAL: *(To perform a practical task)*

LABELS

Understanding the Genre
- Understand that labels can add important information
- Understand that a writer or illustrator can add labels to help readers

Writing in the Genre
- Write labels for objects in the classroom
- Add words to pictures
- Create labels for illustrations that accompany written pieces
- Make label books as one type of book

FRIENDLY LETTERS *(notes, cards, invitations, email)*

Understanding the Genre
- Understand how to write notes, cards, and invitations from looking at examples
- Understand that the receiver and sender must be clearly shown
- Understand notes, cards, invitations, and email as written communication among people
- Understand that invitations must include specific information
- Understand that the form of written communication is related to the purpose

Writing in the Genre
- Write notes, cards, invitations, and emails to others
- Write to a known audience or a specific reader
- Write with the specific purpose in mind
- Include important information in the communication
- Write with a friendly tone (conversational language)

LISTS AND PROCEDURES *(how-to)*

Understanding the Genre
- Understand lists as a functional way to organize information
- Understand that the form of a list is usually one item under another and it may be numbered
- Understand procedural writing (how-to) as a list of sequential directions for how to do something and lists of what is needed
- Understand that pictures can accompany the writing to help readers understand the information
- Understand that captions can be written under pictures to give readers more information

Writing in the Genre
- Place items in the list that are appropriate for its purpose or category
- Make lists in the appropriate form with one item under another
- Use drawings in the process of drafting, revising, or publishing procedural writing
- Write captions under pictures
- Use lists to plan activities or support memory
- Write sequential directions in procedural or how-to books

WRITING ABOUT READING (ALL GENRES)

(See the Writing About Reading continuum, pages 94–95.)

Writing

❑ **Selecting Goals:** *Behaviors to Notice, Teach, and Support*

CRAFT

ORGANIZATION

Text Structure
- Include facts and details in informational writing
- Put together the related details on a topic in a text
- Put the facts or information in order
- Write stories that have a beginning, a series of things happening, and an ending
- Write a title and the author's name on the cover of a story or book
- Write an author page at the beginning or end of a book that tells details about the author (picture, writing)
- Dedicate a story to someone and write the dedication on the inside of the cover, on the title page or copyright page, or on a page of its own
- Create a picture book as one form of writing

Beginnings, Endings, Titles
- Use a variety of beginnings to engage the reader
- Use endings that are interesting, leave the reader satisfied, or get the reader to think more about a story or topic
- Select an appropriate title for a poem, story, or informational book

Presentation of Ideas
- Tell about experiences or topics the way one would talk about them to others
- Present ideas in logical sequence
- Introduce ideas followed by supportive details and examples
- Show steps in enough detail that a reader can follow a sequence
- Tell one part, idea, or group of ideas on each page of a book
- Use time appropriately as an organizing tool

Idea Development
- Communicate clearly the main points intended for the reader to understand
- Provide supportive description, details, or examples to explain the important ideas

Language Use
- Understand that the writer is using language to communicate meaning
- Show evidence of using book language or language from other texts

Word Choice
- Learn new words or phrases from reading and try them out in writing
- Use vocabulary appropriate for the topic
- Vary word choice to create interesting description and dialogue

Voice
- Write with a unique perspective
- Write in the way one would speak about the experience, event, or topic
- State information in a unique or surprising way
- Share one's thoughts and feelings about a topic
- Write about what is known and remembered

CONVENTIONS

TEXT LAYOUT
- Understand that the print and pictures can be placed in a variety of places on the page within a book
- Place words in lines, starting left to right, top to bottom
- Place titles and headings in the appropriate place on a page
- Use underlining and bold print to convey meaning
- Understand that layout of print and illustrations are important in conveying the meaning of a text
- Use spaces between words

GRAMMAR

Sentence Structure
- Use conventional sentence structure (noun + verb)

Parts of Speech
- Use noun and verb agreement (*I can*)
- Use prepositional phrases (*to the bus, on the bus*)
- Use modifiers (*red dress; ran fast*)

Tense
- Write in past tense (*I went home yesterday.*)
- Write in future tense (*I'm going to go . . .*)

CAPITALIZATION
- Demonstrate knowledge of the use of upper-and lowercase letters of the alphabet
- Capitalize *I*
- Show awareness of the first place position of capital letters in words
- Use uppercase letters in titles
- Use a capital letter for the first word of a sentence
- Use capital letters in the beginning position in a few familiar, known proper nouns

PUNCTUATION
- Use periods, exclamation points, and question marks as ending marks
- Notice the use of punctuation marks in books and try them out in own writing
- Read one's writing aloud and think where punctuation would go

Writing

❑ **Selecting Goals:** *Behaviors to Notice, Teach, and Support (cont.)*

SPELLING

- Use conventional symbols to write words
- Spell one hundred or more high-frequency words conventionally
- Say words to break them into syllables to spell them
- Use some phonogram patterns to generate words
- Attempt unknown words through sound analysis
- Say words slowly to hear a sound and write a letter that represents it
- Write some words with consonant letters appropriate for sounds in words (beginning and ending)
- Write a letter for easy-to-hear vowel sounds
- Represent several sounds, including beginning and ending
- Use some inflectional endings such as *s* and *ing.*
- Represent many short and long vowel sounds in words
- Spell words with regular consonant-sound relationships and with regular short vowel patterns correctly
- Represent many consonant sounds or vowel sounds with letters
- Attempt unknown words using known word parts
- Construct phonetic spellings that are readable
- Include a vowel in each word
- Represent consonant blends and digraphs with letter clusters in words
- Use simple resources to check spelling (word walls, personal word lists)

HANDWRITING/WORD-PROCESSING

- Leave appropriate space between words
- Hold pencil or pen with satisfactory grip
- Return to the left margin to start a new line
- Use a preferred hand consistently for writing
- Write left to right in lines
- Write letters and words that can be easily read
- Write letters in groups to form words
- Form upper-and lowercase letters efficiently in manuscript print
- Form upper-and lowercase letters proportionately in manuscript print
- Access and use simple programs on the computer (easy word-processing, games)
- Locate letter keys on a computer keyboard to type simple messages

WRITING PROCESS

REHEARSING/PLANNING

Purpose

- Think about the purpose for writing each text
- Write for a specific purpose
- Consider how the purpose affects the kind of writing
- Choose type of text to fit the purpose (for example, poem, factual book, alphabet book, photo book, label book, story with pictures)
- Choose paper to match genre and organization
- Write name and date on writing
- Tell whether a piece of writing is a story or an informational text

Audience

- Write with an understanding that it is meant to be read by others
- Think about the people who will read the writing and what they will want to know
- Include information that the readers will need to understand the text

Oral Language

- Generate and expand ideas through talk with peers and teacher
- Look for ideas and topics in personal experiences, shared through talk
- Use storytelling to generate and rehearse language (that may be written later)
- Tell stories in chronological order
- Retell stories in chronological order

Gathering Seeds/Resources/Experimenting with Writing

- Make a list of ideas on topics for writing
- Gather information for writing
- Record information in words or drawings
- Make lists to plan for writing
- Use drawings to share or remember thinking

Content, Topic, Theme

- Choose topics that one knows about or cares about
- Choose topics that are interesting
- Select information that will support the topic
- Observe carefully (objects, animals, people, places, actions) before writing about them
- Select topics for story or poem writing
- Select own topics for informational writing and state what is important about the topic
- Stay focused on a topic

Writing

❏ **Selecting Goals:** *Behaviors to Notice, Teach, and Support (cont.)*

Inquiry/Research
- Ask questions and gather information on a topic
- Take notes or make sketches to help in remembering information
- Remember important information about a topic in order to write about it
- Participate actively in experiences and remember details that contribute to writing and drawing
- Remember important labels for drawings

Genre/Form
- Select from a variety of forms the kind of text that will fit the purpose (books with illustrations and words; books with illustrations only; alphabet books; label books; poetry books; question and answer books; illustration-only books)

DRAFTING/REVISING

Understanding the Process
- Understand the role of the writing conference in helping writers
- Understand that writers can get help from other writers
- Understand that writers can change writing in response to peer or teacher feedback

Producing a Draft
- Use drawings to tell about a topic or tell a story
- Uses words and drawings to compose a story
- Write a continuous message on a simple topic

Rereading
- Reread writing each day (or during writing on the same day) before continuing to write
- Reread stories to be sure the meaning is clear
- Reread the text to be sure there are no missing words or information
- Review drawings to revise by adding (or deleting) information

Adding Information
- Add words, phrases, or sentences to make the writing more interesting or exciting to read
- Add words, phrases, or sentences to provide more information to readers
- Add dialogue to provide information or provide narration (in quotes or speech balloons)

Deleting Information
- Delete words or sentences that do not make sense
- Delete extra words or sentences
- Reorder pages by laying them out and reassembling them

Reorganizing Information
- Move sentences from one part to another to make the sequence better
- Reorder writing by cutting apart or laying out pages
- Reorder drawings by cutting apart or laying out pages

Changing Text
- Mark parts that are not clear and provide more information

Using Tools and Techniques
- Add letters, words, phrases, or sentences using a caret or sticky note
- Add words, phrases, or sentences using spider legs or an extra piece of paper glued, taped, or stapled to the piece
- Add pages to a book or booklet
- Remove pages from a book or booklet
- Cross out words or sentences with pencil or marker

Writing

❏ **Selecting Goals:** *Behaviors to Notice, Teach, and Support (cont.)*

EDITING AND PROOFREADING

Understanding the Process
- Understand that the writer shows respect to the reader by applying what is known to correct errors
- Understand that the better the spelling and space between words, the easier it is for the reader to read it

Editing for Conventions
- Check and correct letter formation or orientation
- Edit for spelling errors by making another attempt
- Edit for spelling errors by circling words that do not look right and trying to spell them another way
- Edit for the spelling of known words (should be spelled conventionally)
- Recognize that the teacher is the final editor who will make the edits the writer has not yet learned how to do prior to publishing

Using Tools
- Use beginning reference tools (for example, word walls or personal word lists to assist in word choice or checking spelling)

PUBLISHING
- Create drawings for pieces of writing
- Share writing by reading it to the class
- Put several stories or poems together
- Select a poem, story, or informational book to publish
- Use labels and captions on drawings that are displayed

SKETCHING AND DRAWING
- Use drawing to plan, draft, revise, or publish writing
- Create drawings that are related to the written text and increase readers' understanding and enjoyment
- Use drawings to represent people, places, things, and ideas
- Add or remove details to drawings to revise information

VIEWING SELF AS A WRITER
- Take risks as a writer
- View self as writer
- Have a list of topics in mind to write about
- Think about what to work on next in writing
- Select best pieces of writing from own collection
- Self-evaluate own writing and talk about what is good about it and what techniques were used
- Produce a quantity of writing within the time available (for example, one or two pages per day)
- Keep working independently rather than waiting for teacher instructions
- Make attempts to solve own problems
- Take on writing independently
- Try out techniques other writers used

Writing

A first grader's memoir

Writing

worked together to cach
it and we COT IT, "Woha" 8

I said, thats so cool,
I no!!!! evreione else 9

said, Lets bring it back
to the lodge I said. 10

Good ide said my
Aunt. Weslowly moved 11

back thow the cove back
to the lodge and out the 12

turtul in the turtul cage.
We shoud ranalleb and 13

Grandpa Steve. then let
it go. "Bye turtel weal!" 14

said, It sliped back into the
water. The end 15

Oral, Visual, and Technological Communication

❏ **Selecting Goals:** *Behaviors and Understandings to Notice, Teach, and Support*

LISTENING AND SPEAKING

LISTENING AND UNDERSTANDING

- Listen with attention and understanding to directions (multiple steps)
- Demonstrate the ability to remember and follow simple directions
- Listen actively to others read or talk about their writing and give feedback
- Show interest in listening to and talking about stories, poems, or informational texts
- Listen with attention and understanding to oral reading of stories, poems, and informational texts
- Compare personal knowledge with what is heard

SOCIAL INTERACTION

- Engage in imaginary play
- Enter into dramatic dialogue in play or role play contexts
- Use polite conversational conventions (*please, thank you,* greetings)
- Speak at an appropriate volume—not too loud but loud enough to be heard and understood by others
- Adjust volume as appropriate for different contexts
- Speak clearly enough to be understood by others in conversation
- Enter a conversation appropriately
- Engage in the turn-taking of conversation
- Sustain a conversation with a variety of audiences, including peers, teacher, and family

EXTENDED DISCUSSION

- Follow the topic and add to the discussion
- Build on the statements of others
- Engage actively in routines (for example, turn and talk)
- Form clear questions to gain information
- Participate actively in whole-class discussion or with peers, as partners, or in a small group
- Use grade level-appropriate specific vocabulary when talking about texts (title, author)

CONTENT

- Begin to verbalize reasons for problems, events, and actions
- Explain cause-and-effect relationships
- Express opinions and explain reasoning (*because . . .*)
- Predict future events in a story
- Offer solutions and explanations for story problems
- Explain and describe people, events, places, and objects
- Describe similarities and differences among people, places, events, and objects
- Report interesting information from background experience or reading
- Ask many questions, demonstrating curiosity
- Initiate and join in on songs, rhymes, and chants
- Share knowledge of story structure by describing setting, characters, events, or ending
- Show interest in the meaning of words
- Express and reflect on feelings of self and others

PRESENTATION

VOICE

- Speak about a topic with enthusiasm
- Talk with confidence
- Tell stories in an interesting way

CONVENTIONS

- Speak at appropriate volume to be heard
- Look at the audience while talking
- Speak at an appropriate rate to be understood by the audience
- Enunciate words clearly

ORGANIZATION

- Have the topic or story in mind before starting to speak
- Show knowledge of story structure
- Tell personal experiences in a logical sequence
- Have an audience in mind before starting to speak
- Have a clear purpose
- Present ideas and information in a logical sequence

Oral, Visual, and Technological Communication

❑ **Selecting Goals:** *Behaviors and Understandings to Notice, Teach, and Support (cont.)*

WORD CHOICE

- Use language from stories when retelling them
- Use words that describe (adjectives and adverbs)

IDEAS AND CONTENT

- Recite short poems and songs
- Tell stories and retell familiar stories
- Tell personal experiences
- Make brief oral reports that demonstrate understanding of a topic

MEDIA

- Use props, illustrations, images, or other digital media to extend the meaning of a presentation
- Perform plays and puppet shows that involve speaking as a character

TECHNOLOGY

COMPUTER LITERACY

- Find buttons and icons on the computer screen to use simple programs that require interaction (e.g., math, literacy, drawing)
- Use mouse and keyboard effectively
- Use email for conversation

ONLINE READING AND INFORMATION LITERACY

- Search for and locate approved websites and use them for entertainment or to get information

Phonics, Spelling, and Word Study

❑ **Selecting Goals:** *Behaviors and Understandings to Notice, Teach, and Support*

EARLY LITERACY CONCEPTS

- Locate the first and last letters of words in continuous text
- Recognize one's name in isolation and in continuous text
- Understand that you say one word for one group of letters when you read
- Understand the concept of *sentence* (as a group of words with ending punctuation)
- Understand the concepts of *letter* and *word* (as a single character or a group of letters)
- Understand the concepts of *first* and *last* in written language
- Use left-to-right directionality of print and return to left in reading and writing
- Use one's name to learn about words and make connections to words
- Use spaces between words when writing
- Match one spoken to one written word while reading and writing

PHONOLOGICAL AWARENESS

- Segment sentences into words
- Hear and recognize word boundaries
- Hear, say, connect, and generate rhyming words (*fly, high, buy, sky*)
- Blend two to four phonemes in words (*d-o-g, dog, t-e-n-t*)
- Segment words into phonemes (*b-a-t, t-e-n-t*)
- Connect words by the sounds (*Mom, my*)
- Manipulate phonemes (cat-at, and, sand)
- Hear and say beginning phonemes (sounds) in words (*run/race, mom/make*) and ending (*win/fun, get/sit*)
- Hear and say syllables (*to-ma-to, can-dy, um-brel-la*)

LETTER KNOWLEDGE

- Categorize letters by features—by slant lines (*v, w, x*) and straight lines (*p, l, b, d*); by circles (*o, b, g, p*) and no circles (*k, x, w, r*); by tunnels (*n, h*); by tails (*y, p, g*); by no tails (*r, s*); by dots/no dots; by tall/ short; by consonants/vowels
- Distinguish letter forms
- Make connections between words by recognizing letters (*bat, big, ball*), letter clusters (*feat, meat, heat*), and letter sequences
- Recognize and produce the names of most of the upper-and lowercase letters
- Identify a word that begins with the sound of each letter
- Recognize consonants and vowels
- Recognize letters that are embedded in words and in continuous text
- Recognize uppercase and lowercase letters
- Understand alphabetical order
- Understand special uses of letters (capital letters, initials)
- Use efficient and consistent motions to form letters when writing

LETTER/SOUND RELATIONSHIPS

- Recognize and use beginning consonant sounds and the letters that represent them to read and write words
- Recognize that letter clusters (blends and digraphs: *st, pl sh, ch, th*) represent consonant sounds
- Hear and identify long (*make, pail, day*) and short (*can, egg, up*) vowel sounds in words and the letters that represent them

- Recognize and use other vowel sounds (*oo* as in *moon, look; oi* as in *oil; oy* as in *boy; ou* as in *house; ow* as in *cow; aw* as in *paw*)

SPELLING PATTERNS

- Recognize and use a large number of phonograms (VC, CVC, CVCe, VCC)
- Recognize that words have letter patterns that are connected to sounds (phonograms and other letter patterns)
- Recognize and use the consonant-vowel-consonant (CVC) pattern (*cab, fad, map*)

HIGH-FREQUENCY WORDS

- Write a core of at least fifty high-frequency words (*a, all, am, an, and, are, at, be, but, came, come, can, do, for, from, get, got, had, have, he, her, him, his, I, if, in, is, it, like, me, my, no, of, on, one, out, said, saw, see, she, so, that, the, their, then, there, they, this, to, up, was, we, went, were, with, you, your*)
- Read a core of at least fifty high-frequency words (*a, all, am, an, and, are, at, be, but, came, come, can, do, for, from, get, got, had, have, he, her, him, his, I, if, in, is, it, like, me, my, no, of, on, one, out, said, saw, see, she, so, that, the, their, then, there, they, this, to, up, was, we, went, were, with, you, your*)

WORD MEANING

CONCEPT WORDS

- Recognize and use concept words (color names, number words, days of the week, months of the year)

COMPOUND WORDS

- Recognize and use simple compound words (*into, myself, itself, cannot, inside, maybe, nobody*)

SYNONYMS AND ANTONYMS

- Recognize and use synonyms (words that mean about the same: *begin/start, close/shut, fix/mend, earth/world, happy/glad, high/tall, jump/leap*)
- Recognize and use antonyms (words that mean the opposite: *hot/ cold, all/none, break/fix, little/big, long/short, sad/glad, stop/start*)

HOMOGRAPHS AND HOMOPHONES

- Recognize and use simple homophones (sound the same, different spelling and meaning: *to/too/two, here/hear, blue/blew, there/their/ they're*)

WORD STRUCTURE

SYLLABLES

- Understand the concept of syllables and demonstrate by clapping (*horse, a-way, farm-er, morn-ing, bi-cy-cle, to-geth-er, ev-er-y*)
- Understand how vowels appear in syllables (every syllable has a vowel)

Phonics, Spelling, and Word Study

❑ **Selecting Goals:** *Behaviors and Understandings to Notice, Teach, and Support (cont.)*

PLURALS

- Understand the concept of plurals and plural forms: adding -s (*dogs, cats, apples, cans, desks, faces, trees, monkeys*); adding -es (when words end in *x, ch, sh, s, ss, tch, zz*)

VERB ENDINGS

- Recognize and use endings that add -s to a verb to make it agree with the subject (*skate/skates, run/runs*)
- Recognize and use endings that add -ing to a verb to denote the present participle (*play/playing, send/sending*)
- Recognize and use endings that add -ed to a verb to make it past tense (*walk/walked, play/played, want/wanted*)

CONTRACTIONS

- Recognize and understand contractions with *am* (*I'm*), *is* (*he's*), *will* (*I'll*), *not* (*can't*)

POSSESSIVES

- Recognize and use possessives that add an apostrophe and an *s* to a singular noun (*dog/dog's, woman/woman's, girl/girl's, boy/boy's*)

BASE WORDS

- Remove the ending from a base word to make a new word (*running, run*)

WORD-SOLVING ACTIONS

- Use known words to help in spelling new words
- Make connections between names and other words
- Recognize and locate words (names)
- Recognize and spell known words quickly
- Use the letters in names to read and write words (*Chuck/chair, Mark/make*)
- Use known words to monitor reading and spelling
- Use letters and relationships to sounds to read and write words
- Use known words and word parts to help in reading and spelling new words (*can, candy*)
- Change beginning, middle, and ending letters to make new words (*sit/hit, day/play, hit/hot, sheet/shirt, car/can/cat*)
- Change the onset or rime to make a new word (*bring/thing, bring/brown*)
- Break words into syllables to read or write them

GRADE 2

Interactive Read-Aloud and Literature Discussion

❏ **Selecting Texts:** *Characteristics of Texts for Reading Aloud and Discussion*

GENRES/FORMS

Genres
- Poems
- Traditional literature (cumulative, *pourquoi,* beasts, cyclical, fables, tall tales)
- Fantasy
- Realistic fiction
- Informational texts
- Simple biographies on well-known subjects
- Memoir
- Special types of genres: mystery
- Hybrid texts (a text in one genre with a simple form of another genre embedded in it)

Forms
- Oral stories
- Informational picture books
- Picture story books
- Beginning chapter books
- Beginning series books

TEXT STRUCTURE
- Informational texts with simple description on each page—sometimes repeating patterns
- Factual texts that incorporate sequence (for example, life cycles and how-to books)
- Factual texts that include description, temporal sequence, and compare and contrast
- Factual texts with clearly defined categories
- Traditional folk-and-fairy tales with more repeating patterns
- Simple structure with beginning, series of episodes, and an ending
- A few stories with repeating patterns

CONTENT
- Content that verifies as well as extends students' experiences
- Some scientific and technical topics (human body, wide variety of animals—many not in children's common experiences, how-to books, technology)
- Many texts centering on problems related to family, friends, and school
- Themes and content that reflect a full range of cultures

THEMES AND IDEAS
- Humor that is obvious
- Themes important to second graders (friendship, family, neighborhood)
- Most themes explicitly stated or easy to derive

LANGUAGE AND LITERARY FEATURES
- Longer plots with more episodes
- Stories with multiple characters
- Characters that develop over time, learning from mistakes and creating relationships
- Literary language, including some use of metaphor and simile, as well as description
- A few literary devices (for example a story within a story)
- A variety of dialogue between more than one of two characters
- Some informational texts with categories and subcategories

SENTENCE COMPLEXITY
- Some long and complex sentences that require attention to follow
- A variety of sentence structures

VOCABULARY
- Some words of high interest that will be memorable to children
- Many words that are in children's speaking vocabulary
- New commonly used vocabulary words that are explained in the text or shown in illustrations
- Increased amount of technical vocabulary in informational text
- Some complex vocabulary words that are understandable given students' background knowledge

ILLUSTRATIONS
- Labeled drawings or photographs
- Pictures with legends
- Simple graphics, clearly labeled
- More complex illustrations that have detail and add more to the meaning of the text
- Chapter books with just a few black-and-white illustrations
- Picture books with illustrations that reflect the theme and writer's tone and make a coherent work of art
- Illustrations that help the reader understand the mood of the story

BOOK AND PRINT FEATURES
- Title, author, and illustrator on cover and title page
- Some simple chapter books with titles on each chapter
- A few simple navigational tools (table of contents, chapter titles)

Interactive Read-Aloud and Literature Discussion

❏ **Selecting Goals:** *Behaviors and Understandings to Notice, Teach, and Support*

Thinking *Within* the Text

- Notice and remember facts, concepts, or ideas from a text
- Provide an oral summary of a text
- Notice and remember the events of a story in sequence
- Notice and understand the problem of a story and how it is solved
- Self-monitor understanding and ask questions when meaning is lost
- Notice and derive information from pictures
- When joining in on refrains or repetitive text, mimic the teacher's intonation and stress
- Notice and respond to word stress and tone of voice while listening and afterward
- Recognize new meanings for known words by using context
- Recognize and actively work to solve new vocabulary words
- Add new vocabulary words to known words and use them in discussion and in writing
- Follow multiple events in a story to understand the plot

Thinking *Beyond* the Text

- Bring background knowledge to understanding characters and their problems
- Make connections to prior knowledge
- Infer characters' intentions or feelings
- Infer characters' feelings and motivations from description, what they do or say, and what others think about them
- Interpret illustrations and discuss how they make readers feel
- Use evidence from the text to support predictions (*I think . . . because . . .*)
- Support thinking beyond the text with specific evidence based on personal experience or knowledge or evidence from the text
- Make predictions using information from the text
- Predict what will happen after the end
- Make connections to other texts by topic, major ideas, authors' styles, and genres
- Specify the nature of connections in discussion
- Develop new concepts and ideas from listening to and discussing texts
- Think about and interpret the significance of events in a story
- Relate important ideas in the text to each other and to ideas in other texts

Thinking *About* the Text

- Recognize and identify some aspects of text structure, such as beginning, events in sequential order, most exciting point in a story, and ending
- Discuss the characteristics of the work of some authors and illustrators
- Notice the writer's use of language (for example, word choice)
- Notice similarities and differences among texts that are by the same author or are on the same topic
- Talk about the connections between the illustrations and the text
- Recognize how the writer or illustrator has placed ideas in the text and in the graphics
- Form and state the basis for opinions about authors, illustrators, and texts (tell why)
- Understand fiction as stories that are not real and nonfiction as texts that provide real information
- Understand realistic fiction as stories that could be real and fantasy as stories that could not be real
- Understand biography as the story of a person's life
- Compare different versions of the same story, rhyme, or traditional tale
- Use specific vocabulary to talk about texts: *author, illustrator, cover, wordless picture book, picture book, character, problem, solution, series book, dedication, endpapers, book jacket, title page, chapters, resolution, main character, setting, fiction, nonfiction, informational book, literary nonfiction, poetry*

Shared and Performance Reading

❑ **Selecting Texts:** *Characteristics of Texts for Sharing and Performing*

GENRES/FORMS

Genres

- Simple fantasy—many with talking animals
- Factual texts—simple informational books, some organized as sophisticated ABC books
- Longer poems of all kinds
- Songs and traditional rhymes from many cultures
- Traditional folktales
- Realistic fiction

Forms

- Readers' theater scripts
- Plays
- Texts produced through shared writing—stories, poems, descriptions, story retellings, directions, informational reports
- Enlarged poems
- Individual poetry anthologies
- Enlarged picture books

TEXT STRUCTURE

- Informational texts with description, compare/contrast, sequence
- Many traditional tales with particular structures (cumulative tales, circular stories, use of "three's")

CONTENT

- Nonsensical characters (animal and human)
- Language and word play—rhymes, nonsense, alliteration
- Many topics centering on problems related to family, friends, school
- Some scientific and technical topics—human body, wide variety of animals (many not in children's common experiences), "how-to" books, space and technology

THEMES AND IDEAS

- Obvious humor—silly situations, and language play
- Themes important to second graders—making friends, playing fair, helping the family, belonging
- Most themes explicitly stated or easy to derive

LANGUAGE AND LITERARY FEATURES

- Figurative language and play on words
- Stories with multiple episodes offering selection for readers' theater
- Many texts with rhyme and rhythm
- Characters who learn and change
- Dialogue that lends itself to readers' theater
- Predictable plots and stories

SENTENCE COMPLEXITY

- A few sentences that are long with many embedded phrases and clauses
- Sentences that are more complex than children would use in oral conversation

VOCABULARY

- New content words related to concepts children are learning that are easy to explain
- Words to assign dialogue that guide readers in interpretation of the text (*cried, shouted, whispered*)
- Many synonyms, antonyms, and homophones
- Many words that are in children's speaking vocabulary
- Some words of high interest that will be memorable to children

WORDS

- A full range of plurals
- A full range of words with inflectional endings and suffixes
- Many high-frequency words that help the reading of the text to move along
- Many multisyllable words that offer opportunities to notice word structure

ILLUSTRATIONS

- Many poems and other texts that have no pictures
- Illustrations that offer high support for comprehending
- Large, clear, colorful illustrations in a variety of media

BOOK AND PRINT FEATURES

- Most texts on charts or in big books with enlarged print that the entire group can see
- Some words in bold and italics to assist in using word stress
- Up to about 20 lines on a page
- Full range of punctuation
- Title, author, and illustrator on cover and title page for books
- Title at the top of poems and other pieces
- Some reading from individual copies of plays or scripts
- Ample space between words and between lines for both common and individual texts
- Variation in layout across a text

Shared and Performance Reading

❑ **Selecting Goals:** *Behaviors and Understandings to Notice, Teach, and Support*

Thinking *Within* the Text

- Track print left to right and top to bottom with only line indication from the teacher's pointer
- Acquire understanding of new words through repeated reading
- Understand the meaning of the words during reading
- Use high-frequency words to monitor accuracy of reading and gain momentum
- Read with high accuracy rate
- Read aloud with fluency
- Reflect meaning with the voice through pause, stress, and phrasing
- Recognize and use a range of punctuation, reflecting it in the voice while reading (period, question mark, exclamation mark, comma, quotation marks)
- Self-correct intonation, phrasing, and pausing while reading aloud
- Use multiple sources of information to monitor reading accuracy, pronunciation, and understanding of words
- Participate in more complex reading with alternate parts, recognizing turn by cues from the text
- Remember and emphasize important information in a text while reading it aloud
- Talk about characters, problems, and events in a story in a discussion of how to read it

Thinking *Beyond* the Text

- Make predictions as to what will happen next or what characters might do as preparation for reading
- Show interpretation of character's intentions or feelings in the voice while reading
- Show anticipation in the voice when reading
- Express personal connections through discussion
- Make connections between texts that they have read or heard before
- Use background knowledge and experience to contribute to text interpretation
- Use details from illustrations to contribute to text interpretation
- Infer a character's feelings or motivations as preparation for reading in the character's voice

Thinking *About* the Text

- Recognize and identify parts of stories, such as beginning, series of events, and endings
- Understand and discuss title, author, and illustrator
- Notice language that has potential for shared and performance reading
- Recognize when texts are realistic, fantasy, or true informational texts and read them differently as appropriate
- Compare different versions of the same story, rhyme, or traditional tale
- Begin to understand the subtle changes in meaning that a writer can convey through word choice
- Notice when the writer has used words with different connotations and reflect understanding in the voice
- Notice characters that have memorable traits and would be good for performance reading
- Notice how layout of pictures or print affects the way you read it—for example, larger font or bold

Writing About Reading

❑ **Selecting Genres and Forms:** *Students learn different ways to share their thinking about reading in explicit minilessons. Using modeled or shared writing, the teacher may demonstrate the process and engage the students in the construction of the text. Often the teacher and students read several examples of a form, identify its characteristics, and try out the type of response. Then students can select from the range of possible forms when responding to reading (usually in a reader's notebook). By the end of second grade they will be able to demonstrate conventional spelling and write about reading in a variety of genres.*

FUNCTIONAL WRITING

- Sketches or drawings that assist in remembering a text, interpreting a character or event, or representing content of a text
- Short-writes responding to a text in a variety of ways (for example, a prediction, an opinion, or an interesting aspect of the text)
- Lists to support memory (characters, events in a story)
- Notes to remember something about a text or to record interesting information or details, or record interesting language or words
- Simple charts or webs (graphic organizers) to show comparison or sequence
- Grids to show relationships among different kinds of information
- Letters to other readers or to authors and illustrators (including dialogue letters in a reader's notebook)
- Labels for photographs or any kind of drawing
- Written directions (sometimes with drawings) that show a simple sequence of actions based on a text
- Directions or how-to descriptions drawn from a text

NARRATIVE WRITING

- Drawings showing the sequence of events in a text (sometimes with speech bubbles to show dialogue)
- Graphic representations of stories
- Simple statements summarizing a text
- Innovations on known texts (for example, new endings or similar plots with different characters)

INFORMATIONAL WRITING

- List of facts from a text supported by illustrations
- Headings that show subtopics or information to follow
- Sentences reporting some interesting information from a text
- A few sentences with information about an author
- A few sentences with information about an illustrator
- Representations (through writing and drawing) of a sequence of actions or directions from a text
- Labeling of drawings that represent interesting information from a text

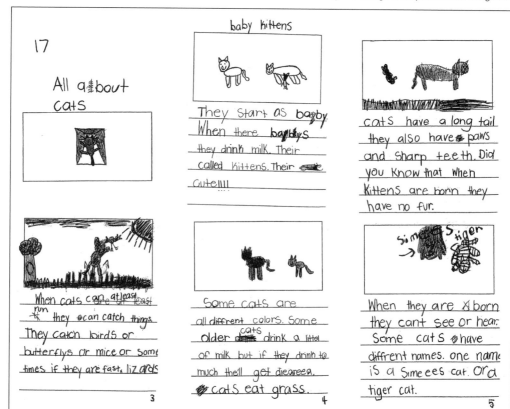

A second grader writes about what she has learned about cats

Writing About Reading

❑ **Selecting Goals:** *Behaviors and Understandings to Notice, Teach, and Support*

Thinking *Within* the Text

- Accurately reflect information from a text
- Represent information, concepts, setting, events, characters, and story problems through drawing and/or writing
- Notice and sometimes use new words from a text
- Use new vocabulary words appropriately to reflect meaning
- Reread to remember what has been written
- Reread to assure meaningfulness, accuracy of sentence structure, and appropriate word use
- Report information from a text or summarize it in a few sentences
- Write summaries that reflect literal understanding of a text
- Represent important information about a fiction text (characters, events) or informational text
- List significant events in a story or ideas in an informational text
- Write and/or draw about facts

Thinking *Beyond* the Text

- Provide specific examples and evidence from personal experience or the text
- Express connections to prior knowledge, to other texts, and to personal background or experience
- Predict what will happen next in a text or what a character will do
- Describe or illustrate characters' feelings and motivations, inferring them from the text
- Produce innovations on a text by changing ending, series of events, the characters, or the setting
- Make notes of new information and understandings
- Write about and illustrate new information
- Express opinions about new learning or interesting facts
- Use drawings to relate important ideas in a text to each other or to other texts
- Write or draw about something in the reader's own life when prompted by a text

Thinking *About* the Text

- Create texts that have some of the characteristics of published texts (cover, title, author, illustrator, illustrations, beginning, ending, events in a sequence, about the author page)
- Sometimes borrow the style or language of a writer
- Describe the relationships between illustrations and text
- Write opinions about a text and back them up with specific information or reasons
- Notice the way a text is organized and sometimes apply organization to writing (for example, sequence of events or established sequence such as numbers or days of the week)
- Show awareness of temporal sequence, compare and contrast, and cause and effect
- Identify and record whether a text is fiction or nonfiction
- Notice and sometimes use interesting language from a text
- Produce some simple graphic representations of a story (for example, story map or timeline)
- Compare different versions of the same story or traditional tale with graphic organizers, drawings, or in sentences
- Use specific vocabulary to write about texts: *cover, endpapers, title, author, illustrator, table of contents, character, fiction, nonfiction, biography, informational texts, problem and solution*

Writing

❑ **Selecting Purpose and Genre:** *Most second graders will have learned to produce simple narratives and other genres through composing and writing. They will continue to benefit from using drawing to extend their thinking and express their ideas. By the end of the year they will demonstrate the use of some literary language as well as the structure of narratives (exposition of problem and solution). Using mentor texts will help them to refine their writing and make it more interesting. They will be able to write many words using conventional spelling and produce more complex sentences.*

NARRATIVE: *(To tell a story)*

MEMOIR *(personal narrative, autobiography)*

Understanding the Genre
- Understand how to craft personal narratives and memoirs from mentor texts
- Understand personal narrative as a story from the author's life, usually told in first person
- Understand memoir as a reflection of a memorable experience or a person

Writing in the Genre
- Write an engaging beginning and a satisfying ending to stories
- Select "small moments" or experiences and share thinking and feeling about them
- Describe a setting and how it is related to the writer's experiences
- Use dialogue as appropriate to add to the meaning of the story
- Use words that show the passage of time
- Tell details about the most important moments in a story or experience while eliminating unimportant details
- Describe characters by what they do, say, and think and what others say about them
- Use some literary language that is different from oral language
- Write in a way that shows the significance of the story
- Usually write in first person to achieve a strong voice
- Select meaningful topics
- Reveal something important about self or about life

SHORT FICTION *(short story, short realistic fiction, or historical fiction)*

Understanding the Genre
- Understand how to craft fiction by using mentor texts as models
- Understand fiction as a short story about an event in the life of the main character
- Understand that fiction may be realism or fantasy (animal fantasy, tall tales, fable)
- Understand the elements of fiction, including setting, problem, characters, and problem resolution

Writing in the Genre
- Describe characters by how they look and what they do
- Describe the setting with appropriate detail
- Write simple fictional stories (realism or fantasy)

INFORMATIONAL: *(To explain or give facts about a topic)*

LITERARY NONFICTION

Understanding the Genre
- Understand how to write literary nonfiction from studying mentor texts
- Understand literary nonfiction as a text that helps people learn something and is interesting to read
- Understand that writers write informational texts for readers to learn about a topic
- Understand that the writer of literary nonfiction works to help readers become interested in a topic
- Understand that nonfiction can tell a story and give information
- Understand that to write literary nonfiction, the writer needs to become very knowledgeable about the topic
- Understand that a report usually has several subtopics related to the main topic

Writing in the Genre
- Write pieces that are interesting and enjoyable to read
- Use headings, labeled drawings and diagrams, table of contents, or other features of informational text to guide the reader
- Write about a topic keeping the audience and their interests and knowledge in mind
- Provide interesting details around a topic
- Introduce information in categories
- Provide supporting details in each category
- Use some vocabulary specific to the topic
- Provide information that teaches readers about a topic
- Use a narrative structure to help readers understand information and interest them in a topic

Writing

❑ **Selecting Purpose and Genre:** *(cont.)*

POETIC: *(To express feelings, sensory images, ideas, or stories)*

POETRY *(free verse, rhyme)*

Understanding the Genre

- Understand poetry as a unique way to communicate about and describe feelings, sensory images, ideas, or stories
- Understand the way print works in poems
- Understand that poems can take a variety of shapes
- Understand that poems can be created from other kinds of texts
- Understand the importance of specific word choice in poetry
- Understand that there are different kinds of poems
- Understand that poems do not have to rhyme

Writing in the Genre

- Write a variety of poems
- Notice and use line breaks and white space as they are used in poetry
- Observe closely to select topics or content and write with detail
- Shape words on the page to look like a poem
- Remove extra words to clarify the meaning and make the writing more powerful
- Use poetic language to communicate meaning

FUNCTIONAL: *(To perform a practical task)*

FRIENDLY LETTERS *(notes, cards, invitations, email)*

Understanding the Genre

- Understand that the form of written communication is related to the purpose
- Understand notes, cards, invitations, friendly letters, and email as written communication among people
- Understand how to write effective notes, invitations, emails, cards, and friendly letters by studying examples
- Understand that invitations need to include specific information about the time and place of the event
- Understand a friendly letter as a more formal kind of communication between people
- Understand that a friendly letter has parts (date, salutation, closing, signature, and sometimes P.S.)
- Understand notes and cards need to include short greetings and relevant information

Writing in the Genre

- Write to a known audience or a specific reader
- Address the audience appropriately
- Write a card, note, invitation, or friendly letter with the purpose in mind
- Write notes, cards, invitations, and email for a variety of purposes
- Include important information in the communication
- Write a friendly letter with all parts

LISTS AND PROCEDURES *(how-to)*

Understanding the Genre

- Understand lists are a functional way to organize information
- Understand that the form of a list or procedure is usually one item under another and it may be numbered
- Understand procedural writing (how-to) as a list of directions for how to do something and a list of what is needed
- Understand how to craft procedural writing from mentor texts
- Understand how drawings can help the reader understand information

Writing in the Genre

- Make lists in the appropriate form with one item under another
- Use lists to plan activities or support memory
- Use a list to inform writing (poems or informational)
- Use number words or transition words
- Make lists with items that are appropriate to the purpose of the list
- Write procedural or how-to books
- Write steps of a procedure with appropriate sequence and explicitness
- Include pictures to illustrate the steps in a procedure

TEST WRITING *(extended response, short answer)*

Understanding the Genre

- Understand that test writing often requires writing about an assigned topic Understand that test writing is a particular kind of writing used when taking tests
- Understand that some writing serves the purpose of demonstrating what a person knows or can do as a writer
- Understand that test writing often requires writing about something real

Writing in the Genre

- Analyze the prompt to understand the purpose, genre, and audience for the writing
- Read and internalize the criteria for an acceptable response
- Write focused responses to questions and to prompts
- Write concisely and to the direction of the question or prompt
- Elaborate on important points
- Exclude extraneous details
- Incorporate one's knowledge of craft in shaping response

WRITING ABOUT READING *(all genres)*

(See the Writing About Reading continuum, pages 114–115.)

Writing

❑ **Selecting Goals:** *Behaviors to Notice, Teach, and Support*

CRAFT

ORGANIZATION

Text Structure
- Organize texts in different ways
- Write a text that is narrative ordered by time
- Understand that an informational text is ordered by logic (categories, sequences, ideas related to each other)
- Begin to use underlying structures (description, compare and contrast, sequence, problem and solution)
- Write an author page at the beginning or end of a book to give information about the author
- Dedicate a story to someone and write the dedication inside the cover, on the title page or copyright page, or on a page of its own
- Create a picture book as one kind of writing

Beginnings, Endings, Titles
- Use a variety of beginnings to engage the reader
- Use a variety of endings to engage and satisfy the reader (for example, surprise, circular story)
- Use a variety of beginning, middle, and ending structures appropriate to the genre
- Select an appropriate title for a poem, story, or informational book

Presentation of Ideas
- Tell one part, idea, or group of ideas on each page of a book
- Present ideas clearly
- Organize information into categories for presentation
- Show major topics by using headings
- Use headings, a table of contents, and other features to help the reader find information and understand how facts are related
- Use time appropriately as an organizing tool
- Show steps in enough detail that a reader can follow a sequence
- Bring a piece to closure through an ending or summary statement
- Order the writing in ways that are characteristic to the genre (narrative or informational)
- Use graphics (diagrams, illustrations, photos) to provide information
- Use some vocabulary specific to the topic or content

IDEA DEVELOPMENT
- Communicate main points clearly to readers
- Provide supporting information or examples that are accurate, relevant, and helpful
- Gather and internalize information and then write it in own words

LANGUAGE USE
- Borrow a word, phrase, or a sentence from another writer
- Use memorable words or phrases
- Show through language instead of telling
- Use examples to make meaning clear to readers

WORD CHOICE
- Show ability to vary the text by choosing alternative words (for example, alternatives for *said*)
- Learn new words from reading and try them out in writing
- Use transitional words for time flow (*after, then*)
- Use vocabulary appropriate for the topic

VOICE
- Write with a unique perspective
- Write in a way that speaks directly to the reader
- State information in a unique or surprising way
- Use punctuation to make the text interesting and effective

CONVENTIONS

TEXT LAYOUT
- Arrange print on the page to support the text's meaning and to help the reader notice important information
- Understand that layout of print and illustrations are important in conveying the meaning of a text
- Understand how to use layout, spacing, and size of print to create titles, headings, and subheadings

GRAMMAR

Sentence Structure
- Write complete sentences
- Use a range of complete sentences (declarative, interrogative, exclamatory)

Parts of Speech
- Use subject and verb agreement in simple sentences (*we were*)
- Use nouns and pronouns that are in agreement (*Mike/he*)
- Use prepositional phrases, adjectives, and adverbs correctly

Tense
- Write in past tense (*I went home yesterday.*)
- Write in present tense (*Owls love to . . .*)
- Write in future tense (*I'm going to go . . .*)

CAPITALIZATION
- Use a capital letter for the first word of a sentence
- Use capital letters appropriately to capitalize days, months, cities, states
- Use capitals for names of people and places
- Use all capital letters for a head or for emphasis
- Use capitals to start the first letter in the first word, last word, and most other words in titles

Writing

❏ **Selecting Goals:** *Behaviors to Notice, Teach, and Support (cont.)*

PUNCTUATION

- Understand and use ellipses to show pause or anticipation, usually before something surprising
- Use dashes and ellipses for emphasis or to slow down the text for readers
- Use periods, exclamation points, and question marks as ending marks
- Use quotation marks around the speaker's exact words
- Use periods after abbreviations
- Notice the use of punctuation marks in books and try them out in own writing
- Use apostrophes in contractions and possessives
- Use commas to identify a series

SPELLING

- Correctly spell familiar high-frequency words (200+), words with regular letter-sound relationships (including consonant blends and digraphs and some vowel patterns), and commonly used endings
- Take apart multisyllable words to spell the parts accurately or close to accurately
- Use knowledge of phonogram patterns to generate multisyllable words
- Spell simple and some complex plurals
- Use simple rules for adding inflectional endings to words (drop *e*, double letter)
- Spell simple possessives
- Spell most contractions
- Spell words that have been studied (spelling words)
- Write easy compound words accurately
- Spell many one-syllable words that have vowel and *r* correctly

HANDWRITING/WORD-PROCESSING

- Begin to develop efficient keyboarding skills
- Form upper-and lowercase letters efficiently and proportionately in manuscript print
- Use word processor to plan, draft, revise, edit, and publish
- Make changes on the screen to revise and edit, and publish documents

WRITING PROCESS

REHEARSING/PLANNING

Purpose

- Write for a specific purpose: to inform, entertain, persuade, reflect, instruct, retell, maintain relationships, plan
- Understand how the purpose of the writing influences the selection of genre
- Select the genre for the writing based on the purpose
- Tell whether a piece of writing is a story or an informational text

Audience

- Write with a specific reader or audience in mind
- Understand how the writing meets the needs of a specific reader or audience
- Plan and organize information for the intended reader(s)
- Understand audience as all readers rather than just the teacher

Oral Language

- Generate and expand ideas through talk with peers and teacher
- Look for ideas and topics in personal experiences, shared through talk
- Explore relevant questions in talking about a topic
- Identify the meaning to convey a message
- Use talk and storytelling to generate and rehearse language (that may be written later)
- Use language in stories that is specific to a topic
- Tell stories in chronological order
- Retell stories in chronological order

Gathering Seeds/Resources/Experimenting with Writing

- Use a writer's notebook or booklet as a tool for collecting ideas, experimenting, planning, sketching, or drafting
- Reread a writer's notebook to select topics
- Use sketching, webs, lists, and freewriting to think about, plan for, and try out writing
- Try out beginnings

Content, Topic, Theme

- Observe carefully events, people, settings, and other aspects of the world to gather information on a topic
- Get ideas from other books and writers about how to approach a topic
- Choose a topic that is significant
- Decide what is most important about the topic or story
- Use resources, including the Internet, to get information on a topic
- Select own topics for informational writing and state what is important about the topic
- Stay focused on a topic
- Select details that will support the topic

Inquiry/Research/Exploration

- Form questions to answer about a topic
- Take notes or make sketches to help in remembering or generating information
- Participate actively in experiences and remember details that contribute to writing and drawing
- Select the most important information about a topic or story
- Gather information (with teacher assistance) about a topic from books or other print and media resources while preparing to write about it

Writing

❑ **Selecting Goals:** *Behaviors to Notice, Teach, and Support (cont.)*

Genre/Form

- Select from a variety of forms the kind of text that will fit the purpose (book with illustrations and words; alphabet book; label book; poetry book; question and answer book; illustration-only book)
- Understand that illustrations play different roles in a text (increase reader's enjoyment, add information, show sequence)

DRAFTING/REVISING

Understanding the Process

- Understand the role of the writer, teacher, or peer writer in conference
- Understand that other writers can be helpful in the process
- Change writing in response to peer or teacher feedback

Producing a Draft

- Write a draft or discovery draft (write fast and as much as possible on a topic)
- Engage the reader with a strong lead
- Bring the piece to closure with an ending or final statement
- Establish an initiating event and follow with a series of events in a narrative
- Maintain control of a central idea across the piece
- Present ideas in logical order across the piece

Rereading

- Recognize and point out the most important part of a piece of writing
- Reread and revise the draft or rewrite a section to clarify meaning
- Reread each day before writing more

Adding Information

- Add information to the middle to clarify meaning for readers
- Expand information through adding details or examples
- Add dialogue to provide information, provide narration, or show thoughts and feelings (in quotes or speech balloons)

Deleting Information

- Take out repetitive words, phrases, or sentences, or add to meaning
- Delete words or sentences that do not make sense
- Take out unnecessary words, phrases, or sentences

Reorganizing Information

- Move sentences around for better sequence
- Move information from one part of the text to another to make a text clearer

Changing Text

- Identify vague parts and provide specificity
- Change words to make the writing more interesting

Using Tools and Techniques

- Add letters, words, phrases, or sentences using a caret or sticky note with an asterisk
- Use a spider leg or piece of paper taped on to insert text
- Use a number to identify place to add information and an additional paper with numbers to write the information to insert
- Reorder a piece by cutting it apart or laying out the pages

EDITING AND PROOFREADING

Understanding the Process

- Understand that the writer shows respect to the reader by applying what is known to correct errors
- Understand that the better the spelling and space between words, the easier it is for the reader to read it
- Know how to use an editing and proofreading checklist

A second grader's book about how to travel

Writing

❏ **Selecting Goals:** *Behaviors to Notice, Teach, and Support (cont.)*

Editing for Conventions

- Check and correct letter formation
- Edit for conventional spelling of important words (for publication)
- Edit for the spelling of known words (should be spelled conventionally)
- Edit for spelling errors by circling or underlining words that do not look right and making another attempt
- Understand that the teacher will be final spelling editor for the published piece (after the student has used everything known)
- Edit for capitalization and end punctuation
- Edit for sentence sense

Using Tools

- Use simple spell check programs on the computer
- Use beginning reference tools (for example, word walls, personal word lists, or word cards to assist in word choice or checking spelling)

PUBLISHING

- Select a poem, story, or informational book to publish
- Include graphics or illustrations as appropriate to the text
- Generate multiple titles to arrive at the most suitable and interesting
- Select a title that fits the content of the piece to publish (or complete as final draft)
- Share a text with peers by reading it aloud
- Add to the text during the publishing process (for example, illustrations and other graphics, cover spread, title, dedication, table of contents, about the author piece)
- Attend to layout of text in final publication
- Use labels and captions on drawings that are displayed
- Understand publishing as the sharing of a piece of writing with an audience

SKETCHING AND DRAWING

- Create drawings that are related to the written text and increase readers' understanding and enjoyment
- Use sketching to support memory and help in planning
- Use drawing to capture details important to a topic
- Provide important information in illustrations
- Use drawings and sketches to represent people, places, things, and ideas in the composing, revising, and publishing process
- Add labels or sentences to drawings as needed to explain them
- Add details to drawings to add information or increase interest
- Create drawings that employ careful attention to color or detail

VIEWING SELF AS A WRITER

- Write in a variety of genres across the year
- Understand writing as a vehicle to communicate meaning
- Take risks as a writer
- View self as writer
- Write with independence
- Write with initiative and investment
- Produce a reasonable quantity of writing within the time available
- Attend to the language and craft of other writers in order to learn more as a writer
- Show ability to discuss what is being worked on as a writer in a conference
- Seek feedback on writing
- Be willing to work at the craft of writing, incorporating new learning from instruction
- Select best pieces of writing from own collection and give reasons for the selections
- Self-evaluate own writing and talk about what is good about it and what techniques were used
- Compare previous to revised writing and notice and talk about the differences
- State what was learned from each piece of writing

Play with your toys while you wait. You might want to right a book.

Oral, Visual, and Technological Communication

❑ **Selecting Goals:** *Behaviors and Understandings to Notice, Teach, and Support*

LISTENING AND SPEAKING

LISTENING AND UNDERSTANDING

- Listen to remember, and follow directions (multiple steps)
- Listen actively to others read or talk about their writing and give feedback
- Listen with attention during lessons and respond with statements and questions
- Listen with attention and understanding to oral reading of stories, poems, and informational texts
- Listen attentively to presentations by the teacher and fellow students and be able to identify the main idea
- Understand and interpret information presented in visual media

SOCIAL INTERACTION

- Use conventions of respectful speaking
- Speak at an appropriate volume—not too loud but loud enough to be heard and understood by others
- Speak at appropriate volume in different contexts
- Speak clearly enough to be understood by others in conversation
- Engage in the turn-taking of conversation
- Use appropriate ways to get a turn
- Actively participate in conversation; listening and looking at the person who is speaking

EXTENDED DISCUSSION

- Listen to and build on the talk of others
- Engage actively in routines (for example, turn and talk)
- Ask clear questions during small-group and whole-class discussion
- Ask questions for clarification to gain information
- Participate actively in small-group and whole-class discussion
- Use grade level-appropriate specific vocabulary when talking about texts (*title, author*)
- Relate or compare one's own knowledge and experience with information from other speakers

CONTENT

- Describe cause-and-effect relationships
- Provide reasons and argue for a point, using evidence
- Predict and recall stories or events
- Offer solutions and explanations for story problems
- Explain and describe people, events, places, and objects
- Describe similarities and differences among people, places, events, and objects
- Categorize objects, people, places, and events
- Report interesting information from background experience or reading

Oral, Visual, and Technological Communication

❑ **Selecting Goals:** *Behaviors and Understandings to Notice, Teach, and Support (cont.)*

PRESENTATION

VOICE

- Show enthusiasm while speaking about a topic
- Show confidence when presenting
- Vary the voice to emphasize important aspects of events or people
- Tell stories in an interesting way
- Present facts in an interesting way

CONVENTIONS

- Speak at appropriate volume to be heard when addressing large and small groups
- Look at the audience while talking
- Speak at an appropriate rate to be understood by the audience
- Enunciate words clearly
- Correctly pronounce all words except for a few sophisticated new content words (with the understanding that there will be variations based on children's home language or dialect)
- Use intonation and word stress to emphasize important ideas
- Vary language according to purpose

ORGANIZATION

- Have the topic or story in mind before starting to speak
- Have an audience in mind before starting to speak
- Maintain a clear focus on the important or main ideas
- Present ideas and information in a logical sequence
- Have a clear beginning and conclusion
- Have a plan or notes to support the presentation

WORD CHOICE

- Use language from stories and informational texts when retelling stories or making a report
- Use words that describe (adjectives and adverbs)
- Use language appropriate to oral presentation words (rather than literary language or slang)
- Use content-specific words when needed to explain a topic

IDEAS AND CONTENT

- Recite some poems from memory
- Recite poems or tell stories with effective use of intonation and word stress to emphasize important ideas, engage listeners' interest, and show character traits
- Engage in role play of characters or events encountered in stories
- Make brief oral reports that demonstrate understanding of a topic
- Demonstrate understanding of a topic by providing relevant facts and details

MEDIA

- Use props, illustrations, images, or other digital media to extend the meaning of a presentation
- Identify and acknowledge sources of the information included in oral presentations

TECHNOLOGY

COMPUTER LITERACY

- Use mouse or keyboard effectively to navigate the computer and search for information
- Use effective keyboarding movements for efficient use of the computer
- Send and respond to email messages
- Understand basic controls of a web browser, including how to initiate a search and bookmark favorite websites
- Use spell check, monitoring each suggested substitution

ONLINE READING AND INFORMATION LITERACY

- Use a simple search engine to find information from approved and accessible sites
- Locate and identify specific information (text, pictures, animation) within approved and accessible websites
- Download (or copy and paste) selected information from websites and document the original source of the material

COMPOSING AND PUBLISHING DIGITAL TEXTS

- Use simple word-processing programs to draft and prepare some pieces for publication
- Include scanned or digital images in word-processed documents
- Understand the affordances of different spaces for publishing digital texts
- Create simple multimedia projects such as digital videos, podcasts, or slideshows that may include voice, images, and text

Phonics, Spelling, and Word Study

❑ **Selecting Goals:** *Behaviors and Understandings to Notice, Teach, and Support*

LETTER/SOUND RELATIONSHIPS

- Recognize and use the full range of consonant letters and letter clusters (*st, ch*) in beginning, middle, and ending position in words
- Recognize and use long and short vowel sounds in words
- Recognize and use letter combinations that represent long vowel sounds (*ai, ay, ee, ea, oa, ow*)
- Recognize and use vowel sounds in open syllables (CV: *ho-tel*)
- Recognize and use vowel sounds in closed syllables (CVC: *lem-on*)
- Recognize and use vowel sounds with *r* (*car, first, hurt, her, corn, floor, world, near*)
- Recognize and use letters that represent no sound in words (*lamb, light*)

SPELLING PATTERNS

- Recognize and use a large number of phonogram patterns (VC, CVC, CVCe, VCC, VVC, VVCC, VVCe, VCCC, VVCCC)

HIGH-FREQUENCY WORDS

- Write and read 150 to 200 high-frequency words automatically
- Employ self-monitoring strategies for continually accumulating ability to read and write accurately a large core of high-frequency words (working toward automatic knowledge of the five hundred most frequent)

WORD MEANING

COMPOUND WORDS

- Recognize and use a variety of compound words (*into, myself, itself, cannot, inside, maybe, nobody, outside, sunshine, today, together, upset, yourself, without, sometimes, something*)

SYNONYMS AND ANTONYMS

- Recognize and use synonyms (words that mean about the same: *begin/start, close/shut, fix/mend, earth/world, happy/glad, high/tall, jump/leap*)
- Recognize and use antonyms (words that mean the opposite: *hot/ cold, all/none, break/fix, little/big, long/short, sad/glad, stop/start*)

HOMOGRAPHS AND HOMOPHONES

- Recognize and use homophones (sound the same, different spelling and meaning: *to/too/two, here/hear, blue/blew, there/their/they're*)
- Recognize and use homographs (same spelling and different meaning: *bat/bat, well/well, wind/wind*)
- Recognize and use words with multiple meanings (*play/play*)

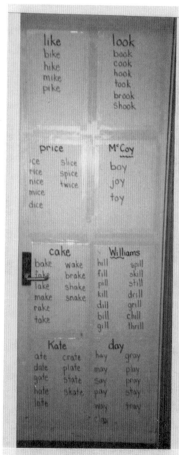

Phonics, Spelling, and Word Study

❏ **Selecting Goals:** *Behaviors and Understandings to Notice, Teach, and Support (cont.)*

WORD STRUCTURE

SYLLABLES

- Understand how vowels appear in syllables (every syllable has a vowel)
- Recognize and use syllables in words with double consonants (*lad-der*) and in words with the VV pattern (*ri-ot*)

PLURALS

- Understand the concept of plurals and plural forms: adding *-s* (*dogs, cats, apples, cans, desks, faces, trees, monkeys*); adding *-es* (when words end in *x, ch, sh, s, ss, tch, zz*); changing spelling (*foot/feet, goose/geese, man/men, mouse/mice, woman/women*)

VERB ENDINGS

- Recognize and form present and past tense by using endings (*-es, -ed: like, likes, liked*); form present participle by adding *-ing* (*liking*); make a verb past tense (*-ed, d: played, liked*)
- Recognize and use endings: *-er* to a verb to make a noun (*read/reader, play/player, jump/jumper*), *-er* to a verb that ends with a short vowel and a consonant (*dig/digger, run/runner*), *-r* to a verb that ends in silent *r* (*bake/baker, hike/hiker*), *-er* to a verb ending in *y* (*carry/carrier*)

ENDINGS FOR ADJECTIVES

- Recognize and use endings that show comparisons (*-er, -est*)
- Contractions
- Recognize and understand contractions with *am* (*I'm*), *is* (*he's*), *will* (*I'll*), *not* (*can't*)

POSSESSIVES

- Recognize and use possessives that add an apostrophe and an *s* to a singular noun (*dog/dog's, woman/woman's, girl/girl's, boy/boy's*)

BASE WORDS

- Remove the ending from a base word to make a new word (*running, run*)

PREFIXES

- Recognize and use common prefixes (*re-, un-*)

WORD-SOLVING ACTIONS

- Use known words to monitor reading and spelling
- Use letters and relationships to sounds to read and write words
- Break words into syllables to read or write them
- Add, delete, and change letters (*in/win, bat/bats*), letter clusters (*an/plan, cat/catch*), and word parts to make new words
- Take apart compound words or join words make compound words (*into/in-to, side-walk/sidewalk*)
- Use letter-sound knowledge to monitor reading and spelling accuracy
- Use the parts of compound words to solve a word and derive the meaning
- Use known words and word parts (onsets and rimes) to help in reading and spelling new words (*br-ing, cl-ap*)
- Notice patterns and categorize high-frequency words to assist in learning them quickly
- Recognize base words and remove prefixes and suffixes to break them down and solve them

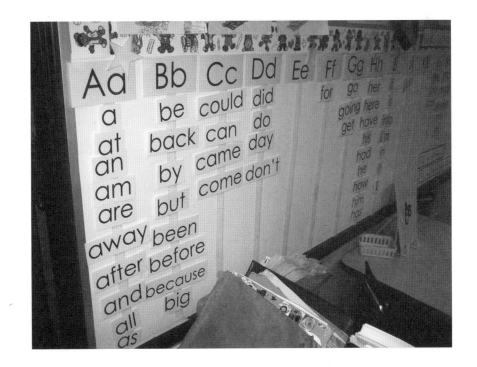

Guided Reading

- ❑ **Level Pre-A**
- ❑ **Level A**
- ❑ **Level B**
- ❑ **Level C**
- ❑ **Level D**
- ❑ **Level E**
- ❑ **Level F**
- ❑ **Level G**
- ❑ **Level H**
- ❑ **Level I**
- ❑ **Level J**
- ❑ **Level K**
- ❑ **Level L**
- ❑ **Level M**
- ❑ **Level N**

Readers at **Pre-A Level:**

Typically, children at this level are in prekindergarten or kindergarten. They are beginning to notice aspects of print in the environment and in books. Supportive teachers engage them in shared reading and group writing of enlarged texts that they read with the support of the teacher. Teachers point out directionality, letter formation, spaces, words, and aspects of language. Often, they have students locate words that begin with particular letters, for example, those that begin like their names. They engage in drawing and approximated writing every day so they begin to produce letter-like forms, particular letters, and even words and share much of their thinking through drawing.

After shared reading of a poem or other text, children may use a pointer to read it independently or with a partner. If little versions of the shared text are available, some children will be able to point and read them. In all of this reading, they depend on picture information, memory, and awareness of language; but they are also learning visual signposts, especially if they are having lessons on letters and sounds and engaging in writing.

Some of the children will move from this supported choral reading of simple texts to actual reading of Level A books. While we do not recommend formal guided reading lessons in prekindergarten, you may want to sit down for about five minutes with particular individuals or very small groups of children who show interest and guide them through the shared reading (chorally) of a Level A text while you observe their careful pointing.

The text factors that are appropriate for teacher supported reading by the children are the same as those listed for Level A.

Prekindergarten Children

Most prekindergarten children will be at pre-A level. We have not provided curriculum goals for guided reading for prekindergarten children; but you will want to notice and encourage important emergent literacy behaviors such as those listed under Early Reading Behaviors on the Phonics, Spelling, and Word Study continuum. If you are working with a prekindergarten group reading at level A, consult the Level A continuum for behaviors to notice, teach, and support, but we would not consider these goals for the end of prekindergarten. It is more important to build a strong oral language foundation, to engage students in a wide variety of excellent read-aloud texts, and provide many opportunities for exploring writing and drawing.

Readers at **Level A:**

At Level A, readers are just beginning to learn how print works and to construct the *alphabetic principle* (understand that there are relationships between sounds and letters). They are learning to look (aided by the finger) left to right across words and across one line of print. They are learning to search for and use information from pictures and to use simple language structures to help them learn about print. They differentiate print from pictures and begin to notice the distinctive features of letters, attaching names to them. They are learning to read one line sentences with simple words and on familiar topics. They are learning how to match one spoken word with one word in print. As they read, they begin to learn some easy, high-frequency words, to notice and use visual signposts of some words, and to notice mismatches. They use what they know (for example, a sound and related letter) to begin to self-monitor reading. Reading and rereading these very simple texts will help them gain gradual control of ways to look at and work with print.

Selecting Texts: Characteristics of Texts at This Level

GENRE/FORMS

Genre
- Some simple factual texts
- Animal fantasy
- Realistic fiction

Forms
- Picture books

TEXT STRUCTURE

Fiction
- Very simple narratives with stories carried by pictures

Nonfiction
- Focused on a single idea or one simple topic
- Underlying text structure (description)
- Present one simple category of information
- Some texts with sequential information

CONTENT
- Familiar, easy content (family, play, pets, school)
- All concepts supported by picture information

THEMES AND IDEAS
- Very familiar themes and ideas

LANGUAGE AND LITERARY FEATURES
- Mostly nameless, flat characters
- Repeating language patterns (simple three to six words on each page)
- Texts with familiar settings close to children's experience
- A few simple elements of fantasy (for example, talking animals)

SENTENCE COMPLEXITY
- Short, predictable sentences that are close to oral language
- Simple sentences (no embedded phrases or clauses)
- Subject preceding verb in most sentences
- Simple sentences (subject and predicate)

VOCABULARY
- Almost all vocabulary familiar to children and likely to be used in their oral language
- Word meanings illustrated by pictures

I can kick.

4

5

WORDS

- Mostly one-syllable words with very easy and predictable letter-sound relationships
- Some simple plurals
- Repeated use of a few easy high-frequency words
- Some words with -s and -ing
- Many words with easy, predictable letter-sound relationships (decodable)
- Words with easy spelling patterns

ILLUSTRATIONS

General

- Illustrations that match print very closely
- Clear illustrations that fully support meaning
- Illustrations that support each page of text
- Very simple illustrations with no distracting detail
- Consistent layout of illustrations and print

BOOK AND PRINT FEATURES

Length

- One line of text on each page
- Very short, usually eight pages of print and illustrations

Print and Layout

- Ample space between words and lines
- Print in large plain font
- Print clearly separated from pictures
- Consistent placement of print (layout)

Punctuation

- Period only punctuation in most texts

Selecting Goals: Behaviors and Understandings to Notice, Teach, and Support

Thinking *Within* the Text

Solving Words
- Recognize most words quickly with the support of meaning and language structure
- Say a word and predict its first letter before locating it
- Say a word slowly to hear and identify the first sound and connect to a letter
- Recognize a few easy high-frequency words
- Locate easy high-frequency words in a text
- Locate familiar, easy high-frequency words by noticing anything about the word
- Slow down speech to assist in voice-print match

Monitoring and Correcting
- Reread the sentence to problem solve, self-correct, or confirm
- Reread to search for/use information from language or meaning
- Self-monitor and self-correct using language structure
- Use voice-print match to self-monitor and self-correct
- Show evidence of close attention to print
- Use known words to self-monitor and self-correct

Searching for and Using Information
- Read left to right across one line of print
- Match one spoken word with one printed word
- Search for information in the print and pictures or photographs
- Use oral language in combination with pointing, matching voice with words on the page (indicated by crisp pointing)
- Search for and use information from pictures
- Reread to search for information
- Use language structure and meaning to learn about print

Summarizing
- Remember what the story is about during reading
- Remember information to help in understanding the end of a story
- Remember important information

Maintaining Fluency
- Point crisply and read at a steady rate slow enough to match voice to print but without long pauses
- Notice and use end punctuation and reflect it in voice

Adjusting
- Slow down to problem solve words and resume reading with momentum

Planning for Word Work after Guided Reading

One- to three-minute demonstrations and active student engagement using a chart or easel, white board, magnet letters, or pencil and paper can develop fluency and flexibility in visual processing. Plan for explicit work in specific visual processing areas that need support.

Examples:

- Recognize a few easy high-frequency words (for example, *the, a, I, and, is, can, in, it*) quickly
- Recognize a few easy CVC words (*can, get*) quickly
- Make a few easy CVC words (*cat, pin, sat, hot, can*)
- Make a few easy high-frequency words (*it, is, in, we, me, to, the*)
- Write a few easy CVC words (*can, sit, cat, run*)

- Write a few easy high-frequency words (*a, an, the, me, to*)
- Match/sort pictures by initial/final sounds (*girl, glass*)
- Match or sort pictures by rhyming sound at the end (*man, fan, can*)
- Match or sort letters by a variety of features (uppercase or lowercase; tall or short; with and without sticks, circles, tails, dots, tunnels)
- Match lowercase letters with speed

- Clap the syllables in one- and two-syllable words (from pictures)
- Search for and locate letters by name quickly
- Read the Alphabet Linking Chart by letter names, pictures and words, and in different ways (all vowels, all consonants, letters only, backwards order, every other letter)

Thinking *Beyond* the Text

Predicting
- Use knowledge of language structure to anticipate the text
- Make predictions based on information in the pictures
- Predict the ending of a story based on reading the beginning and middle
- Make predictions based on personal experiences and knowledge

Making Connections
- Talk about own experiences in relation to the text
- Make connections between texts on the same topic or with the same content
- Identify recurring characters or settings when applicable

Synthesizing
- Talk about what the reader already knows relative to text information
- Identify new information in text or pictures

Inferring
- Talk about characters' feelings
- Talk about the pictures, revealing interpretation of a problem or of characters' feelings

Thinking *About* the Text

Analyzing
- Understand how the ideas in a book are related to each other
- Understand how the ideas in a text are related to the title

Critiquing
- Share opinions about a text
- Share opinions about illustrations

Readers at **Level B:**

At Level B, readers are learning how print works, particularly developing the concepts of left-to-right directionality across words and across lines of print. They are firming up voice-print match while reading texts with two or more lines of print. Readers may recognize repeating language patterns in texts that have very simple stories and focus on a single idea, as well as learn more about the distinctive features of letters and the connections between sounds and letters. It is very important that they begin to self-monitor their reading and attempt to self-correct as they notice the mismatches and check one source of information against another. They are beginning to notice and use visual signposts and are expanding their core of simple high-frequency words.

Selecting Texts: Characteristics of Texts at This Level

GENRE/FORMS

Genre
- Some simple factual texts
- Animal fantasy
- Realistic fiction

Forms
- Picture books

TEXT STRUCTURE

Fiction
- Simple narratives with stories carried by pictures

Nonfiction
- Focused on a single idea or one simple topic
- Underlying text structure (description)
- Present one simple category of information
- Some texts with sequential information

CONTENT
- Familiar, easy content (family, play, pets, school)
- All concepts supported by picture information

THEMES AND IDEAS
- Very familiar themes and ideas

LANGUAGE AND LITERARY FEATURES
- Mostly nameless, flat characters
- Repeating language patterns (simple three to seven words in a sentence)
- Texts with familiar settings close to children's experience
- A few simple elements of fantasy (for example, talking animals)

SENTENCE COMPLEXITY
- Short, predictable sentences that are close to oral language
- Mostly simple sentences (no embedded phrases or clauses)
- Subject preceding verb in most sentences
- Simple sentences (subject and predicate often with phrases at the end)

VOCABULARY
- Almost all vocabulary familiar to children and likely to be used in their oral language
- Word meanings illustrated by pictures

My little dog likes
to run with me.

6

7

WORDS
- Mostly one-syllable words with very easy and predictable letter-sound relationships
- Some simple plurals
- Repeated use of a few easy high-frequency words
- Some words with -s and -ing
- Many words with easy, predictable letter-sound relationships (decodable)
- Words with easy spelling patterns

ILLUSTRATIONS

General
- Illustrations that match print very closely
- Clear illustrations that fully support meaning
- Illustrations that support each page of text
- Very simple illustrations with little distracting detail
- Consistent layout of illustrations and print

BOOK AND PRINT FEATURES

Length
- Very short, usually eight pages of print and illustrations
- Two or more lines of text on each page

Print and Layout
- Ample space between words and lines
- Print in large plain font
- Sentences turn over one or more lines
- Print clearly separated from pictures
- Consistent placement of print and illustrations (layout)
- Line breaks match ends of phrases and sentences

Punctuation
- Period only punctuation in most texts

Selecting Goals: Behaviors and Understandings to Notice, Teach, and Support

Thinking *Within* the Text

Solving Words
- Recognize most words quickly with the support of meaning and language structure
- Use the first letter of a word in connection with meaning or language syntax to solve it
- Locate unknown words by identifying the first letter
- Say a word slowly to hear and identify the first sound and connect to a letter
- Recognize a few easy high-frequency words
- Locate high-frequency words in a text
- Use knowledge of syllables to help in voice-print match
- Slow down speech to assist in voice-print match

Monitoring and Correcting
- Reread the sentence to problem solve, self-correct, or confirm
- Use first letters of words (and related sounds) to monitor and self-correct
- Use prior knowledge to monitor and self-correct
- Self-monitor and self-correct using language structure
- Begin to cross-check one kind of information against another to monitor and self-correct reading (for example, meaning with visual information)
- Self-monitor and self-correct using meaning in text and pictures
- Use voice-print match to self-monitor and self-correct
- Show evidence of close attention to print
- Use known words to self-monitor and self-correct

Searching for and Using Information
- Read left to right across more than one line of print
- Return to the left to read the next line of print
- Match one spoken word with one printed word (voice-print match indicated by crisp pointing under each word)
- Search for and use information in print (letters and sounds, known words)
- Ask questions to clarify meaning or get information
- Search for and use information in pictures and language
- Reread to search for and use information from pictures or language
- Remember and use language patterns to help in reading a text

Summarizing
- Remember what the story is about during reading
- Remember details while reading
- Remember information to help in understanding the end of a story
- Discuss the text after reading, remembering important information or details of a story

Maintaining Fluency
- Point and read at a steady rate slow enough to match but without long pauses
- Notice and use ending punctuation and reflect it in the voice

Adjusting
- Slow down to problem solve words and resume reading with momentum

Planning for Word Work after Guided Reading

One- to three-minute demonstrations and active student engagement using a chart or easel, white board, magnet letters, or pencil and paper can develop fluency and flexibility in visual processing. Plan for explicit work in specific visual processing areas that need support.

Examples:

- Recognize a few easy high-frequency words (for example, *the, and, my, like, see, is, can, in, it*) quickly
- Recognize and make a few CVC words (*hit, cut, man, dog, pet*)
- Write a few CVC words (*run, can, pet*)
- Write a few easy high-frequency words (for example, *can like, the, me, we, is*)

- Match or sort pictures by initial sounds (*bear, bike, bone*)
- Match or sort pictures by ending sounds (*horse, glass, dress*)
- Match or sort letters by a variety of features quickly (uppercase or lowercase; tall or short; with and without sticks, circles, tails, dots, tunnels)

- Match or sort pictures with rhyming sounds (*pen, ten, hen*)
- Match or sort upper- and lowercase letters quickly (*Aa, Dd*)
- Clap the syllables in words with one, two, or three parts
- Recognize letters by name and locate them quickly in words
- Read Alphabet Linking Chart in different ways (sing, read consonants, read letter names, read pictures, backwards order, every other letter)

Thinking *Beyond* the Text

Predicting
- Use knowledge of language structure to anticipate the text
- Make predictions using language structure
- Make predictions based on the information in pictures
- Predict the ending of a story based on reading the beginning and middle
- Make predictions based on personal experiences and knowledge

Making Connections
- Discuss personal experiences in relation to the text
- Make connections between texts on the same topic or with the same content
- Identify recurring characters when applicable

Synthesizing
- Identify what the reader already knows relative to information in the text, prior to reading
- Identify new information in text or pictures

Inferring
- Understand characters' feelings and reveal through talk or drawing
- Understand the pictures reveal interpretation of a problem or of characters' feelings

Thinking *About* the Text

Analyzing
- Notice and appreciate humor (and show by verbal or nonverbal means)
- Realize stories have a beginning and an end
- Understand how the ideas in a book are related to each other
- Understand how the ideas in a text are related to the title

Critiquing
- Share opinions about books
- Share opinions about illustrations

Readers at Level C:

At Level C, readers encounter simple stories and familiar topics in texts that usually have two to six lines of print on each page. They smoothly and automatically move left to right across words and across lines of print, sweeping back to the left margin for each new line and reading print on both left and right pages. Reading is becoming smooth, allowing for some expression, and the eyes are taking over the process of matching the spoken word to the printed word. Readers are moving away from needing to point and are showing phrased reading. Readers are noticing quotation marks and reflecting dialogue with the voice. They are developing a larger core of high-frequency words that they recognize quickly and easily. At this level, readers are consistently monitoring their reading and cross-checking one source of information against another. Overt self-correction reveals readers' growing control of the ability to process print.

Selecting Texts: Characteristics of Texts at This Level

GENRE/FORMS

Genre
- Some simple factual texts
- Animal fantasy
- Realistic fiction

Forms
- Picture books

TEXT STRUCTURE

Fiction
- Simple narratives with several episodes (usually similar or repetitive)

Nonfiction
- Focused on a single idea or one simple topic
- Underlying text structure (description)
- Present one simple category of information
- Some texts with sequential information

CONTENT
- Familiar, easy content (family, play, pets, school)
- All concepts supported by pictures

THEMES AND IDEAS
- Familiar themes and ideas

LANGUAGE AND LITERARY FEATURES
- Amusing one-dimensional characters
- Repeating natural language patterns
- Texts with familiar settings close to children's experience
- Simple dialogue (assigned by *said* in most texts)
- A few simple elements of fantasy (for example, talking animals)

SENTENCE COMPLEXITY
- Simple, predictable sentence structure but varied patterns
- Sentences that are questions
- Many sentences with prepositional phrases and adjectives
- Subject preceding verb in most sentences
- Simple sentences (subject and predicate)

VOCABULARY
- Almost all vocabulary familiar to children and likely to be used in their oral language
- Word meanings illustrated by pictures
- Some variation in words used to assign dialogue (mostly *said*)

She was sleeping
on the rug.
I said,
"Wake up, Socks!"

8

9

WORDS
- Mostly one or two-syllable words
- Simple plurals
- Some simple contractions and possessives (words with apostrophes)
- Greater range of easy high-frequency words
- Some words with -s and -ing
- Many words with easy, predictable letter-sound relationships (decodable)
- Some words used in different language structures (*said Mom; Mom said*)
- Words with easy spelling patterns

ILLUSTRATIONS

General
- Illustrations that match print very closely
- More meaning carried in the text and less with picture support
- Illustrations on every page or every other page
- Very simple illustrations with little distracting detail
- Consistent layout of illustrations and print

BOOK AND PRINT FEATURES

Length
- Very short, usually eight pages of print
- Two to five lines of text on each page

Print and Layout
- Ample space between words and lines
- Print in large plain font
- Some words in bold or larger font for emphasis
- Print clearly separated from pictures
- Consistent placement of print (layout)
- Line breaks match ends of phrases and sentences

Punctuation
- Ellipses in some texts to create expectation
- Periods, commas, quotation marks, exclamation points, and question marks in most texts

Selecting Goals: Behaviors and Understandings to Notice, Teach, and Support

Thinking *Within* the Text

Solving Words
- Recognize easy high-frequency words and simple regular words easily with support of meaning and language structure
- Locate the first and last letters of words in continuous text
- Notice the beginning letter of a word, connect to a sound, and say the first sound of a word
- Use letter-sound information in coordination with meaning and language structure to solve words
- Say words slowly to identify first sound, connect to letter, and locate the word in a text
- Recognize ten or more high-frequency words within continuous text
- Make connections between words by letters, sounds, or spelling patterns
- Use known words to make connections and solve words

Monitoring and Correcting
- Reread the sentence to problem solve, self-correct, or confirm
- Self-monitor and self-correct reading using initial letters and connections to sounds
- Self-monitor and self-correct using language structure
- Cross-check one kind of information against another to monitor and self-correct reading (for example, meaning with visual information)
- Self-monitor and self-correct using meaning in text and pictures
- Use known words to self-monitor and self-correct

Searching for and Using Information
- Read left to right across more than one line of print and return to the left to read the next line of print
- Search for and use information in print (letters, sounds, known words)
- Search for and use information from pictures
- Process texts with simple dialogue, all assigned to speakers
- Reread to search for/use information from language or meaning
- Remember and use language patterns to help in reading a text

Summarizing
- Remember information to help in understanding the end of a story
- Remember and use details when discussing a story after reading
- Understand and identify a simple sequence of events in a story

Maintaining Fluency
- Reflect language syntax by putting words together in phrases
- Notice and use ending punctuation and reflect it in the voice
- Reflect understanding of words in bold by saying the word louder (in fiction texts)
- Notice and use quotation marks and reflect dialogue with the voice
- Demonstrate appropriate stress on words in a sentence

Adjusting
- Slow down to problem solve words and resume reading with momentum

Planning for Word Work after Guided Reading

One- to three-minute demonstrations and active student engagement using a chart or easel, white board, magnet letters, or pencil and paper can develop fluency and flexibility in visual processing. Plan for explicit work in specific visual processing areas that need support.

Examples:

- Recognize a few easy high-frequency words (e.g., *the, and, like, here, look, see, is, can, in, it*)
- Make several CVC words (*cat, but, can, hot, get*)
- Break apart CVC words (*s-un, n-ot, g-et*)
- Recognize several CVC words (for example, *get, sun, man, not*)

- Write/make several easy high-frequency words
- Sort letters quickly by a variety of features (uppercase or lowercase; tall or short; with and without sticks, circles, tails, dots, tunnels)
- Match/sort words with rhymes (using pictures)
- Match pictures with letters using beginning or ending sounds

- Say and clap syllables in one-, two-, and three-syllable words (from pictures)
- Locate words rapidly using first letter and related sounds
- Say words slowly and write letters related to sounds
- Read the Alphabet Linking Chart in a variety of ways (for example, all consonants, all vowels, every other letter)

Thinking *Beyond* the Text

Predicting
- Use knowledge of language structure to anticipate the text
- Make predictions using information from pictures
- Predict the ending of a story based on reading the beginning and middle
- Make predictions based on personal experiences and knowledge
- Make predictions based on information gained through reading

Making Connections
- Make and discuss connections between texts and reader's personal experiences
- Make connections between texts that are alike in some way (topic, ending, characters)

Synthesizing
- Identify what the reader already knows relative to information in the text
- Identify new information in text or pictures
- Remember new information for discussion
- Talk about what the reader already knows about a topic or character prior to reading

Inferring
- Talk about characters' feelings and motives
- Show evidence in the print or pictures to support inference

Thinking *About* the Text

Analyzing
- Notice and point out connections between text and pictures
- Realize stories have a beginning and an end
- Understand how the ideas in a text are related to the title

Critiquing
- Share opinions about the text as a whole (beginning, characters, ending)
- Share opinions about illustrations

Readers at **Level D:**

At Level D, readers follow simple stories of fiction and fantasy and easy informational texts. They can track print with their eyes (not pointing) over two to six lines per page and process texts with more varied language patterns (and those patterns that exist are more complex). They notice and use a range of punctuation and read dialogue, reflecting the meaning through phrasing. Readers can solve many regular easy two-syllable words, usually those with inflectional endings (-*ing*) and simple compound words. Voice-print match is smooth and automatic, and pointing is rarely needed (only at difficulty). The core of known high-frequency words is expanding. Readers consistently monitor their reading and cross-check one source of information with another.

Selecting Texts: Characteristics of Texts at This Level

GENRE/FORMS

Genre
- Some simple factual texts
- Animal fantasy
- Realistic fiction
- A few very simple retellings of traditional tales

Forms
- Picture books

TEXT STRUCTURE

Fiction
- Simple narratives with several episodes (usually similar or repetitive)

Nonfiction
- Focused on a single idea or one simple topic
- Underlying text structure (description)
- Present one simple category of information
- Some texts with sequential information

CONTENT
- Familiar, easy content (family, play, pets, school)
- Most concepts supported by pictures

THEMES AND IDEAS
- Familiar themes and ideas

LANGUAGE AND LITERARY FEATURES
- Amusing or engaging one-dimensional characters
- More complex repeating language patterns
- Greater variety of language structures
- Texts with familiar settings close to children's experience
- Simple dialogue and some split dialogue
- Simple dialogue assigned to speaker
- Variety in assignment to speaker (other than *said*)
- Simple sequence of events (often repeated)
- A few simple elements of fantasy (for example, talking animals)

SENTENCE COMPLEXITY
- Some longer sentences (some with more than six words)
- Some sentences that are questions
- Many sentences with prepositional phrases and adjectives
- A few sentences beginning with phrases
- Mostly simple sentences (subject and predicate)

VOCABULARY
- Almost all vocabulary familiar to children and likely to be used in their oral language
- Word meanings illustrated by pictures
- Variation in words used to assign dialogue
- Greater range of vocabulary and multi-syllable words
- Large numbers of high-frequency words
- Complex word solving required to understand meaning

WORDS
- Mostly one- to two-syllable words
- Simple plurals
- Many high-frequency words
- Some words with -*s* and -*ing*
- Some words with inflectional endings (-*ing*)
- Many words with easy, predictable letter-sound relationships (decodable)
- Some words used multiple times in different language structures (*said Mom; Mom said*)
- Mostly simple spelling patterns

The pig went
in the little house.
The pig said,
"What a nice
little house!"

6

7

ILLUSTRATIONS

General
- Highly supportive illustrations that generally match the text
- Illustrations on every page or every other page
- More details in the illustrations

BOOK AND PRINT FEATURES

Length
- Very short, usually eight pages of print
- Mostly two to six lines of print per page (but variable)

Print and Layout
- Ample space between words and lines
- Print in large plain font
- Some words in bold or larger font for emphasis
- Some sentences that turn over one or more lines
- Sentences beginning on the left in most texts
- Print clearly separated from pictures
- Line breaks match ends of phrases and sentences

Punctuation
- Ellipses in some texts to create expectation
- Periods, commas, quotation marks, exclamation points, and question marks

Selecting Goals: Behaviors and Understandings to Notice, Teach, and Support

Thinking *Within* the Text

Solving Words
- Recognize a large number of regular words and easy high-frequency words quickly with the support of the meaning and language structure
- Locate the first and last letters of words in continuous text
- Say words slowly to identify first sound, connect to letter, and locate the word in a text
- Take apart words by using the sounds of individual letters in words with CVC patterns
- Recognize twenty or more high-frequency words within continuous text quickly
- Make connections between words by letters, sounds, or spelling patterns

Monitoring and Correcting
- Reread a sentence to problem solve, self-correct, or confirm
- Self-monitor accuracy and self-correct using known words, letter-sound information, and word parts
- Cross-check one kind of information against another to monitor and self-correct reading (for example, meaning with visual information)
- Use two or more sources of information (meaning, language structure, visual information) to self-monitor and self-correct reading
- Use known words to self-monitor and self-correct

Searching for and Using Information
- Notice details in pictures or photographs and use information to understand the text
- Process texts with simple dialogue and some pronouns, all assigned to speakers
- Reread to search for and use information
- Notice, search for, remember, and discuss information that is important to understanding
- Use text meaning and language structure to solve new words

Summarizing
- Remember information to help in understanding the end of a story
- Recall and retell the important information in or events from the text
- Understand and talk about a simple sequence of events or steps

Maintaining Fluency
- Identify and read phrases as word groups
- Reflect words in bold with the voice
- Notice and use quotation marks and reflect dialogue with the voice
- Reflect punctuation through appropriate pausing and intonation while reading orally
- Demonstrate appropriate stress on words in a sentence

Adjusting
- Slow down to problem solve and resume good rate of reading
- Anticipate and use language patterns when available but do not depend on them

Planning for Word Work after Guided Reading

One- to three-minute demonstrations and active student engagement using a chart or easel, white board, magnet letters, or pencil and paper can develop fluency and flexibility in visual processing. Plan for explicit work in specific visual processing areas that need support.

Examples:

- Recognize a few easy high-frequency words quickly (for example, *at, an, am, do, go, he, in, like, me, my, no, see, so, to, up, we*)
- Review high-frequency words from previous levels
- Write or make several high-frequency words quickly
- Add *-s* to words to make a plural and read them (*cat/cats*)

- Recognize several CVC words easily and quickly (*hot, bug, pin*)
- Make several CVC words (*cat, but, can, hot, get*) quickly
- Break apart CVC words (*m-an, d-og, r-un*)
- Write several CVC words quickly
- Sort letters quickly by a variety of features (uppercase or lowercase; tall or short; with and without sticks, circles, tails, dots, tunnels)
- Match pictures with letters using beginning sounds

- Change the beginning letter to make a one-syllable word (*man/can*)
- Change ending letters to make a new one-syllable word (*cat/can*)
- Say and clap the syllables in one-, two-, three-, and four-syllable words (from pictures)
- Read the Alphabet Linking Chart in a variety of ways (sing, read letter names, read words, read pictures, read every other letter)

Thinking *Beyond* the Text

Predicting
- Use knowledge of language structure to anticipate the text
- Make predictions using picture information
- Predict the ending of a story based on reading the beginning and middle
- Make predictions based on personal experiences and knowledge
- Make predictions based on information gained through reading

Making Connections
- Make and discuss connections between texts and reader's personal experiences or knowledge
- Make connections between texts that are alike in some way (topic, ending, characters)
- Recognize and apply attributes of recurring characters where relevant

Synthesizing
- Identify what reader already knows relative to information in the text
- Identify new information in text or pictures
- Acquire and report new information from text
- Talk about what the reader already knows about a topic or character prior to reading
- Show evidence in the text of new ideas or information

Inferring
- Infer and talk about characters' feelings, motives, and attributes
- Show evidence in the print, pictures, or photographs to support inference

Thinking *About* the Text

Analyzing
- Notice how the writer has made a story funny or surprising
- Identify and appreciate humor in a text
- Notice and comment on the connections between the print and the pictures
- Understand that a story has a beginning, a series of events, and an end
- Understand and discuss how writers use interesting characters and situations

Critiquing
- Share opinions about the text as a whole (beginning, characters, ending)
- Share opinions about illustrations or photographs
- Identify the text type as fiction or informational

Readers at Level E:

At Level E, readers encounter texts that usually have three to eight lines of print per page. They are flexible enough to process texts with varied placement of print and a full range of punctuation. Texts have more subtle ideas and complex stories and require more attention to understand, but other processes are becoming automatic for readers. They take apart longer words with inflectional endings and read some sentences that carry over two to three lines or even across two pages. Readers are relying much more on the print as they encounter texts with less supportive pictures. Left-to-right directionality and voice-print match are automatic and effortless, and oral reading demonstrates fluency and phrasing with appropriate stress on words. They read without pointing, bringing in the finger only occasionally at point of difficulty. They recognize a large number of high-frequency words and easily solve words with regular letter-sound relationships as well as a few irregular words.

Selecting Texts: Characteristics of Texts at This Level

GENRE/FORMS

Genre
- A variety of informational texts on easy topics
- Animal fantasy
- Realistic fiction
- Some very simple retellings of traditional tales

Forms
- Picture books
- Simple plays

TEXT STRUCTURE

Fiction
- Narrative texts with clear beginning, series of events, and ending

Nonfiction
- Focused on a single idea or one simple topic
- Underlying text structure (description)
- Present one simple category of information
- Some texts with sequential information

CONTENT

- Familiar content that expands beyond home, neighborhood, and school
- Most concepts supported by pictures

THEMES AND IDEAS

- Themes related to typical experiences of children
- Many light, humorous stories, typical of childhood experiences
- Concrete, easy-to-understand ideas

LANGUAGE AND LITERARY FEATURES

- Amusing or engaging one-dimensional characters
- More literary stories and language
- Texts with familiar settings close to children's experience
- Both simple and split dialogue, speaker usually assigned
- Some longer stretches of dialogue
- Simple sequence of events (often repeated)
- A few simple elements of fantasy (for example, talking animals)

SENTENCE COMPLEXITY

- Some longer sentences (some with more than ten words)
- Some sentences that are questions
- Some complex sentences with variety in order of clauses
- Some sentences with prepositional phrases and adjectives
- Some sentences with verb preceding subject
- Use of commas to set words apart (addressee in dialogue, qualifiers, etc.)
- Simple sentences (subject and predicate)
- Language structures of text not repetitive

VOCABULARY

- Almost all vocabulary familiar to children and likely to be used in their oral language
- Word meanings illustrated by pictures
- Variation in use of words to assign dialogue in some texts (*said, cried, shouted*)
- Greater range of vocabulary and multi-syllable words
- Large numbers of high-frequency words
- Complex word solving required to understand meaning

You can see giraffes
at the zoo.
Giraffes are tall animals.
They can eat leaves from the
tops of trees.

10

WORDS
- Mostly one- to two-syllable words
- Some three-syllable words
- Simple plurals and possessives
- Many high-frequency words
- Some words with inflectional endings (-*ing*)
- Mostly words with easy predictable letter-sound relationships and spelling patterns (decodable)
- Some words used multiple times in different language structures (*said Mom; Mom said*)
- Variety of easy spelling patterns
- Easy contractions

ILLUSTRATIONS

General
- Highly supportive illustrations that generally match the text
- Illustrations on every page or every other page
- More details in the Illustrations

BOOK AND PRINT FEATURES

Length
- Short, eight to sixteen pages of print
- Most texts two to eight lines per page

Print and Layout
- Ample space between words and lines
- Print in large plain font
- Some words in bold or larger font for emphasis
- Some sentences turn over one line
- Sentences beginning on the left in most texts
- Sentences carrying over two to three lines and some over two pages
- Print in most texts clearly separated from pictures
- Line breaks match ends of phrases and sentences
- Some limited variation in print placement

Punctuation
- Periods, commas, quotation marks, exclamation points, question marks, and ellipses

Selecting Goals: Behaviors and Understandings to Notice, Teach, and Support

Thinking *Within* the Text

Solving Words
- Recognize many regular words and high-frequency words quickly and easily
- Use beginning and ending parts of words to solve them
- Use sounds related to vowels to solve words
- Use sounds related to consonants and consonant clusters to solve words
- Recognize and use word parts (onsets and rimes) to solve words while reading
- Make connections between words by letters, sounds, or spelling patterns
- Use what is known about a word to solve an unknown word while reading
- Take apart many new words "on the run"
- Take apart compound words to solve them

Monitoring and Correcting
- Reread the sentence or beginning of a phrase to problem solve, self-correct, or confirm
- Use sounds related to consonants and consonant clusters to monitor and correct reading
- Use meaning, language structure, and visual information to monitor and self-correct reading
- Use known words to self-monitor and self-correct

Searching for and Using Information
- Notice details in pictures and use information to understand the text
- Process texts with simple dialogue and some pronouns, all assigned to speakers
- Reread to search for and use information from language structure or meaning
- Use all sources of information together to solve new words while reading
- Notice, search for, remember, and discuss information that is important to understanding

Summarizing
- Remember information to help in understanding the end of a story or topic
- Recall important details while reading a text
- Notice a series of events in order to link them
- Understand a simple sequence or events or steps
- Remember new and important information about a topic

Maintaining Fluency
- Demonstrate phrased, fluent oral reading
- Reflect language syntax and meaning through phrasing and expression
- Reflect punctuation through appropriate pausing and intonation while reading orally
- Demonstrate appropriate stress on words in a sentence

Adjusting
- Slow down to problem solve and resume good rate of reading
- Have expectations for reading fiction and nonfiction texts
- Reread to solve words or think about ideas and resume good rate of reading

Planning for Word Work after Guided Reading

One- to three-minute demonstrations and active student engagement using a chart or easel, white board, magnet letters, or pencil and paper can develop fluency and flexibility in visual processing. Plan for explicit work in specific visual processing areas that need support.

Examples:

- Recognize many easy high-frequency words (for example, *at, an, am, do, go, he, in, like, me, my, no, see, so, to, up, we, look, hers, this*)
- Write or make many high-frequency words (for example, *this, here, look, like, but*)
- Review high-frequency words from previous levels
- Add *-s* or *-es* to a word to make it plural (*bike/bikes, glass/glasses*)
- Make words using VC (*is*), CVC (*cat*), and CVCe (*take*) patterns

- Break apart one syllable words that begin with consonants or consonant clusters (*p-an, pl-ay, sp-in, h-at*)
- Use parts of known words to read new words (*today*)
- Read simple compound words (*into, airplane*)
- Using phonogram patterns, make new words by changing first and last letters to make new words (*pin/pit/hit*)

- Build words quickly with magnetic letters
- Change beginning, middle, or ending of a word to make a new word (*hop/stop, stop/stay, hot/hit*)
- Use what is known about words to read new words (*no, go; get, wet*)
- Say words slowly to write them letter by letter
- Read the Consonant Cluster Linking Chart in a variety of ways (all words, every other box, backwards order)

Thinking *Beyond* the Text

Predicting
- Use knowledge of language structure to anticipate the text
- Predict the ending of a story based on reading the beginning and middle
- Make predictions based on personal experiences and knowledge
- Make predictions based on information gained through reading

Making Connections
- Make and discuss connections between texts and reader's personal experiences
- Make connections between the text and other texts that have been read or heard
- Recognize and apply attributes of recurring characters where relevant

Synthesizing
- Identify what the reader already knows relative to information in the text
- Identify new information in text or pictures
- Acquire new information while reading a text
- Talk about what the reader already knows about a topic or character prior to reading
- Show evidence in the text of new ideas or information
- Understand the central message in a story

Inferring
- Infer and talk about characters' feelings, motives, and attributes
- Infer and talk about causes for feelings, motives, or actions
- See changes in characters across time and articulate possible reasons for development
- Show evidence in the print or pictures to support inference
- Infer causes and effects as implied in the text
- Show evidence in the print or pictures to support inferences

Thinking *About* the Text

Analyzing
- Recognize how the author or illustrator has created humor
- Recognize whether a text is fiction or nonfiction
- Discuss the difference between photographs and drawings
- Recognize and discuss how print layout or features are used to reflect meaning (such as large or bold words)
- Understand that a story has a beginning, a series of events, and an end
- Recognize when the writer is presenting a sequence of events, a set of directions, or simple factual information
- Understand how writers use interesting characters and situations
- Identify who is telling the story

Critiquing
- Share opinions about the text as a whole (beginning, characters, ending topic)
- Express opinions about the quality of the illustrations or photographs
- Express opinions about the information in a text
- Make judgments about characters or events in a text

Readers at **Level F:**

At Level F, readers are beginning to build knowledge of the characteristics of different genres of texts. They can read stretches of both simple and split dialogue. They quickly and automatically recognize a large number of high-frequency words and use letter-sound information to take apart simple, regular words as well as some multisyllable words while reading. They recognize and use inflectional endings, plurals, contractions, and possessives. They can also process and understand syntax that largely reflects patterns particular to written language, as well as stories that have multiple episodes. In fiction, they are beginning to meet characters that are more developed, as well as some literary language. In informational texts, they are learning more new facts about topics. They read without pointing and with appropriate rate, phrasing, intonation, and word stress.

Selecting Texts: Characteristics of Texts at This Level

GENRE/FORMS

Genre
- A variety of informational texts on easy topics
- Animal fantasy
- Realistic fiction
- Some very simple retellings of traditional tales

Forms
- Picture books
- Simple plays

TEXT STRUCTURE

Fiction
- Narrative texts with clear beginning, series of events, and ending

Nonfiction
- Focused on a single idea or one simple topic
- Underlying text structure (description, comparison and contrast)
- Present one simple category of information
- Some texts with sequential information

CONTENT
- Familiar content that expands beyond home, neighborhood, and school
- Concepts accessible through text and illustrations

THEMES AND IDEAS
- Themes related to typical experiences of children
- Many light, humorous stories, typical of childhood experiences
- Concrete, easy-to-understand ideas

LANGUAGE AND LITERARY FEATURES
- Amusing or engaging one-dimensional characters
- More literary stories and language
- Texts with familiar settings close to children's experience
- Both simple and split dialogue, speaker usually assigned
- Some longer stretches of dialogue
- Simple sequence of events (often repeated)
- A few simple elements of fantasy (for example, talking animals)

SENTENCE COMPLEXITY
- Some long sentences (more than ten words) with prepositional phrases, adjectives, and clauses
- Some sentences that are questions in simple sentences and in dialogue
- Some complex sentences with variety in order of clauses
- Sentences with prepositional phrases and adjectives
- Variation in placement of subject, verb, adjectives, and adverbs
- Use of commas to set words apart (addressee in dialogue, qualifiers, etc.)
- Some compound sentences conjoined by *and*
- Language structures of text not repetitive

VOCABULARY
- Most vocabulary words familiar to children and likely to be used in their oral language
- Variation in use of words to assign dialogue in some texts (*said, cried, shouted*)
- Greater range of vocabulary and multi-syllable words
- Large numbers of high-frequency words
- Complex word solving required to understand meaning

WORDS
- Mostly one- to two-syllable words
- Some three-syllable words
- Plurals, contractions, and possessives
- Many high-frequency words
- Many words with inflectional endings
- Mostly words with easy predictable letter-sound relationships and spelling patterns (decodable)
- Some complex letter-sound relationships in words
- Some words used multiple times in different language structures (*said Mom; Mom said*)
- Variety of easy spelling patterns
- Easy contractions

"I am ready for school,"
said Anna.
She had a new red backpack
and new shoes.

"We have one more thing to
do," said her mom. "You may
need to get some glasses."

ILLUSTRATIONS

General

- Highly supportive illustrations that generally match the text
- Illustrations that support the text but do not carry all important aspects of meaning
- Illustrations on every page or every other page in most texts
- More details in the illustrations

BOOK AND PRINT FEATURES

Length

- Short, eight to sixteen pages of print
- Most texts three to eight lines of print per page

Print and Layout

- Ample space between words and lines
- Print in large plain font
- Some words in bold or larger font for emphasis
- Some sentences turn over one line
- Sentences carrying over two to three lines and some over two pages
- Longer sentences starting on left margin
- Some short sentences, starting middle of a line
- Print in most texts clearly separated from pictures
- Many texts with layout supporting phrasing
- Some limited variation in print placement

Punctuation

- Periods, commas, quotation marks, exclamation points, question marks, and ellipses

Selecting Goals: Behaviors and Understandings to Notice, Teach, and Support

Thinking *Within* the Text

Solving Words
- Recognize most words quickly
- Remove the ending from base words to solve new words
- Use letter-sound analysis from left to right to read a new word
- Use sounds related to vowels to solve words
- Use sounds related to consonants and consonant clusters to solve words
- Recognize fifty or more high-frequency words within continuous text automatically
- Use word parts (onsets and rimes) to efficiently take words apart while reading for meaning
- Make connections between words by letters, sounds, or spelling patterns
- Use language structure, meaning, and visual information in a coordinated way to solve words
- Take apart many easy new words "on the run" while reading for meaning
- Take apart compound words to solve them

Monitoring and Correcting
- Self-correct closer to the point of error
- Reread a phrase to problem solve, self-correct, or confirm
- Use letter-sound relationships and word parts to monitor and self-correct reading
- Use meaning, language structure, and visual information to self-monitor and self-correct reading
- Use known words to self-monitor and self-correct

Searching for and Using Information
- Reread to search for and use information or confirm reading
- Use all sources of information together to solve words while reading
- Use simple organizational features (titles and headings)
- Notice and use readers' tools, such as table of contents, where applicable
- Process texts with simple dialogue and some pronouns, all assigned to speakers
- Search for specific facts in informational text
- Notice, search for, remember, and discuss information that is important to understanding

Summarizing
- Remember information to help in understanding the end of a story
- Notice a series of events in order to link them
- Understand a simple sequence of events or steps
- Provide an oral summary with appropriate details in sequence
- Identify and talk about important information about a topic or story

Maintaining Fluency
- Demonstrate phrased, fluent oral reading
- Reflect language syntax and meaning through phrasing and expression
- Reflect punctuation through appropriate pausing and intonation while reading orally
- Demonstrate appropriate stress on words in a sentence

Adjusting
- Slow down or repeat to think about the meaning of the text and resume normal speed
- Have expectations for reading realistic fiction, animal fantasy, simple traditional tales, and easy informational books
- Reread to solve words or think about ideas and resume good rate of reading

---

Planning for Word Work after Guided Reading

One- to three-minute demonstrations and active student engagement using a chart or easel, white board, magnet letters, or pencil and paper can develop fluency and flexibility in visual processing. Plan for explicit work in specific visual processing areas that need support.

Examples:

- Recognize many easy high-frequency words (for example, *all, are, be, but, for, got, had, of, on, then, this, your*)
- Write many high-frequency words quickly
- Review high-frequency words from previous levels
- Change words to add simple inflectional endings (*-ed, -ing; stopped, stopping*)
- Change words to make plurals by adding *-es* (*box/boxes, glass/glasses*)
- Recognize words that have short (CVC: *pet*) and long (CVCe: *bike*) vowel patterns

- Recognize, make or write words using phonograms with CVCe patterns (*take*) and phonograms with double vowel letters (*moon, green*)
- Take apart compound words (*doghouse, butterfly*)
- Change beginning, middle, and ending letters—single consonants and vowels as well as blends and digraphs—to make new words (*call/ball, ball/bell, bell/best*)
- Use what is known about words to read or write new words (*we, me; on, in*)
- Recognize words that begin with consonant digraphs (*she, chin, what*)

- Take apart words that begin with initial consonants, consonant clusters, and consonant digraphs (*s-ell, sm-ell, sh-ell*)
- Read, write, or sort words with consonant clusters that blend two or three consonant sounds (*tree, stream*)
- Read words with double consonant letters in middle from white board (*better*)
- Take apart and make contractions with am (*I'm*) and not (*don't*)
- Read the Consonant Cluster Linking Chart a variety of ways

Thinking *Beyond* the Text

Predicting
- Use knowledge of language structure to anticipate the text
- Predict the ending of a story based on reading the beginning and middle
- Make predictions based on personal experiences and knowledge
- Make predictions based on information gained through reading
- Make predictions based on knowledge of characters or type of story

Making Connections
- Make and discuss connections between texts and reader's personal experiences
- Make connections between the text and other texts that have been read or heard
- Recognize and apply attributes of recurring characters where relevant
- Use specific examples to support thinking

Synthesizing
- Discuss prior knowledge of content prior to reading
- Identify new information in text or pictures
- Notice and acquire new information while reading a text
- Show evidence from the text to indicate new ideas or information

Inferring
- Infer and discuss characters' feelings, motives, and attributes
- Interpret causes for feelings, motives, or actions
- Show empathy for characters and infer their feelings and motivations
- Show evidence in the print or pictures to support inferences
- Infer causes and effects as implied in the text

Thinking *About* the Text

Analyzing
- Understand what the writer has done to make a text surprising, funny, or interesting
- Recognize whether a text is fiction or nonfiction
- Recognize whether a text is realistic fiction or fantasy
- Recognize an informational text by its features
- Recognize and discuss how print layout or features are used to reflect meaning (such as large or bold words)
- Understand that a story has a beginning, a series of events, and an end
- Identify chronological sequence were applicable
- Notice how the writer has selected interesting information for factual texts

Critiquing
- Share opinions about the text as a whole (beginning, characters, ending)
- Express opinions about a text and state reasons
- Express opinions about the quality of the illustrations
- Express opinions about the information in a text
- Make judgments about characters or events in a text

Readers at Level G:

At Level G, readers encounter a wider range of texts and continue to internalize knowledge of different genres. They are still reading texts with three to eight lines of print per page, but print size is slightly smaller and there are more words on a page. With early reading behaviors completely under control and quick and automatic recognition of a large number of high-frequency words, they have attention to give to slightly more complex story lines and ideas. They are able to use a range of word-solving strategies (letter-sound information, making connections between words, and using word parts) as they go while attending to meaning. They read texts with some content-specific words, but most texts have only a few challenging vocabulary words. In their oral reading they demonstrate (without pointing) appropriate rate, phrasing, intonation, and word stress.

Selecting Texts: Characteristics of Texts at This Level

GENRE/FORMS

Genre
- A variety of informational texts on easy topics
- Animal fantasy
- Realistic fiction
- Traditional literature (mostly folktales)

Forms
- Picture books
- Simple plays

TEXT STRUCTURE

Fiction
- Narrative texts with straightforward structure (beginning, series of episodes, ending) but more episodes included

Nonfiction
- Focused on a single idea/topic or series of related ideas/topics
- Include underlying text structures (description, comparison and contrast)
- Largely focused on one category of information
- Some longer texts with repeating longer and more complex patterns
- Some unusual formats, such as letters or questions followed by answers

CONTENT
- Accessible content that expands beyond home, neighborhood, and school
- Concepts accessible through text and illustrations

THEMES AND IDEAS
- Themes related to typical experiences of children
- Many light, humorous stories, typical of childhood experiences
- Concrete, easy-to-understand ideas

LANGUAGE AND LITERARY FEATURES
- Amusing or engaging one-dimensional characters
- More literary stories and language
- Some texts with settings that are not typical of many children's experience
- Variety in presentation of dialogue (simple with pronouns, split, direct, with some longer stretches of dialogue)
- Simple sequence of events (often repeated)
- A few simple elements of fantasy (for example, talking animals)

SENTENCE COMPLEXITY
- Some long sentences (more than ten words) with prepositional phrases, adjectives, and clauses
- Some sentences that are questions in simple sentences and in dialogue
- Sentences with clauses and embedded phrases, some introductory
- Some complex sentences with variety in order of clauses, phrases, subject, verb, and object
- Language structures of text not repetitious

VOCABULARY
- Most vocabulary words familiar to children and likely to be used in their oral language
- Some content-specific words introduced, explained, and illustrated in the text
- Variation in use of words to assign dialogue in some texts (*said, cried, shouted*)
- Greater range of vocabulary and multi-syllable words
- Large numbers of high-frequency words
- Complex word solving required to understand meaning

"I **can't** go to sleep,"
said Nick.
"Will you open the door?"
he asked.

Nick's mom opened the door.
Light came into the room.

12

"Good night, Nick," his mom said.

13

WORDS

- Mostly one- to two-syllable words
- Some three-syllable words
- Plurals, contractions, and possessives
- Many high-frequency words
- Many words with inflectional endings
- Some complex letter-sound relationships in words
- Some words used multiple times in different language structures (*said Mom; Mom said*)
- Wide variety of easy spelling patterns
- Easy contractions

ILLUSTRATIONS

General
- Illustrations that support and extend meaning but do not carry all of the important information in the print
- Illustrations on every page or every other page in most texts
- Complex illustrations depicting multiple ideas

BOOK AND PRINT FEATURES

Length
- Short, eight to sixteen pages of print
- Most texts three to eight lines of print per page

Print and Layout
- Ample space between words and lines
- Some texts in smaller font size
- Some words in bold or larger font for emphasis
- Sentences carrying over two to three lines and some over two pages
- Longer sentences starting on left margin
- Some short sentences, starting middle of a line
- Print in most texts clearly separated from pictures
- Many texts with layout supporting phrasing
- Some limited variation in print placement

Punctuation
- Periods, commas, quotation marks, exclamation points, question marks, and ellipses

Selecting Goals: Behaviors and Understandings to Notice, Teach, and Support

Thinking *Within* the Text

Solving Words
- Recognize most words quickly and easily
- Remove the ending from base words to solve new words
- Use letter clusters (blends and digraphs) to solve words
- Use left to right letter-sound analysis to read a word
- Use consonant and vowel sound-letter relationships to solve words
- Quickly and automatically recognize seventy-five or more high-frequency words within continuous text
- Use known words and word parts (including onsets and rimes) to solve unknown words
- Make connections between words by letters, sounds, or spelling patterns
- Connect words that mean the same or almost the same to derive meaning from the text
- Use context and pictures to derive the meaning of unfamiliar vocabulary
- Solve easy new words quickly
- Take apart compound words to solve them

Monitoring and Correcting
- Self-correct close to the point of error (reread a phrase or word)
- Reread to problem solve, self-correct, or confirm
- Use relationships between sounds and letters, letter clusters, and large parts of words to monitor accuracy of reading
- Use meaning, language structure, and visual information to monitor and self-correct reading
- Realize when more information is needed to understand a text
- Use known words to self-monitor and self-correct

Searching for and Using Information
- Search for and use all sources of information in the text
- Use all sources of information together to solve new words
- Notice and use labels for pictures
- Use simple organizational features (titles and headings)
- Notice and use readers' tools, such as table of contents, where applicable
- Process texts with some split dialogue, all assigned to speakers
- Search for specific facts in informational text
- Notice, search for, remember, and discuss information that is important to understanding

Summarizing
- Remember information to help in understanding the end of a story
- Remember the important information from a factual text
- Understand and talk about a simple sequence of events or steps
- Follow and reflect in discussion the multiple events of a story
- After reading, provide an oral summary with appropriate details in sequence after reading

Maintaining Fluency
- Demonstrate phrased, fluent oral reading
- Reflect language syntax and meaning through phrasing and expression
- Reflect punctuation through appropriate pausing and intonation while reading orally
- Demonstrate appropriate stress on words to reflect the meaning

Adjusting
- Slow down or repeat to think about the meaning of the text and resume normal speed
- Have expectations for reading realistic fiction, animal fantasy, simple traditional tales, and easy informational books
- Reread to solve words or think about ideas and resume good rate of reading

Planning for Word Work after Guided Reading

One- to three-minute demonstrations and active student engagement using a chart or easel, white board, magnet letters, or pencil and paper can develop fluency and flexibility in visual processing. Plan for explicit work in specific visual processing areas that need support.

Examples:

- Recognize many high-frequency words (for example, *all, are, be, but, for, got, had, of, on, then, this, your*)
- Review high-frequency words from previous levels
- Change words to add simple inflectional endings (*-ed, -ing; stopped, stopping*)
- Change words to make plurals by adding *-es* (*churches, foxes, dishes*)
- Take apart and read words using phonograms with VCe (*tale*) patterns and phonograms with double vowel letters (*meet*)

- Read, write, or make words that have short (CVC: *let*) and long (CVCe: *make*) vowel patterns
- Take apart compound words (*door-bell*)
- Change beginning, middle, and ending letters—single consonants and vowels as well as blends and digraphs—to make new words (*can/than, thin/thick*)
- Use what is known about words to read new words (*not, got; and, hand*)
- Recognize words that begin with consonant digraphs (*thin, shell*)

- Solve words using letter-sound analysis from left to right (*st-e-p*)
- Take apart or make words that begin with initial consonants, consonant clusters, and consonant digraphs (*tr-uck, sp-lash, m-eet, str-eam*)
- Take apart or make words with double consonant letters in middle from white board (*lad-der, sum-mer*)
- Read Consonant Cluster Linking Chart in a variety of ways

Thinking *Beyond* the Text

Predicting
- Use knowledge of language structure to anticipate the text
- Predict the ending of a story based on reading the beginning and middle
- Make predictions based on personal experiences and knowledge
- Make predictions based on information gained through reading
- Make predictions based on knowledge of characters or type of story
- Support predictions with evidence from the text or personal experience and knowledge

Making Connections
- Make and discuss connections between texts and reader's personal experiences
- Make connections between the text and other texts that have been read or heard
- Recognize and apply attributes of recurring characters where relevant

Synthesizing
- Relate the content of the text to what is already known
- Identify new information in text or pictures
- Identify new information from simple informational texts and incorporate into personal knowledge

Inferring
- Infer and interpret characters' feelings, motives, and attributes
- Infer causes for feelings, motives, or actions
- Show empathy for characters
- Use and interpret information from pictures without depending on them to construct meaning
- Infer causes and effects as implied in the text
- Justify inferences with evidence from the text

Thinking *About* the Text

Analyzing
- Identify what the writer has done to make a text surprising, funny, or interesting
- Recognize whether a text is fiction or nonfiction
- Identify characteristics of genres (simple animal fantasy, easy factual texts, realistic fiction, traditional literature, plays)
- Notice how writers or illustrators use layout and print features for emphasis
- Identify parts of a text (beginning, series of episodes, end)
- Notice writer's use of specific words to convey meaning (for example, *shouted, cried*)
- Identify a point in the story when the problem is resolved
- Discuss whether a story (fiction) could be true and tell why

Critiquing
- Share opinions about the text as a whole (beginning, characters, ending)
- Express opinions about the quality of a text
- Express opinions about the quality of the illustrations
- Agree or disagree with the ideas in a text
- Make judgments about characters or events in a text

Readers at **Level H:**

At Level H, readers encounter challenges similar to those at Level G; but the language and vocabulary are even more complex, the stories longer and more literary, and there is less repetition in the episodic structure. They process a great deal of dialogue and reflect it through appropriate word stress and phrasing in oral reading. Readers will find that plots and characters are more elaborate but are still simple and straightforward. They solve a large number of multisyllable words (many words with inflectional endings), plurals, contractions, and possessives. Readers automatically read a large number of high-frequency words in order to meet the demands for more in-depth thinking and also to solve words with complex spelling patterns. In order to achieve efficient and smooth processing, readers will begin to read more new texts silently. In oral reading, they demonstrate (without pointing) appropriate rate, phrasing, intonation, and word stress.

Selecting Texts: Characteristics of Texts at This Level

GENRE/FORMS

Genre
- Informational texts
- Animal fantasy
- Realistic fiction
- Traditional literature (mostly folktales)

Forms
- Picture books
- Simple plays

TEXT STRUCTURE

Fiction
- Narrative texts organized in predictable ways (beginning, series of repeated episodes, ending)
- Narratives with more episodes and less repetition

Nonfiction
- Focused on a single idea/topic or series of related ideas/topics
- Include underlying structures clearly (description, comparison and contrast, temporal sequence, problem and solution)
- Largely focused on one category of information
- Some longer texts with repeating longer and more complex patterns
- Some unusual formats, such as letters or questions followed by answers

CONTENT

- Accessible content that expands beyond home, neighborhood, and school
- Concepts accessible through text and illustrations

THEMES AND IDEAS

- Many light, humorous stories, typical of childhood experiences
- Greater variety in themes (going beyond everyday events)

LANGUAGE AND LITERARY FEATURES

- Amusing or engaging one-dimensional characters
- Some stretches of descriptive language
- Some texts with settings that are not typical of many children's experience
- Almost all dialogue assigned to speaker
- Full variety in presentation of dialogue (simple, simple using pronouns, split, direct)
- Use of dialogue for drama
- Multiple episodes taking place across time
- Simple, traditional elements of fantasy

SENTENCE COMPLEXITY

- Some long sentences (more than ten words) with prepositional phrases, adjectives, and clauses
- Some sentences that are questions in simple sentences and in dialogue
- Some complex sentences with variety in order of clauses, phrases, subject, verb, and object
- Variation in placement of subject, verb, adjectives, and adverbs

VOCABULARY

- Most vocabulary words known by children through oral language or reading
- Some content-specific words introduced, explained, and illustrated in the text
- Wide variety in words used to assign dialogue to speaker
- Large numbers of high-frequency words
- Complex word solving required to understand meaning

This truck picks up trash.
The trash goes in the back
of the truck.
The truck crushes the trash
to make it smaller.
Then the truck
carries the trash away.

6

7

WORDS
- Mostly one- to two-syllable words
- Some three-syllable words
- Plurals, contractions, and possessives
- Wide range of high-frequency words
- Many words with inflectional endings
- Some complex letter-sound relationships in words
- Some complex spelling patterns
- Multisyllable words that are generally easy to take apart or decode
- Some easy compound words

ILLUSTRATIONS

General
- Complex illustrations depicting multiple ideas
- Illustrations on every page or every other page in most texts

Fiction
- Some texts with only minimal illustrations
- Illustrations that support interpretation, enhance enjoyment, set mood but are not necessary for understanding

Nonfiction
- One kind of graphic on a page
- Some simple graphics (illustrations with labels)

BOOK AND PRINT FEATURES

Length
- Short, eight to sixteen pages of print
- Most texts three to eight lines of print per page
- A few easy chapter books with more pages

Print and Layout
- Ample space between words and lines
- Italics indicating unspoken thought
- Some texts in smaller font size
- Words in bold and italics that are important to meaning and stress
- Sentences carrying over two to three lines and some over two pages
- Longer sentences starting on left margin
- Some short sentences, starting in the middle of a line
- Print in most texts clearly separated from pictures
- Many texts with layout supporting phrasing
- Some limited variation in print placement

Punctuation
- Periods, commas, quotation marks, exclamation points, question marks, dashes, and ellipses in some texts

Selecting Goals: Behaviors and Understandings to Notice, Teach, and Support

Thinking *Within* the Text

Solving Words
- Use letter-sound relationships in sequence to solve more complex new words
- Use consonant and vowel sound-letter relationships to solve words
- Recognize one hundred or more high-frequency words within continuous text quickly and automatically
- Use known words and word parts (including onsets and rimes) to solve unknown words
- Make connections between words by letters, sounds, or spelling patterns
- Connect words that mean the same or almost the same to derive meaning from the text
- Demonstrate knowledge of flexible ways to solve words (taking it apart, using meaning, etc.)
- Break apart a longer word into syllables in order to decode manageable units
- Use context and pictures to derive the meaning of unfamiliar vocabulary
- Use context to derive meaning of new words
- Take apart compound words to solve them
- Demonstrate competent, active word solving while reading at a good pace—less overt problem solving

Monitoring and Correcting
- Self-correct close to the point of error
- Reread (at the phrase or word) to problem solve, self-correct, or confirm when needed but less frequently than in previous levels
- Use multiple sources of information to monitor and self-correct (language structure, meaning, and letter-sound information)
- Realize when more information is needed to understand a text
- Use known words to self-monitor and self-correct

Searching for and Using Information
- Use multiple sources of information together to solve words
- Use some simple graphics, labeled pictures, that add information to the text
- Use a table of contents to locate information in a text
- Process texts with some split dialogue, all assigned to speakers
- Notice, search for, remember, and discuss information that is important to understanding

Summarizing
- Remember information to help in understanding the end of a story
- Demonstrate understanding of sequence when summarizing a text
- Identify and understand a set of related ideas in a text
- Summarize narratives with multiple episodes as part of the same simple plot
- Provide an oral summary with appropriate details in sequence after reading

Planning for Word Work after Guided Reading

One- to three-minute demonstrations and active student engagement using a chart or easel, white board, magnet letters, or pencil end-paper can develop fluency and flexibility in visual processing. Plan for explicit work in specific visual processing areas that need support.

Examples:

- Recognize and write many high-frequency words (for example, *come, came, from, her, him, his, one, out, said, saw, she, that, their, there, they, was, went, were, with*)
- Review high-frequency words from previous levels
- Change words to add simple inflectional endings (*-ed, -ing; stopped, stopping*)
- Change words to make plurals by adding *-es* (*dresses, crashes*)
- Make or take apart words using phonograms with VCe patterns (*sale, rule*) and phonograms with double vowel letters (*spoon, keep*)
- Write words with inflectional endings, plurals, VCe patters, etc.

- Read, make, or take apart words that have short (CVC: *hat*) and long (CVCe: *game*) vowel patterns
- Take apart compound words (*every-one*)
- Change beginning, middle, and ending letters—single consonants and vowels as well as blends and digraphs—to make new words (*cot/cat, cash/trash*)
- Make possessives by adding an apostrophe and an *s* to a singular noun (*the dog's bone*)
- Solve words using letter-sound analysis from left to right (*s-t-r-ea-m*)
- Use what is known about words to read new words (*but, butter; in, spin*)

- Take apart words that begin with initial consonants, consonant clusters, and consonant digraphs (*ch-air, sp-in, spr-ing*)
- Take apart words with consonant clusters at the beginning—both blends and digraphs (*cr-ib, while*)
- Take apart words with double consonant letters in middle (*but-ter*)
- Read contractions with *is* (*he's, she's*) or not (*don't*)
- Read Consonant Cluster Chart in a variety of ways

Maintaining Fluency
- Demonstrate phrased, fluent oral reading
- Reflect language syntax and meaning through phrasing and expression (including dialogue)
- Demonstrate awareness of the function of the full range of punctuation
- Demonstrate appropriate stress on words to reflect the meaning
- Use multiple sources of information (language structure, meaning, fast word recognition) to support fluency and phrasing

Adjusting
- Slow down or repeat to think about the meaning of the text and resume normal speed
- Have expectations for reading realistic fiction, animal fantasy, simple traditional tales, and easy informational books
- Reread to solve words or think about ideas and resume good rate of reading

Thinking *Beyond* the Text

Predicting
- Use knowledge of language structure to anticipate the text
- Use understanding of text structure to make predictions about what will happen next
- Make predictions based on knowledge of characters or type of story
- Use background information, personal experience, and information from the text to make predictions
- Support predictions with evidence from the text or personal experience and knowledge

Making Connections
- Bring knowledge from personal experiences to the interpretation of characters and events
- Bring background knowledge to the understanding of a text before, during, and after reading
- Make connections between the text and other texts that have been read or heard
- Recognize and apply attributes of recurring characters where relevant

Synthesizing
- Differentiate between what is known and new information
- Identify new information and incorporate it into present understandings
- Demonstrate learning new content from reading

Inferring
- Show empathy for characters and infer their feelings and motivations
- Interpret and talk about causes for feelings, motives, or actions
- Use and interpret information from pictures without depending on them to construct the meaning derived from reading words
- Infer causes and effects as implied in the text
- Justify inferences with evidence from the text

Thinking *About* the Text

Analyzing
- Understand what the writer has done to make a text surprising, funny, or interesting
- Discuss characteristics of genres (simple animal fantasy, easy factual texts, realistic fiction, traditional literature, plays)
- Differentiate between informational and fiction texts
- Understand, talk about, write, or draw when a writer has used description or compare and contrast
- Notice and discuss how writers or illustrators use layout and print features for emphasis
- Identify parts of a text (beginning, series of episodes, end)
- Notice writer's use of specific words to convey meaning (for example, *shouted, cried*)
- Identify a point in the story when the problem is resolved
- Discuss whether a story (fiction) could be true and tell why

Critiquing
- Share opinions about the text as a whole (beginning, characters, ending)
- Express opinions about the quality of a text
- Express opinions about the quality of the illustrations
- Notice how the illustrations are consistent (or inconsistent) with meaning and extend the meaning
- Agree or disagree with the ideas in a text
- Make judgments about characters or events in a text

Readers at Level I:

At Level I, readers will be processing texts that are mostly short (eight to sixteen pages), as well as some easy illustrated chapter books (forty to sixty pages) that require them to sustain attention and memory over time. They will meet some long sentences of more than ten words that contain prepositional phrases, adjectives, and clauses. They will also encounter compound sentences. They can effectively process complex sentences when required by a text. In addition to automatically recognizing a large number of words, they are using word-solving strategies for complex spelling patterns, multisyllable words, and many words with inflectional endings, plurals, contractions, and possessives. They read many texts silently, following the text with their eyes and without pointing. In oral reading, they reflect appropriate rate, word stress, intonation, phrasing, and pausing.

Selecting Texts: Characteristics of Texts at This Level

GENRE/FORMS

Genre
- Informational texts
- Animal fantasy
- Realistic fiction
- Traditional literature (mostly folktales)

Forms
- Picture books
- Simple plays

TEXT STRUCTURE

Fiction
- Narratives with multiple episodes and little repetition of similar episodes
- Narratives with more elaborated episodes
- Some very short chapter books with the same characters across chapters

Nonfiction
- Focused on a single idea/topic or series of related ideas/topics
- Underlying structures used and presented clearly (description, comparison and contrast, temporal sequence, problem and solution)
- Texts organized into a few simple categories
- Some longer texts that repeat longer and more complex patterns
- Some unusual formats, such as letters or questions followed by answers

CONTENT
- Familiar content and some new content that typically children would not know
- Concepts accessible through text and illustrations

THEMES AND IDEAS
- Many light, humorous stories, typical of childhood experiences
- Some ideas that are new to most children
- Themes accessible given typical experiences of children
- A few abstract ideas which are highly supported by text and illustrations

LANGUAGE AND LITERARY FEATURES
- Amusing or engaging one-dimensional characters
- More elaborated description of character attributes
- Language characteristic of traditional literature in some texts
- Some texts with settings that are not typical of many children's experience
- Variety of dialogue (between more than two characters in many texts)
- Multiple episodes taking place across time
- Simple, traditional elements of fantasy

- Most texts told from a single point of view with some texts showing more than one

SENTENCE COMPLEXITY
- Some long sentences (more than ten words) with prepositional phrases, adjectives, and clauses
- Many sentences with embedded clauses and phrases
- Variation in placement of subject, verb, adjectives, and adverbs
- Use of commas to set words apart (addressee in dialogue, qualifiers, etc.)
- Sentences with nouns, verbs, adjectives, and adverbs in series, divided by commas
- Many compound sentences

VOCABULARY
- Most vocabulary words known by children through oral language or reading
- Some content-specific words introduced, explained, and illustrated in the text
- Wide variety of words to assign dialogue (*said, cried, shouted, thought, whispered*) and adjectives describing the dialogue (*quietly, loudly*)

WORDS
- Many two- to three-syllable words
- Plurals, contractions, and possessives
- Wide range of high-frequency words
- Many words with inflectional endings
- Some complex letter-sound relationships in words
- Some complex spelling patterns
- Multisyllable words that are generally easy to take apart or decode
- Some easy compound words

Koalas do not drink water.
There is water
in the leaves koalas eat.
They get food and water
at the same time.

8

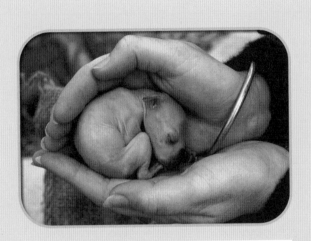

This is a baby koala.
A young koala is called a joey,
just like a baby kangaroo.
When a joey is born,
it has no hair.

9

ILLUSTRATIONS

General

- Two or more kinds of graphics on a page
- Some illustrations complex with many ideas

Fiction

- Some texts with no illustrations, black and white minimal illustrations, or symbolic illustrations
- Some texts requiring readers to infer the story from pictures with minimal text or dialogue only
- Illustrations that support interpretation, enhance enjoyment, set mood but are not necessary for understanding

Nonfiction

- One or two kinds of graphics on a page
- Some simple graphics (illustrations with labels)

BOOK AND PRINT FEATURES

Length

- Short, eight to sixteen pages of print
- Most texts three to eight lines of print per page
- Some easy illustrated chapter books of fifty to sixty pages

Print and Layout

- Ample space between words and lines
- Print in large plain font
- Italics indicating unspoken thought
- Some texts in smaller font size
- Words in bold and italics that are important to meaning and stress
- Sentences carrying over two to three lines and some over two pages
- Longer sentences starting on left margin
- Some short sentences, starting middle of a line
- Print in most texts clearly separated from pictures
- Some limited variation in print placement

Punctuation

- Periods, commas, quotation marks, exclamation points, question marks, dashes, and ellipses

Tools

- Some informational texts with a table of contents
- Some informational texts with a simple glossary

Selecting Goals: Behaviors and Understandings to Notice, Teach, and Support

Thinking *Within* the Text

Solving Words
- Use letter-sound relationships in sequence to solve more complex new words
- Use consonant and vowel sound-letter relationships to solve words
- Recognize one hundred or more high-frequency words within continuous text quickly and automatically
- Use known words and word parts (including onsets and rimes) to solve unknown words
- Make connections between words by letters, sounds, or spelling patterns
- Connect words that mean the same or almost the same to help in understanding a text and acquiring new vocabulary
- Demonstrate knowledge of flexible ways to solve words (taking it apart, using meaning, use letter sequence, etc.)
- Break down a longer word into syllables in order to decode manageable units
- Use context and pictures to derive the meaning of unfamiliar vocabulary
- Use context to derive meaning of new words
- Take apart compound words to solve them
- Use meaning, structure, and visual information to solve words
- Demonstrate competent, active word solving while reading at a good pace—less overt problem solving

Monitoring and Correcting
- Self-correct at point of error (or before overt error)
- Use multiple sources of information to monitor and self-correct (language structure, meaning, and letter-sound information)
- Realize when more information is needed to understand a text
- Reread to confirm word solving by checking other sources of information
- Use known words to self-monitor and self-correct

Searching for and Using Information
- Use multiple sources of information together to solve words
- Notice and use graphics such as labels and captions for pictures and simple diagrams
- Use simple readers' tools (table of contents, index, glossary) to find information in texts
- Process texts with some split dialogue, all assigned to speakers
- Notice, search for, remember, and discuss information that is important to understanding

Summarizing
- Follow and remember a series of events over a longer text in order to understand the ending
- Report episodes in a text in the order they happened
- Identify and understand a set of related ideas in a text
- Summarize a longer narrative text with multiple episodes
- Identify important ideas in a text and report them in an organized way, either orally or in writing
- Understand the problem of a story and its solution

Planning for Word Work after Guided Reading

One- to three-minute demonstrations and active student engagement using a chart or easel, white board, magnet letters, or pencil and paper can develop fluency and flexibility in visual processing. Plan for explicit work in specific visual processing areas that need support.

Examples:

- Recognize a few easy high-frequency words (select from list of one hundred high-frequency words)
- Review high-frequency words from previous levels
- Change words to add simple inflectional endings (*-ed, -ing; stopped, stopping*)
- Change words to make plurals by adding *-es* (*buses*)
- Read plural and singular forms for words that change the spelling (*child/children, foot/feet*)
- Recognize homophones (same pronunciation, different spelling and meaning) (*write, right*)

- Take apart words with double vowel patterns (*fe-et, r-oom, br-own*)
- Take apart compound words (*every-thing*)
- Take apart and make one-syllable words with a variety of phonogram patterns (*cl-ay, dr-ip*)
- Take apart two-syllable words (*drag-on, le-mon*)
- Change beginning, middle and ending letters—single consonants and vowels as well as blends and digraphs—to make new words (*band/sand/send/sent*)
- Make possessives by adding an apostrophe and an *s* to a singular noun (*the girl's shoe*)

- Use what is known about words to read new words (*tree, top, treetop; ape, shape*)
- Take apart, make, or write words with initial consonant clusters and consonant digraphs (*pr-int, sh-ake*)
- Read words with double consonant letters in middle (*ladder*)
- Read, write, or make words with consonant clusters—both blends and digraphs (*drip, ring, crash, shape*)
- Read, write, or make words with consonant clusters that blend two or three consonant sounds (*steam, street*)
- Read contractions with *is* and *not* (*she's, can't*)

Maintaining Fluency
- Demonstrate phrased, fluent oral reading
- Read dialogue with phrasing and expression that reflects understanding of characters and events
- Demonstrate awareness of the function of the full range of punctuation
- Demonstrate appropriate stress on words to reflect the meaning
- Use multiple sources of information (language structure, meaning, fast word recognition) to support fluency and phrasing
- Solve most words in the text quickly and automatically to support fluency
- Read silently at a good rate

Adjusting
- Slow down to search for information and resume normal pace of reading again
- Demonstrate different ways of reading a variety of fiction and nonfiction texts
- Reread to solve words or think about ideas and resume good rate of reading

Thinking *Beyond* the Text

Predicting
- Use knowledge of language structure to anticipate the text
- Use text structure to predict the outcome of a narrative
- Make predictions based on knowledge of characters or type of story
- Make predictions about the solution to the problem of a story
- Make predictions based on personal experiences, content knowledge, and knowledge of similar texts
- Search for and use information to confirm or disconfirm predictions
- Justify predictions using evidence

Making Connections
- Bring knowledge from personal experiences to the interpretation of characters and events
- Bring background knowledge to the understanding of a text before, during, and after reading
- Make connections between the text and other texts that have been read or heard
- Recognize and apply attributes of recurring characters where relevant

Synthesizing
- Differentiate between what is known and new information
- Demonstrate learning new content from reading
- Express changes in ideas after reading a text

Inferring
- Infer and discuss characters' feelings and motivations through reading their dialogue
- Demonstrate understandings of characters, using evidence from text to support statements
- Infer cause and effect in influencing characters' feelings or underlying motives
- Infer causes of problems or of outcomes in fiction and nonfiction texts

Thinking *About* the Text

Analyzing
- Notice some characteristics of genre (for example, traditional language, literary language, descriptive language)
- Differentiate between informational and fiction texts
- Understand and talk about when a writer has used underlying structures (description, compare and contrast, temporal sequence, problem and solution)
- Notice the relationship between pictures and text
- Notice how writers or illustrators use layout and print features for emphasis
- Notice and speculate why the writer has selected information to present in particular ways (photograph, caption, boxes, pictures)
- Identify a point in the story when the problem is resolved
- Discuss whether a story (fiction) could be true and tell why

Critiquing
- Express opinions about the quality of a text
- Notice how the illustrations are consistent (or inconsistent) with meaning and extend the meaning
- Discuss the quality of illustrations or graphics
- Agree or disagree with the ideas in a text and give reasons
- Hypothesize how characters could have behaved differently
- Judge the text as to whether it is interesting, humorous, or exciting, and specify why

Readers at **Level J:**

At Level J, readers process a variety of texts, including short informational texts on familiar topics, short fiction texts, and longer illustrated narratives that have short chapters. They adjust their reading strategies to process not only realistic fiction and informational texts but to read very simple biographies. In fiction, characters generally do not change since the plots are relatively simple and texts are not long. Readers process an increased number of longer and more complex sentences (those with more than ten words containing prepositional phrases, adjectives, clauses, and many compound sentences). Readers are able to automatically recognize a large number of words, and can quickly apply word-solving strategies to multisyllable words with inflectional endings, suffixes, and prefixes. They can read a wide range of plurals, contractions, and possessives. In oral reading, they reflect appropriate rate, word stress, intonation, phrasing, and pausing (recognizing and using a range of punctuation). They read silently in independent reading and while reading individually in guided reading

Selecting Texts: Characteristics of Texts at This Level

GENRE/FORMS

Genre
- Informational texts
- Animal fantasy
- Realistic fiction
- Traditional literature (mostly folktales)
- Some simple biographies on familiar subjects

Forms
- Picture books
- Plays
- Beginning chapter books with illustrations
- Some series books
- Some graphic texts

TEXT STRUCTURE

Fiction
- Narratives with little repetition of similar episodes
- Narratives with more elaborated episodes
- Some beginning chapter books with short chapters
- Chapters connected by character
- Chapters usually connected to a longer plot

Nonfiction
- Focused on a single idea/topic or series of related ideas/topics
- Underlying structures used and presented clearly (description, comparison and contrast, temporal sequence, problem and solution)
- Texts organized into a few simple categories of information
- Some longer texts with repeating longer and more complex patterns
- Some unusual formats, such as letters or questions followed by answers

CONTENT
- Familiar content and some new content that typically children would not know
- New content accessible through text and illustrations

THEMES AND IDEAS
- Many light, humorous stories, typical of childhood experiences
- Some ideas new to most children
- Themes accessible given typical experiences of children
- A few abstract ideas that are highly supported by text and illustrations
- Some texts (graphic novels) requiring readers to infer the story from pictures with minimal text or dialogue only

LANGUAGE AND LITERARY FEATURES
- Amusing or engaging characters, some of which have more than one dimension
- Elaborated description of character traits
- Language characteristic of traditional literature in some texts
- Some texts with settings that are not typical of many children's experience
- Variety of dialogue (may be between more than two characters in many texts)
- Multiple episodes taking place across time
- Simple, traditional elements of fantasy
- Most texts told from a single point of view, with some having several points of view

SENTENCE COMPLEXITY
- Many longer (more than ten words), more complex sentences (prepositional phrases, introductory clauses, lists of nouns, verbs, or adjectives)
- Many sentences with embedded clauses and phrases
- Occasional use of parenthetical material embedded in sentences
- Sentences with nouns, verbs, adjectives, and adverbs in a series, divided by commas
- Variation in placement of subject, verb, adjectives, and adverbs
- Many compound sentences

VOCABULARY
- Most vocabulary words known by children through oral language or reading
- Content words illustrated with pictures or other graphics
- Some new vocabulary and content-specific words introduced that are explained and illustrated in the text
- Wide variety of words to assign dialogue (*said, cried, shouted, thought, whispered*) and adjectives describing the dialogue (*quietly, loudly*)

WORDS
- Many two- to three-syllable words
- Plurals, contractions, and possessives
- Wide range of high-frequency words
- Many words with inflectional endings
- Many words with complex letter-sound relationships
- Some complex spelling patterns

Therapy Dogs

Sometimes people can not stay at home because they are not well. They must stay in a hospital or in a nursing home. They miss their homes and families.

People feel better when they pet a dog.

4

5

- Multisyllable words that are generally easy to take apart or decode
- Some easy compound words

ILLUSTRATIONS

General
- Two or more kinds of graphics on a page
- Some illustrations complex with many ideas

Fiction
- Many texts with minimal illustrations and some with none
- Some complex and artistic illustrations that communicate meaning to match or extend the text

- Illustrations that support interpretation, enhance enjoyment, set mood but are not necessary for understanding

Nonfiction
- More than one kind of graphic on a page
- Many simple graphics (illustrations with labels)

BOOK AND PRINT FEATURES

Length
- Chapter books (most approximately forty to seventy-five pages)
- Many lines of print on a page (approximately three to twelve lines)

- Shorter (most approximately twenty-four to thirty-six pages of print) texts on single topics (usually nonfiction)

Print and Layout
- Ample space between lines
- Italics indicating unspoken thought
- Some texts in smaller font size
- Words in bold and italics that are important to meaning and stress
- Sentences carrying over two to three lines and some over two pages
- Longer sentences starting on left margin in most texts
- Some sentences, starting middle of a line

- Print in most illustrated texts clearly separated from pictures
- Variety in layout, reflecting different genres

Punctuation
- Periods, commas, quotation marks, exclamation points, question marks, dashes, and ellipses

Tools
- Some texts with a table of contents
- Some texts with a simple glossary
- Chapter titles in some books
- Some texts with headings in bold to show sections

Selecting Goals: Behaviors and Understandings to Notice, Teach, and Support

Thinking *Within* the Text

Solving Words

- Use letter-sound relationships in sequence to solve more complex words
- Recognize many high-frequency words within continuous text quickly and automatically
- Use known words and word parts (including onsets and rimes) to solve unknown words
- Make connections between words by letters, sounds, or spelling patterns
- Use multiple sources of information together to solve words
- Connect words that mean the same or almost the same to help in understanding a text and acquiring new vocabulary
- Demonstrate knowledge of flexible ways to solve words (noticing word parts, noticing endings and prefixes)
- Break down a longer word into syllables in order to decode manageable units
- Solve words of two or three syllables, many words with inflectional endings and complex letter-sound relationships
- Use known words to solve new words
- Use context to derive meaning of new words
- Demonstrate competent, active word solving while reading at a good pace—less overt problem solving

Monitoring and Correcting

- Self-correct at point of error (or before overt error)
- When reading aloud, self-correct information when it does not reflect the meaning
- Use multiple sources of information to monitor and self-correct (language structure, meaning, and letter-sound information)
- Realize when more information is needed to understand a text
- Reread to confirm word solving by checking other sources of information
- Use known words to self-monitor and self-correct

Searching for and Using Information

- Use multiple sources of information together to solve new words
- Notice and use graphics such as labels and captions for pictures and simple diagrams
- Use chapter titles or headings to foreshadow content
- Use readers' tools (table of contents, headings, and glossary) to find information
- Process long sentences (ten or more words) with many embedded phrases and clauses
- Process texts with a variety of dialogue, all assigned to speakers
- Understand how to use pictures and symbols to construct meaning in graphic texts

Summarizing

- Follow and remember a series of events over a longer text in order to understand the ending
- Report episodes in a text in the order they happened
- Summarize ideas from a text and tell how they are related
- Summarize a longer narrative text with multiple episodes
- Identify important ideas in a text and report them in an organized way, either orally or in writing
- Understand the problem of a story and its solution

Planning for Word Work after Guided Reading

One- to three-minute demonstrations and active student engagement using a chart or easel, white board, magnet letters, or pencil and paper can develop fluency and flexibility in visual processing. Plan for explicit work in specific visual processing areas that need support.

Examples:

- Recognize or write many high-frequency words (select from list of one hundred high-frequency words)
- Change words to add inflectional endings (-ing, -ed; running, smiled)
- Change words to make plurals by changing y to i and adding -es (bunny, bunnies)
- Write plural and singular forms for a wide range of plurals (cars, boxes, pennies)
- Change words by attaching simple prefixes and suffixes (redo, runner)

- Recognize and connect homophones (same pronunciation, different spelling and meaning) (nose, knows)
- Read or write words that have double vowel patterns (VVC: keep, good) as well as words with y as a vowel (my)
- Change words to create comparatives (-er, -est) (dark/darker/darkest)
- Take apart compound words (some-thing)
- Take apart and make words with two or three syllables (um-brell-a)

- Take apart one-syllable words with a variety of phonogram patterns (sl-eep, dr-eam)
- Read words using letter-sound analysis from left to right (b-e-f-ore)
- Use what is known about words to read new words (and, candy; before, begin)
- Read contractions with am, is, not, and are (I'm, he's, can't, we're)

Maintaining Fluency
- Demonstrate phrased, fluent oral reading
- Read dialogue with phrasing and expression that reflects understanding of characters and events
- Demonstrate awareness of the function of the full range of punctuation
- Demonstrate appropriate stress on words, pausing and phrasing, intonation, and use of punctuation
- Use multiple sources of information (language structure, meaning, fast word recognition) to support fluency and phrasing
- Solve most words in the text quickly and automatically to support fluency
- Read silently at a good rate

Adjusting
- Slow down to search for information and resume normal pace of reading again
- Demonstrate different ways of reading fiction and nonfiction texts
- Demonstrate adjustment of reading for simple biographies
- Reread to solve words or think about ideas and resume good rate of reading

Thinking *Beyond* the Text

Predicting
- Use text structure to predict the outcome of a narrative
- Make predictions about the solution to the problem of a story
- Make predictions based on personal experiences, content knowledge, and knowledge of similar texts
- Search for and use information to confirm or disconfirm predictions
- Justify predictions using evidence
- Predict what characters will do based on the traits revealed by the writer

Making Connections
- Bring knowledge from personal experiences to the interpretation of characters and events
- Bring background knowledge to the understanding of a text before, during, and after reading
- Make connections between the text and other texts that have been read or heard
- Specify the nature of connections (topic, content, type of story, writer)

Synthesizing
- Differentiate between what is known and new information
- Demonstrate learning new content from reading
- Express changes in ideas after reading a text

Inferring
- Demonstrate understandings of characters, using evidence from text to support statements
- Infer characters' feelings and motivations through reading their dialogue
- Infer and discuss understanding of characters' motivations and feelings
- Infer cause and effect in influencing characters' feelings or underlying motives
- Infer and discuss what characters are like from what they say or do
- Infer causes of problems or of outcomes in fiction and nonfiction texts

Thinking *About* the Text

Analyzing
- Notice aspects of genres (fiction, nonfiction, realistic stories, traditional literature and fantasy)
- Understand when a writer has used underlying structures (description, compare and contrast, temporal sequence, problem and solution)
- Notice how pictures are used to communicate meaning in illustrated texts
- Notice the way the writer assigns dialogue
- Notice aspects of a writer's style after reading several texts by the author
- Notice specific writing techniques (for example, question and answer format)
- Notice descriptive language and discuss how it adds to enjoyment or understanding
- Identify a point in the story when the problem is resolved
- Notice and discuss how the writer of a graphic novel has communicated meaning through illustrations and print

Critiquing
- Express opinions about the quality of a text
- Notice how the illustrations are consistent (or inconsistent) with meaning and extend the meaning
- Notice the quality of illustrations or graphics
- Agree or disagree with the ideas in a text
- Hypothesize how characters could have behaved differently
- Judge the text as to whether it is interesting, humorous, or exciting, and specify why

Readers at Level K:

At Level K, readers process a wider range of genres (realistic fiction, animal fantasy, traditional literature, some simple biographies, and more informational texts). They read many illustrated chapter books (including some series books). Most fiction texts have multiple episodes related to a single plot, but the demand on the reader's memory is higher than previous levels. They read about characters that change very little but are at the same time more complex; texts have multiple characters. Readers process a great deal of dialogue, some of it unassigned, and are challenged to read stories based on concepts that are distant in time and space and reflect diverse cultures. Readers solve many content-specific words and some technical words in informational texts. They automatically recognize a large number of words and quickly apply word-solving strategies to multisyllable words with inflectional endings, and to words with suffixes and prefixes. They can read a wide range of plurals, contractions, and possessives. They read silently in independent reading, but when reading orally they demonstrate all aspects of fluent reading.

Selecting Texts: Characteristics of Texts at This Level

GENRE/FORMS

Genre
- Informational texts
- Animal fantasy
- Realistic fiction
- Traditional literature (mostly folktales)
- Some simple biographies on familiar subjects

Forms
- Picture books
- Plays
- Beginning chapter books with illustrations
- Series books
- Some graphic texts

TEXT STRUCTURE

Fiction
- Narratives with many episodes
- Some beginning chapter books with short chapters
- Chapters connected by character or broad theme
- Chapters usually connected to a longer plot
- Simple, straightforward plots

Nonfiction
- Presentation of multiple topics
- Underlying structures (description, comparison and contrast, temporal sequence, problem and solution, cause and effect)

- Texts organized into a few simple categories
- Variety in organization and topic
- Some longer texts with sections presenting different information
- Variety in nonfiction formats (question and answer, paragraphs, boxes, legends, and call-outs)

CONTENT
- Familiar content and some new content that typically children would not know
- New content requiring prior knowledge to understand in some informational texts
- Some texts with plots and situations outside typical experience
- Some texts with settings outside children's typical experience
- New content accessible through text and illustrations

THEMES AND IDEAS
- Many light, humorous stories, typical of childhood experiences
- Some ideas new to most children
- Themes accessible given typical experiences of children
- A few abstract ideas, supported by the text but with less illustration support
- Texts with universal themes illustrating important human issues and attributes (friendship, courage)

- Some texts (graphic novels) requiring readers to infer the story from pictures with minimal text or dialogue only

LANGUAGE AND LITERARY FEATURES
- Some complex and memorable characters
- Some figurative language (metaphor, simile)
- Some texts with settings that are not typical of many children's experience
- Setting important to understanding the plot in some texts
- Complex plots with numerous episodes and time passing
- Simple, traditional elements of fantasy
- Most texts told from a single point of view
- May have more than one point of view within one text

SENTENCE COMPLEXITY
- Variety in sentence length and complexity
- Longer (more than fifteen words), more complex sentences (prepositional phrases, introductory clauses, lists of nouns, verbs, or adjectives)

- Many complex sentences with embedded phrases and clauses
- Variation in placement of subject, verb, adjectives, and adverbs
- Wide variety of words to assign dialogue, with verbs and adverbs essential to meaning

VOCABULARY
- Content words illustrated with pictures or other graphics
- Some new vocabulary and content-specific words introduced, explained, and illustrated in the text
- Wide variety of words to assign dialogue, with verbs and adverbs essential to meaning

WORDS
- Many two- to three-syllable words
- Plurals, contractions, and possessives
- A wide range of high frequency words
- Many words with inflectional endings
- Many words with complex letter-sound relationships
- Some complex spelling patterns
- Multisyllable words that are challenging to take apart or decode
- Some easy compound words

Monday

Touch

If your eyes are closed, how can you tell the difference between a soft chick and rough sandpaper? You use your sense of touch.

6

whiskers

A cat uses its whiskers to feel what is around it.

You use your skin to touch. Cats do, too. But cats also use their whiskers! The touch of the whiskers helps cats know whether they can fit through small openings.

7

ILLUSTRATIONS

General
- Two or more kinds of graphics on a page
- Some long stretches of text with no illustrations or graphics

Fiction
- Some texts with no or only minimal illustrations
- Some texts with illustrations that are essential to interpretation
- Some illustrations that support interpretation, enhance enjoyment, set mood but are not necessary for understanding

Nonfiction
- More than one kind of graphic on a page

- Combination of graphics providing information that matches and extends the text
- In most texts, graphics that are clearly explained (simple diagrams, illustrations with labels, maps, charts)
- Variety in the layout of print in nonfiction texts (question and answer, paragraphs, boxes, legends, call-outs)

BOOK AND PRINT FEATURES

Length
- Many lines of print on a page (three to fifteen lines; more for fiction)

- Chapter books (sixty to one hundred pages of print)

Print and Layout
- Ample space between lines
- Print and font size vary with some longer texts in small fonts
- Use of words in italics, bold, or all capitals to indicate emphasis, level of importance, or signal other meaning
- Variety in print and background color
- Sentences carrying over two to three lines and some over two pages
- Print and illustrations integrated in many texts

- Variety in layout, reflecting different genres
- Usually friendly layout in chapter books, with many sentences starting on the left

Punctuation
- Periods, commas, quotation marks, exclamation points, question marks, dashes, and ellipses in most texts

Tools
- Readers' tools (table of contents, a few headings, glossary, chapter titles, author's notes)

Selecting Goals: Behaviors and Understandings to Notice, Teach, and Support

Thinking *Within* the Text

Solving Words

- Consistent use of multiple sources of information in solving new words
- Connect words that mean the same or almost the same to help in understanding a text and acquiring new vocabulary
- Demonstrate knowledge of flexible ways to solve words (noticing word parts, noticing endings and prefixes)
- Break down a longer word into syllables in order to decode manageable units
- Solve words of two or three syllables, many words with inflectional endings and complex letter-sound relationships
- Solve content-specific words, using graphics and definitions embedded in the text
- Use context to derive meaning of new words
- Understand longer descriptive words
- Demonstrate competent, active word solving while reading at a good pace—less overt problem solving

Monitoring and Correcting

- Self-correct at point of error (or before overt error)
- Self-correct when errors detract from the meaning of the text
- Self-correct information when it does not reflect the meaning
- Use multiple sources of information to monitor and self-correct (language structure, meaning, and letter-sound information)
- Realize when more information is needed to understand a text

Searching for and Using Information

- Search for information in illustrations to support text interpretation
- Search for information in graphics (simple diagrams, illustrations with labels, maps, charts, captions under pictures)
- Use chapter titles as to foreshadow content
- Use readers' tools (table of contents, headings, glossary, chapter titles, and author's notes) to gather information
- Process long sentences (fifteen or more words) with embedded clauses (prepositional phrases, introductory clauses, series of nouns, verbs, or adverbs)
- Process a wide range of dialogue, some unassigned

Summarizing

- Follow and remember a series of events over a longer text in order to understand the ending
- Report episodes in a text in the order they happened
- Summarize ideas from a text and tell how they are related
- Summarize a longer narrative text with multiple episodes
- Identify important ideas in a text and report them in an organized way, either orally or in writing
- Understand the problem of a story and its solution
- Understand how to use pictures to construct meaning in graphic texts

Planning for Word Work after Guided Reading

One- to three-minute demonstrations and active student engagement using a chart or easel, white board, magnet letters, or pencil and paper can develop fluency and flexibility in visual processing. Plan for explicit work in specific visual processing areas that need support.

Examples:

- Recognize, write, or make many high-frequency words
- Review high-frequency words from previous levels
- Change words to add inflectional endings (-ed, -ing; finished, writing)
- Change words to make a full range of plurals by adding -s or -es (faces, dishes, boys, babies, heroes)
- Read, make, or write plural and singular forms for a wide range of plurals (duck/ducks, dish/dishes, fly, flies)
- Change words by attaching simple prefixes and suffixes (untie, hiker)
- Recognize and connect homophones (same pronunciation, different spellings and meanings) (their, they're)

- Read and connect homographs (same spelling, different meanings and sometimes different pronunciations) (read, read; present, present)
- Recognize and pronounce vowel sounds in open (CV: ho-tel) and closed (CVC: lem-on) syllables
- Read words that have double vowel patterns (WC: seem)
- Read words that have vowel sounds with r (corn)
- Take apart, make, and write words with letter combinations representing long vowel sounds (same, say, pail)
- Change words to create comparatives (-er, -est) (long/longer/longest)

- Take apart compound words and discuss how the parts are related to meaning (play-ground)
- Take apart two- and three-syllable words (lit-tle, com-pu-ter)
- Read words using letter-sound analysis from left to right (gl-ance)
- Use what is known about words to read new words (soon, moon; art, party)
- Take apart words with consonant blends and digraphs at the ends of words (h-elp, p-ath)
- Take apart and read words with silent consonants (lamb, light)
- Recognize and take apart the full range of contractions (I'm, that's, he'll, won't, they're, you've)

Maintaining Fluency

- Demonstrate phrased, fluent oral reading
- Read dialogue with phrasing and expression that reflects understanding of characters and events
- Demonstrate awareness of the function of the full range of punctuation
- Demonstrate appropriate stress on words, pausing and phrasing, intonation, and use of punctuation
- Use multiple sources of information (language structure, meaning, fast word recognition) to support fluency and phrasing
- Solve most words in the text quickly and automatically to support fluency
- Read silently at a good rate

Adjusting

- Slow down to search for information and resume normal pace of reading again
- Demonstrate different ways of reading fiction and nonfiction texts
- Demonstrate adjustment of reading for simple biographies
- Reread to solve words or think about ideas and resume good rate of reading

Thinking *Beyond* the Text

Predicting

- Use text structure to predict the outcome of a narrative
- Make predictions about the solution to the problem of a story
- Make predictions based on personal experiences, content knowledge, and knowledge of similar texts
- Search for and use information to confirm or disconfirm predictions
- Justify predictions using evidence
- Predict what characters will do based on the traits revealed by the writer

Making Connections

- Bring knowledge from personal experiences to the interpretation of characters and events
- Bring background knowledge to the understanding of a text before, during, and after reading
- Make connections between the text and other texts that have been read or heard
- Specify the nature of connections (topic, content, type of story, writer)

Synthesizing

- Differentiate between what is known and new information
- Demonstrate learning new content from reading
- Express changes in ideas after reading a text

Inferring

- Demonstrate through talk or writing understandings of characters, using evidence from text to support statements
- Infer and discuss characters' feelings and motivations through reading their dialogue
- Infer and discuss what characters are like from what they say or do
- Infer cause and effect in influencing characters' feelings or underlying motives
- Infer the big ideas or message (theme) of a text
- Infer causes of problems or of outcomes in fiction and nonfiction texts

Thinking *About* the Text

Analyzing

- Notice and discuss aspects of genres (fiction, nonfiction, realistic stories, and fantasy)
- Understand when a writer has used underlying organizational structures (description, compare/contrast, temporal sequence, problem/solution, cause/effect)
- Notice variety in layout (words in bold or larger font, or italics, variety in layout)
- Notice how pictures are used to communicate meaning in illustrated texts
- Notice and discuss the way the writer assigns dialogue
- Notice aspects of a writer's style after reading several texts by the author
- Notice specific writing techniques (for example, question and answer format)
- Notice and interpret figurative language and discuss how it adds to the meaning or enjoyment of a text
- Notice descriptive language and discuss how it adds to enjoyment or understanding
- Understand the relationship between the setting and the plot of a story
- Identify a point in the story when the problem is resolved
- Notice and discuss how the writer of a graphic novel has communicated meaning through illustrations and print

Critiquing

- Express opinions about the quality of a text
- Discuss the quality of illustrations or graphics
- Agree or disagree with the ideas in a text
- Hypothesize how characters could have behaved differently
- Judge the text as to whether it is interesting, humorous, or exciting, and specify why

Readers at Level L:

At Level L, readers process easy chapter books including some series books with more sophisticated plots and few illustrations, as well as shorter informational and fiction books. They adjust their reading to process a range of genres (realistic fiction, simple fantasy, informational texts, traditional literature, and biography, as well as some special types of texts, for example, shorter series books, very simple mysteries, and graphic texts). They understand that chapters have multiple episodes related to a single plot. They learn some new content through reading and are required to bring more prior knowledge to the process; but the content is usually accessible through the text and illustrations. At this level, readers are beginning to recognize themes across texts (friendship, courage), and they understand some abstract ideas. They see multiple perspectives of characters as revealed through description, what they say, think, or do, and what others say about them. They process complex sentences with embedded clauses and figurative language. They recognize and/or flexibly solve a large number of words, including plurals, contractions, possessives, many multisyllable words, many content-specific words, and some technical words. They read silently in independent reading; in oral reading, they demonstrate all aspects of smooth, fluent processing.

Selecting Texts: Characteristics of Texts at This Level

GENRE/FORMS

Genre
- Informational texts
- Simple fantasy
- Realistic fiction
- Traditional literature (folktales, fables)
- Biography, mostly on well-known subjects
- Simple mysteries
- Some graphic novels
- Simple hybrid texts

Forms
- Picture books
- Plays
- Beginning chapter books with illustrations
- Series books
- Graphic texts

TEXT STRUCTURE

Fiction
- Narrative structure including chapters with multiple episodes related to a single plot
- Simple, straightforward plots
- Some embedded genres such as directions or letters

Nonfiction
- Presentation of multiple topics
- Underlying structures (description, comparison and contrast, temporal sequence, problem and solution, cause and effect)
- Texts organized into a few simple categories
- Some longer texts with sections presenting different information
- Variety in organization and topic
- Variety in nonfiction formats (question and answer, paragraphs, boxes, legends, and call-outs)

CONTENT

- New content requiring prior knowledge to understand
- Some texts with plots, settings, and situations outside typical experience
- Some technical content that is challenging and not typically known
- New content accessible through text and illustrations

THEMES AND IDEAS

- Many light, humorous stories, typical of childhood experiences
- Some ideas that are new to most children
- Themes accessible given typical experiences of children

- Texts with universal themes illustrating important human issues and attributes (friendship, courage, challenges)
- Some texts (graphic novels) requiring readers to infer the story from pictures with minimal text or dialogue only

LANGUAGE AND LITERARY FEATURES

- Some complex and memorable characters
- Multiple characters to understand and follow development
- Various ways of showing characters' attributes (description, dialogue, thoughts, others' perspectives)
- Figurative language and descriptive language
- Setting important to understanding the plot in some texts
- Wide variety in showing dialogue, both assigned and unassigned
- Complex plots with numerous episodes and time passing
- Plots with numerous episodes, building toward problem resolution
- Simple, traditional elements of fantasy
- Texts with multiple points of view revealed through characters' behaviors and dialogue

SENTENCE COMPLEXITY

- Variety in sentence length and complexity
- Longer (more than fifteen words), more complex sentences (prepositional phrases, introductory clauses, lists of nouns, verbs, or adjectives)
- Questions in dialogue (fiction) and questions and answers (nonfiction)
- Sentences with nouns, verbs, or adjectives in series, divided by commas
- Assigned and unassigned dialogue

VOCABULARY

- Some new vocabulary and content-specific words introduced, explained, and illustrated in the text
- Wide variety of words to assign dialogue, with verbs and adverbs essential to meaning
- New vocabulary in fiction texts (largely unexplained)
- Words with multiple meanings

Hang On, Baby Monkey

by Donna Latham

Newborn

Deep in the rain forest, a baby monkey is born. His mother is part of a family group called a troop. Monkeys in the troop work together to stay alive.

Monkeys from the troop come close to look at the new baby.

rain forest

Monkeys make their home in the huge Amazon rain forest in South America.

1

WORDS

- Wide variety of high frequency words
- Many two- to three-syllable words
- Some words with more than three syllables
- Words with suffixes and prefixes
- Words with a wide variety of very complex spelling patterns
- Multisyllable words that are challenging to take apart or decode
- Many plurals, contractions, and compound words

ILLUSTRATIONS

General

- A variety of complex graphics, often more than one on a page
- Some long stretches of text (usually a page or two) with no illustrations or graphics

Fiction

- Many texts with no or only minimal illustrations
- Some complex and artistic illustrations that communicate meaning to match or extend the text
- Some texts with illustrations that are essential to interpretation
- Some illustrations that support interpretation, enhance enjoyment, and set mood but are not necessary for understanding
- Much of setting, action, and characters shown in pictures (graphic texts)

Nonfiction

- More than one kind of graphic on a page
- Combination of graphics providing information that matches and extends the text
- Graphics that are clearly explained in most texts
- A variety of graphics: photos, drawings, maps, cutaways, tables, graphs)
- Variety in the layout of print in nonfiction texts (question and answer, paragraphs, boxes, maps, charts, call-outs, illustrations with labels and legends)

BOOK AND PRINT FEATURES

Length

- Chapter books (sixty to one hundred pages of print)
- Shorter texts (most approximately twenty-four to forty-eight pages of print) on single topics (usually nonfiction)
- Many lines of print on a page (five to twenty-four lines; more for fiction)

Print and Layout

- Ample space between lines
- Print and font size varying with some longer texts in small fonts
- Use of words in italics, bold, or all capitals to indicate emphasis, level of importance, or signal other meaning
- Variety in print and background color
- Some sentences continuing over several lines or to the next page
- Print and illustrations integrated in many texts
- Variety in layout reflecting different genres

- Usually friendly layout in chapter books, with many sentences starting on the left
- Bubbles, strips or print, and other print/picture combinations in graphic texts
- Variety in layout of nonfiction formats (question and answer, paragraphs, boxes, legends, call-outs)

Punctuation

- Periods, commas, quotation marks, exclamation points, question marks, dashes, and ellipses in most texts

Tools

- A variety of readers' tools: table of contents, glossary, punctuation guide, titles, labels, headings, subheadings, sidebars, legends

Selecting Goals: Behaviors and Understandings to Notice, Teach, and Support

Thinking *Within* the Text

Solving Words

- Notice new and interesting words, and actively add them to speaking or writing vocabulary
- Connect words that mean the same or almost the same to help in understanding a text and acquiring new vocabulary
- Demonstrate knowledge of flexible ways to solve words (noticing word parts, noticing endings and prefixes)
- Solve words of two or three syllables, many words with inflectional endings and complex letter-sound relationships
- Solve content-specific words, using graphics and definitions embedded in the text
- Recognize multiple meanings of words
- Use context to derive meaning of new words
- Understand longer descriptive words
- Demonstrate competent, active word solving while reading at a good pace
- Derive meaning of words from graphics

Monitoring and Correcting

- Self-correct when errors detract from the meaning of the text
- Self-correct intonation when it does not reflect the meaning when reading aloud
- Use multiple sources of information to monitor and self-correct (language structure, meaning, and letter-sound information)
- Realize when more information is needed to understand a text

Searching for and Using Information

- Use multiple sources of information together to solve new words
- Search for information in illustrations to support text interpretation
- Search for information in graphics (simple diagrams, illustrations with labels, maps, charts, captions under pictures)
- Use chapter titles and section headings as to foreshadow content
- Use readers' tools (table of contents, headings, glossary, chapter titles, and author's notes) to gather information
- Process long sentences (fifteen or more words) with embedded clauses (prepositional phrases, introductory clauses)
- Process sentences with a series of nouns, verbs, or adverbs
- Process a wide range of dialogue, some unassigned
- Follow a sequence of actions from graphics
- Search for important information in pictures

Summarizing

- Follow and remember a series of events over a longer text in order to understand the ending
- Summarize ideas from a text and tell how they are related
- Summarize a longer narrative text with multiple episodes, reporting events in the order they happened
- Identify important ideas in a text and report them in an organized way, either orally or in writing
- Understand the problem of a story and its solution

Planning for Word Work after Guided Reading

One- to three-minute demonstrations with active student engagement using a chart or easel, white board, or pencil and paper can develop fluency and flexibility in visual processing. Plan for explicit work in specific visual processing areas that need support.

Examples:

- Recognize and take apart words with inflectional endings (*painting, skated*)
- Make and change words to add inflectional endings (*-ing, -ed; cry-crying-cried*)
- Change words to make a full range of plurals by adding -s and -es (*stoves, axes, toys, hobbies, echoes*)
- Work flexibly with base words, taking apart and making new words by changing letters and adding prefixes and suffixes (*tie/tied/untie*)
- Recognize word patterns that look the same but sound different (*dear, bear*) and that sound the same but look different (*said, bed*)
- Recognize and connect homophones (same pronunciation, different spellings and meanings) (*dear, deer*)

- Read homographs (same spelling, different meanings, and sometimes different pronunciations) (*bear, bear; bass, bass*)
- Recognize and pronounce vowel sounds in open (CV: *ho-tel*) and closed (CVC: *lem-on*) syllables
- Read words that have double vowel patterns (VVC: *feel*) as well as words that have vowel sounds with r (*march*)
- Take apart and make words using more complex phonograms and long vowel patterns (VVC (*paint*), VVCe (*raise*), VCCe (*large*), VCCC (*lunch*), VVCCC (*health*))
- Make and change words to create comparatives (*-er, -est*) (*light/lighter/lightest*)
- Take apart words with comparatives (*short-er, short-est*)

- Take apart compound words and discuss how the parts are related to meaning (*cook-book*)
- Take apart two- and three-syllable words (*sal-ad, cu-cum-ber*)
- Read words using letter-sound analysis from left to right (*s-l-i-pp-er*)
- Use what is known about words to read new words (*fan, fancy; ate, later*)
- Read words with silent consonants (*sight, knife*)
- Read, take apart, or write words with consonant blends and digraphs at the ends (*spend, splash*)
- Recognize and take apart the full range of contractions (*I'm, that's, he'll, won't, they're, you've*)
- Take apart words with open and closed syllables (*fe-ver, ped-al*)

Maintaining Fluency
- Demonstrate phrased, fluent oral reading
- Read dialogue with phrasing and expression that reflects understanding of characters and events
- Demonstrate awareness of the function of the full range of punctuation
- Demonstrate appropriate stress on words, pausing and phrasing, intonation, and use of punctuation
- Use multiple sources of information (language structure, meaning, fast word recognition) to support fluency and phrasing
- Quickly and automatically solve most words in the text in a way that supports fluency
- Use multiple sources of information in an integrated way to support fluency
- Read silently and orally at an appropriate rate, not too fast and not too slow

Adjusting
- Slow down to search for information or think about ideas and resume normal pace of reading again
- Demonstrate different ways of reading fiction and nonfiction texts
- Demonstrate adjustment to process simple biographies
- Reread to solve words and resume normal rate of reading
- Realize that illustrations carry a great deal of the meaning in graphic texts

Thinking *Beyond* the Text

Predicting
- Use text structure to predict the outcome of a narrative
- Make predictions about the solution to the problem in a story
- Make a wide range of predictions based on personal experiences, content knowledge, and knowledge of similar texts
- Search for and use information to confirm or disconfirm predictions
- Justify predictions using evidence
- Predict what characters will do based on the traits revealed by the writer

Making Connections
- Bring knowledge from personal experiences to the interpretation of characters and events
- Bring background knowledge to the understanding of a text before, during, and after reading
- Make connections between the text and other texts that have been read or heard
- Specify the nature of connections (topic, content, type of story, writer)

Synthesizing
- Differentiate between what is known and new information
- Demonstrate learning new content from reading
- Expresses changes in ideas after reading a text

Inferring
- Demonstrate understandings of characters, using evidence from text to support statements
- Infer characters' feelings and motivations through reading their dialogue
- Show understanding of characters and their traits
- Infer cause and effect in influencing characters' feelings or underlying motives
- Infer the big ideas or message (theme) of a text
- Infer causes of problems or of outcomes in fiction and nonfiction texts
- Infer setting, character's traits and feelings, and plot from illustrations in graphic texts
- Use evidence from the text to support thinking

Thinking *About* the Text

Analyzing
- Notice and discuss aspects of genres (fiction, nonfiction, realistic stories, traditional literature, and fantasy)
- Understand a writer's use of underlying organizational structures (description, compare/contrast, temporal sequence, problem/solution, cause/effect)
- Demonstrate the ability to identify how a text is organized (diagram or talk)
- Identify important aspects of illustrations (design related to the meaning of the text)
- Notice variety in layout (words in bold or larger font, or italics, variety in layout)
- Notice the way the writer assigns dialogue
- Notice aspects of a writer's style after reading several texts by the same author
- Notice specific writing techniques (for example, question and answer format)
- Notice and interpret figurative language and discuss how it adds to the meaning or enjoyment of a text
- Notice descriptive language and discuss how it adds to enjoyment or understanding
- Understand the relationship between the setting and the plot of a story
- Identify a point in the story when the problem is resolved
- Identify the author's explicitly stated purpose
- Notice and discuss how the writer of a graphic text has communicated meaning through illustrations and print

Critiquing
- State opinions about a text and provide evidence to support them
- Discuss the quality of illustrations or graphics
- Hypothesize how characters could have behaved differently
- Judge the text as to whether it is interesting, humorous, or exciting, and specify why

Readers at **Level M:**

At Level M, readers know the characteristics of a range of genres (realistic fiction, simple fantasy, informational texts, traditional literature, and biography). Some fiction texts are chapter books, and readers are becoming interested in special forms, such as longer series books and mysteries. Fiction narratives are straightforward but have elaborate plots and multiple characters that develop and show some change over time. They read shorter nonfiction texts, mostly on single topics, and are able to identify and use underlying structures (description, comparison and contrast, temporal sequence, problem and solution, cause and effect). They can process sentences that are complex, contain prepositional phrases, introductory clauses, lists of nouns, verbs, or adjectives. Word solving is smooth and automatic in both silent and oral reading and children can read and understand descriptive words, some complex content-specific words, and some technical words. They read silently and independently. In oral reading, they demonstrate all aspects of smooth, fluent processing.

Selecting Texts: Characteristics of Texts at This Level

GENRE/FORMS

Genre
- Informational texts
- Simple fantasy
- Realistic fiction
- Traditional literature (folktales, fables, legends, tall tales)
- Biography, mostly on well-known subjects
- Simple mysteries
- Hybrid texts combining more than one genre

Forms
- Picture books
- Plays
- Beginning chapter books with illustrations
- Series books
- Graphic texts

TEXT STRUCTURE

Fiction
- Narrative structure including chapters with multiple episodes related to a single plot
- Simple, straightforward plots
- Much of setting, actions, and characters provided in pictures in graphic texts

Nonfiction
- Presentation of multiple topics
- Underlying structures (description, comparison and contrast, temporal sequence, problem and solution, cause and effect)

- Texts organized into a few simple categories
- Variety in organization and topic
- Variety in nonfiction formats (question and answer, paragraphs, boxes, legends, and call-outs)

CONTENT

- Some technical content that is challenging and not typically known
- Most of content carried by the print rather than pictures
- Content supported or extended by illustrations in most informational texts

THEMES AND IDEAS

- Many light, humorous stories, typical of childhood experiences
- Most ideas supported by the text but with less illustration support
- Texts with universal themes illustrating important human issues and attributes (friendship, courage)
- Some abstract themes requiring inferential thinking to derive
- Some texts (graphic texts) requiring readers to infer the story from pictures with minimal text or dialogue only
- Some texts with moral lessons

LANGUAGE AND LITERARY FEATURES

- Some complex and memorable characters
- Various ways of showing characters' attributes (description, dialogue, thoughts, others' perspectives)
- Multiple characters to understand and notice how they develop and change over time
- Figurative and descriptive language
- Setting important to understanding the plot in some texts
- Various perspectives revealed through dialogue
- Wide variety in showing dialogue, both assigned and unassigned
- Complex plots with numerous episodes and time passing
- Plots with numerous episodes, building toward problem resolution
- Simple, traditional elements of fantasy
- Texts with multiple points of view revealed through characters' behaviors

SENTENCE COMPLEXITY

- Some longer (more than fifteen words), more complex sentences (prepositional phrases, introductory clauses, lists of nouns, verbs, or adjectives)

- Variety in sentence length, with some long and complex sentences
- Questions in dialogue (fiction) and questions and answers (nonfiction)
- Sentences with parenthetical material
- Sentences with nouns, verbs, or adjectives in series, divided by commas

VOCABULARY

- Some new vocabulary and content-specific words introduced, explained, and illustrated in the text
- New vocabulary in fiction texts largely unexplained

WORDS

- Many two- to three-syllable words
- Some words with more than three syllables
- Words with suffixes
- Words with a wide variety of very complex spelling patterns
- Multisyllable words that are challenging to take apart or decode
- Many plurals, contractions, and compound words

Saving Up

by Kitty Colton

I really, really wanted to get a dog. But Mom said I wasn't responsible enough to take care of a pet.

"I'm very responsible!" I said.

"Hmm. Okay, Mr. Responsible. I hate to disagree with you, Danny. But how many times did I tell you to clean your room this week?" asked Mom.

"Well, cleaning my room is totally boring! Taking care of a dog would be totally fun!"

Mom said, "Dogs are a lot of work!" She said I'd have to prove I

1

ILLUSTRATIONS

General
- A variety of complex graphics, often more than one on a page
- Some long stretches of text with no illustrations or graphics

Fiction
- Most texts with no illustrations, minimal black and white illustrations, or symbolic illustrations
- Some highly complex and artistic illustrations that communicate meaning to match or extend the text
- Black and white illustrations in most texts

Nonfiction
- More than one kind of graphic on a page
- Combination of graphics providing information that matches and extends the text
- Variety of graphics (diagrams, labels, cutaways, maps, scales with legends, illustrations with labels, maps, charts)
- In most texts, graphics that are clearly explained
- Variety in the layout of print in nonfiction texts (question and answer, paragraphs, boxes, legends, call-outs)

BOOK AND PRINT FEATURES

Length
- Short texts
- Some chapter books (sixty to one hundred pages of print)

Print and Layout
- Ample space between lines
- Print and font size varying with some longer texts in small fonts
- Use of words in italics, bold, or all capitals to indicate emphasis, level of importance, or signal other meaning
- Variety in print and background color
- Many sentences continuing over several lines or to the next page
- Print and illustrations integrated in many texts
- Captions under pictures that provide important information
- Usually friendly layout in chapter books, with some sentences starting on the left
- Variety in layout of nonfiction formats (question and answer, paragraphs, boxes, legends, call-outs)

Punctuation
- Full range of punctuation, including dashes and ellipses

Tools
- A variety of readers' tools: table of contents, glossary, punctuation guide, titles, labels, headings, subheadings, sidebars, legends

Selecting Goals: Behaviors and Understandings to Notice, Teach, and Support

Thinking *Within* the Text

Solving Words

- Begin to notice new and interesting words, record them, and actively add them to speaking or writing vocabulary
- Connect words that mean the same or almost the same to help in understanding a text and acquiring new vocabulary
- Demonstrate knowledge of flexible ways to solve words (noticing word parts, noticing endings and prefixes)
- Solve words of two or three syllables, many words with inflectional endings and complex letter-sound relationships
- Solve content-specific words, using graphics and definitions embedded in the text
- Use the context of a sentence, paragraph, or whole text to determine the meaning of a word
- Understand longer descriptive words
- Demonstrate competent, active word solving while reading at a good pace— less overt problem solving
- Understand words with multiple meanings
- Derive meaning of new words from graphics

Monitoring and Correcting

- Self-correct when errors detract from the meaning of the text
- When reading aloud, self-correct intonation when it does not reflect the meaning
- Use multiple sources of information to monitor and self-correct (language structure, meaning, and letter-sound information)
- Consistently check on understanding and search for information when meaning breaks down

Searching for and Using Information

- Use multiple sources of information together to solve new words
- Search for information in illustrations to support text interpretation
- Search for information in graphics (simple diagrams, illustrations with labels, maps, charts, captions under pictures)
- Use chapter titles as to foreshadow content
- Use readers' tools (table of contents, headings, glossary, sidebars, captions, chapter titles, and author's notes) to gather information
- Process long sentences (fifteen or more words) with embedded clauses (prepositional phrases, introductory clauses)
- Process sentences with a series of nouns, verbs, or adverbs
- Process a wide range of dialogue, some unassigned
- Understand how to use pictures to construct meaning in graphic texts
- Search for information in pictures

Summarizing

- Follow and remember a series of events over a longer text in order to understand the ending
- Report episodes in a text in the order they happened
- Summarize ideas from a text and tell how they are related
- Summarize a longer narrative text with multiple episodes
- Identify important ideas in a text and report them in an organized way, either orally or in writing
- Understand the problem of a story and its solution

Planning for Word Work after Guided Reading

One- to three-minute demonstrations with active student engagement using a chart or easel, white board, or pencil and paper can develop fluency and flexibility in visual processing. Plan for explicit work in specific visual processing areas that need support.

Examples:

- Take apart words with a variety of endings (*boxful, caring*)
- Add a variety of endings to words (*-ing, -es, -ed, -er; walking, bushes, climbed, hiker*)
- Change words to make a full range of plurals by adding *-s* and *-es* (*pens, fairies, mixes*)
- Take apart words with common prefixes (*un-true, re-play*)
- Remove letters or letter clusters from the beginning of a word to recognize a base word (*un-friend-ly*)
- Work flexibly with base words taking apart and making new words by changing letters and adding prefixes and suffixes (*write/writing/rewrite*)

- Recognize words that have multiple meanings (a form of homograph: *spell, spell*), homographs (look the same, sound different: *present, present*), and homophones (sound the same, look different: *ate, eight*)
- Recognize and pronounce vowel sounds in open (CV: *mo-tel*) and closed (CVC: *rel-ish*) syllables
- Take apart and make words using more complex phonograms and long vowel patterns (VVC (*paint*), VVCe (*raise*), VCCe (*large*), VCCC (*lunch*), VVCCC (*health*))
- Take apart compound words and discuss how the parts are related to meaning (*bath-tub*)

- Take apart multisyllable words to decode manageable units (*sand-wich-es, hap-pi-ly*)
- Read words using letter-sound analysis from left to right (*g-ar-d-en*)
- Use what is known about words to read new words (*mean, clean; van, vanish*)
- Take apart and read the full range of contractions (*I'm, that's, he'll, won't, they're, you've*)

Maintaining Fluency
- Demonstrate phrased, fluent oral reading
- Read dialogue with phrasing and expression that reflects understanding of characters and events
- Demonstrate awareness of the function of the full range of punctuation
- Demonstrate appropriate stress on words, pausing and phrasing, intonation, and use of punctuation
- Use multiple sources of information (language structure, meaning, fast word recognition) to support fluency and phrasing
- Quickly and automatically solve most words in the text in a way that supports fluency
- Use multiple sources of information in a way that supports fluency
- Read silently and orally at an appropriate rate, not too fast and not too slow

Adjusting
- Slow down to search for information and resume normal pace of reading again
- Demonstrate different ways of reading fiction and nonfiction texts
- Demonstrate adjustment of reading for simple biographies
- Reread to solve words or think about ideas and resume good rate of reading
- Realize that meaning must be derived from illustrations (usually combined with print) in graphic texts

Thinking *Beyond* the Text

Predicting
- Use text structure to predict the outcome of a narrative
- Make predictions about the solution to the problem of a story
- Make a wide range of predictions based on personal experiences, content knowledge, and knowledge of similar texts
- Search for and use information to confirm or disconfirm predictions
- Justify predictions using evidence
- Predict what characters will do based on the traits revealed by the writer

Making Connections
- Bring knowledge from personal experiences to the interpretation of characters and events
- Bring background content knowledge to the understanding of a text before, during, and after reading
- Make connections between the text and other texts that have been read or heard
- Specify the nature of connections (topic, content, type of story, writer)

Synthesizing
- Differentiate between what is known and new information
- Demonstrate learning new content from reading
- Expresses changes in ideas after reading a text

Inferring
- Demonstrate understandings of characters, using evidence from text to support statements
- Infer characters' feelings and motivations through reading their dialogue
- Infer cause and effect in influencing characters' feelings or underlying motives
- Infer the big ideas or message (theme) of a text
- Generate or react to alternative understandings of a text
- Infer causes of problems or outcomes in fiction and nonfiction texts
- Identify significant events and tell how they are related to the problem of the story or the solution
- Support all thinking with evidence from the text
- Infer setting, characters' traits and feelings, and plot from illustrations in graphic texts

Thinking *About* the Text

Analyzing
- Notice aspects of genres (fiction, nonfiction, realistic stories, and fantasy)
- Understand when a writer has used underlying organizational structures (description, compare/contrast, temporal sequence, problem/solution, cause/effect)
- Demonstrate the ability to identify how a text is organized (diagram or talk)
- Identify important aspects of illustrations (design related to the meaning of the text)
- Notice variety in layout (words in bold or larger font, or italics, variety in layout)
- Notice the way the writer assigns dialogue
- Notice aspects of a writer's style after reading several texts by the same author
- Notice specific writing techniques (for example, question and answer format)
- Notice and interpret some figurative language and discuss how it adds to the meaning or enjoyment of a text
- Notice descriptive language and discuss how it adds to enjoyment or understanding
- Describe the problem of a story
- Identify author's explicitly stated purpose
- Understand the relationship between the setting and the plot of a story
- Identify a point in the story when the problem is resolved
- Notice and discuss how the writer of a graphic text has communicated meaning through illustrations and print

Critiquing
- State opinions about a text and show evidence to support them
- Discuss the quality of illustrations or graphics
- Hypothesize how characters could have behaved differently
- Judge the text as to whether it is interesting, humorous, or exciting, and specify why

Readers at Level N:

At Level N, readers will process the full range of genres, short fiction stories, chapter books, and shorter informational texts; also, they read special forms such as mysteries and series books. Fiction narratives are straightforward but have more elaborate plots with many episodes and multiple characters who develop and change over time. Some nonfiction texts provide information in categories on several related topics, and readers can identify and use underlying structures (description, compare and contrast, temporal sequence, problem and solution, cause and effect). They continue to read silently at a good rate and automatically use a wide range of word-solving strategies while focusing on meaning. In oral reading, they will continue to read with phrasing, fluency, and appropriate word stress in a way that reflects meaning and recognizes punctuation. Readers will slow down to problem solve or search for information and then resume normal pace; there is little overt problem solving. They can process sentences that are complex, with prepositional phrases, introductory clauses, lists of nouns, verbs, or adjectives. They can read and understand descriptive words, some complex content-specific words, and some technical words. Length of text is no longer a critical factor as students are beginning to read texts that vary greatly. Word solving is smooth and automatic in both silent and oral reading.

Selecting Texts: Characteristics of Texts at This Level

GENRE/FORMS

Genre
- Informational texts
- Simple fantasy
- Realistic fiction
- Traditional literature
- Biography, mostly on well-known subjects
- Historical fiction
- Simple mysteries
- Hybrid texts with embedded genres such as directions, letters, or recipes

Forms
- Picture books
- Plays
- Beginning chapter books with illustrations
- Series books
- Graphic texts

TEXT STRUCTURE

Fiction
- Narrative structure including chapters with multiple episodes related to a single plot
- Plots with detailed episodes

Nonfiction
- Texts organized into categories and subcategories

- Presentation of multiple topics that represent subtopics of a larger content area or theme
- Underlying structures (description, comparison and contrast, temporal sequence, problem and solution, cause and effect)
- Variety in organization and topic
- Variety in nonfiction formats (question and answer, paragraphs, boxes, legends, and call-outs)

CONTENT
- Content requiring prior knowledge to understand in many informational texts
- Most of content carried by the print rather than pictures
- Content supported or extended by illustrations and other graphics in most informational texts
- Content requiring the reader to take on perspectives from diverse cultures and bring cultural knowledge to understanding

THEMES AND IDEAS
- Many light, humorous stories, typical of childhood experiences
- A few abstract ideas, supported by the text but with less illustration support

- Some abstract themes requiring inferential thinking to derive
- Texts with deeper meanings applicable to important human problems and social issues
- Some texts (graphic texts) requiring readers to infer the story from pictures with minimal text or dialogue only

LANGUAGE AND LITERARY FEATURES
- Multiple characters to understand
- Characters and perspectives revealed by what they say, think, and do and what others say or think about them
- Memorable characters who change and develop over time
- Factors related to character change explicit and obvious
- Descriptive and figurative language that are important to understanding the plot
- Setting important to understanding the plot in some texts
- Wide variety in showing dialogue, both assigned and unassigned
- Complex plots with numerous episodes and time passing
- Plots with numerous episodes, building toward problem resolution

- Building suspense through events of the plot
- Simple, traditional elements of fantasy
- Texts with multiple points of view revealed through characters' behaviors

SENTENCE COMPLEXITY
- Variety in sentence length, with some longer (more than fifteen words), more complex sentences (prepositional phrases, introductory clauses, lists of nouns, verbs, or adjectives)
- Questions in dialogue (fiction) and questions and answers (nonfiction)
- Sentences with parenthetical material
- Sentences with nouns, verbs, or adjectives in series, divided by commas

VOCABULARY
- Many complex content-specific words in nonfiction, mostly defined in text, illustrations, or glossary
- New vocabulary in fiction texts largely unexplained
- Some words used figuratively

Dogs at Work

by Misha Kees

Who is your best friend? A best friend can be a classmate, a neighbor, or even a relative. But for some people, their best friend walks on four legs, is covered with fur, and takes them anywhere they need to go. It's a dog! But it's not just any dog—their best friend is a guide dog.

This dog guides its owner through a grocery store.

1

- Some words with connotative meanings that are essential to understanding the text
- Some longer descriptive words (adjectives and adverbs)
- Words that represent abstract ideas

WORDS

- Many words with three or more syllables
- Words with suffixes and prefixes
- Words with a wide variety of very complex spelling patterns
- Multisyllable words that are challenging to take apart or decode
- Some multisyllable proper nouns that are difficult to decode
- Many plurals, contractions, and compound words
- Some words divided (hyphenated) across lines

ILLUSTRATIONS

General
- A variety of complex graphics, often more than one on a page
- Some long stretches of text with no illustrations or graphics

Fiction
- Most texts with no or only minimal illustrations
- Black and white illustrations in most texts
- Some highly complex and artistic illustrations that communicate meaning to match or extend the text (mood, symbolism)
- Much of setting, action, and characters provided in pictures in graphic texts

Nonfiction
- Combination of graphics providing information that matches and extends the text

- Variety of graphics (diagrams, labels, cutaways, maps, scales with legends, illustrations with labels, charts)
- Graphics that are clearly explained in most texts
- Variety in the layout of print in nonfiction texts (question and answer, paragraphs, boxes, legends, call-outs)

BOOK AND PRINT FEATURES

Print and Layout
- Ample space between lines
- Print and font size varying with some longer texts in small fonts
- Use of words in italics, bold, or all capitals to indicate emphasis, level of importance, or signal other meaning
- Variety in print and background color
- Sentences continuing over several lines or to the next page

- Print and illustrations integrated in many texts
- Captions under pictures that provide important information
- Variety in layout, reflecting different genres
- Usually friendly layout in chapter books, with sentences starting on the left
- Variety in layout of nonfiction formats (question and answer, paragraphs, boxes, legends, call-outs)
- Information shown in a variety of picture and print combinations in graphic texts

Punctuation
- Full range of punctuation, including dashes and ellipses

Tools
- A variety of readers' tools: table of contents, glossary, punctuation guide, titles, labels, headings, subheadings, sidebars, legends, author's notes

Selecting Goals: Behaviors and Understandings to Notice, Teach, and Support

Thinking *Within* the Text

Solving Words
- Begin to notice new and interesting words and add them to speaking or writing vocabulary
- Connect words that mean the same or almost the same to help in understanding a text and acquiring new vocabulary
- Demonstrate knowledge of flexible ways to solve words (noticing word parts, noticing endings and prefixes)
- Solve words of two or three syllables, many words with inflectional endings and complex letter-sound relationships
- Solve content-specific words, using graphics and definitions embedded in the text
- Use the context of a sentence, paragraph, or whole text to determine the meaning of a word
- Understand longer descriptive words
- Apply problem-solving strategies to technical words or proper nouns that are challenging
- Realize that words in print are partially defined by illustrations in graphic texts

Monitoring and Correcting
- Continue to monitor accuracy and understanding, self-correcting when errors detract from meaning
- Derive meaning of new words from graphics
- Understand words that stand for abstract ideas

Searching for and Using Information
- Search for information in graphics (simple diagrams, illustrations with labels, maps, charts, captions under pictures)
- Use readers' tools (table of contents, headings, glossary, chapter titles, and author's notes) to gather information and construct meaning

- Process long sentences (fifteen or more words) with embedded clauses (prepositional phrases, introductory clauses, series of nouns, verbs, or adverbs)
- Process a wide range of dialogue, some unassigned
- Respond to plot tension or suspense by reading on to seek resolutions to problems
- Follow a sequence of actions from graphics
- Understand how to use pictures to construct meaning in graphic texts
- Search for information in a sequence of illustrations in graphic texts

Summarizing
- Follow and remember a series of events and the story problem and solution over a longer text in order to understand the ending
- Identify and understand sets of related ideas organized into categories
- Summarize a text at intervals during the reading of a longer text
- Summarize longer narrative texts with multiple episodes either orally or in writing
- Identify important ideas in a text and report them in an organized way, either orally or in writing
- Follow a sequence of actions from graphic texts

Maintaining Fluency
- Demonstrate phrased, fluent oral reading
- Read dialogue with phrasing and expression that reflects understanding of characters and events
- Demonstrate appropriate stress on words, pausing and phrasing, intonation, and use of punctuation
- Use multiple sources of information (language structure, meaning, fast word recognition) to support fluency and phrasing
- Read with high accuracy in a way that supports fluency
- Read silently and orally at an appropriate rate (not too fast and not too slow) for comprehending

Planning for Word Work after Guided Reading

One- to three-minute demonstrations with active student engagement using a chart or easel, white board, or pencil and paper can develop fluency and flexibility in visual processing. Plan for explicit work in specific visual processing areas that need support.

Examples:

- Take apart and make words with a variety of endings (*-ing, -es, -ed,-er*) and discuss changes in spelling and meaning
- Take apart and make a full range of plurals, including irregular plurals and plurals that require spelling changes (*child/children, diary/diaries*)
- Work flexibly with base words, making new words by changing letters and adding prefixes and suffixes (*tip/tie/untie, grew/grow/growing*)

- Recognize words that have multiple meanings (a form of homograph: *train, train*), homographs (look the same, sound different: *lead, lead*), and homophones (sound the same, look different: *meet, meat*)
- Take apart and make words using more complex phonograms and long vowel patterns (VCC (*east*), VCe (*tease*), VCCe (*waste*), VCCC (*branch*), VVCCC (*wealth*))
- Take apart compound words (*mail-box*)

- Take apart multisyllable words to decode manageable units (*free-dom*)
- Solve words using letter-sound analysis from left to right (*r-e-m-e-m-b-er*)
- Use what is known about words to read new words (*reason, unreasonable*)
- Take apart and read the full range of contractions (*I'm, that's, he'll, won't, they're, you've*)
- Take apart words with open (ending in a vowel: *ri-ot*) and closed (ending in a consonant: *riv-er*) syllables

Adjusting
- Demonstrate different ways of reading related to genre, including simple biographies, fantasy, and historical fiction
- Adjust reading to process texts with difficult and complex layout
- Reread to solve words or think about ideas and resume good rate of reading
- Realize that meaning must be derived from illustrations (usually combined with print) in graphic texts

Thinking *Beyond* the Text

Predicting
- Use text structure to predict the outcome of a narrative
- Make a wide range of predictions based on personal experiences, content knowledge, and knowledge of similar texts
- Search for and use information to confirm or disconfirm predictions
- Justify predictions using evidence
- Continue to support predictions with evidence from the text what characters will do based on the traits revealed by the writer

Making Connections
- Bring knowledge from personal experiences to the interpretation of characters and events
- Bring background knowledge to the understanding of a text before, during, and after reading
- Make connections between the text and other texts that have been read or heard and demonstrate in writing
- Specify the nature of connections (topic, content, type of story, writer)

Synthesizing
- Differentiate between what is known and new information
- Through talk or writing, demonstrate learning new content from reading
- Demonstrate changing perspective as events in a story unfold
- Synthesize information across a longer text
- Expresses changes in ideas after reading a text

Inferring
- Demonstrate understanding of characters, using evidence from text to support statements
- Infer characters' feelings and motivations through reading their dialogue
- Infer cause and effect in influencing characters' feelings or underlying motives
- See changes in characters across time and articulate possible reasons for development
- Generate or react to alternative understandings of a text
- Infer causes of problems or of outcomes in fiction and nonfiction texts
- Identify significant events and tell how they are related to the problem of the story or the solution
- Infer the big ideas or message (theme) of a text
- Support all thinking with evidence from the text
- Infer setting, characters' traits and feelings, and plot from illustrations in graphic texts

Thinking *About* the Text

Analyzing
- Notice aspects of genres (realistic and historical fiction, biography and other nonfiction, fantasy)
- Understand when a writer has used underlying organizational structures (description, compare/contrast, temporal sequence, problem/solution, cause/effect)
- Demonstrate the ability to identify how a text is organized
- Identify important aspects of illustrations (design related to the meaning of the text)
- Notice variety in layout (words in bold or larger font, or italics, variety in layout)
- Notice the way the writer assigns dialogue
- Notice aspects of a writer's style after reading several texts by the author
- Notice specific writing techniques (for example, question and answer format)
- Notice and interpret figurative language and discuss how it adds to the meaning or enjoyment of a text
- Notice descriptive language and discuss how it adds to enjoyment or understanding
- Understand the relationship between the setting and the plot of a story
- Describe the problem of a story
- Describe the way the problem was solved
- Identify the author's explicitly stated purpose
- Notice and discuss how the writer of a graphic novel has communicated meaning through illustrations and print
- Compare and contrast characters' points of view in a story
- Explain how illustrations or photographs in a text contribute to the meaning

Critiquing
- State opinions about a text and show evidence to support them
- Discuss the quality of illustrations or graphics
- Hypothesize how characters could have behaved differently
- Evaluate aspects of a text that add to enjoyment (for example, humorous characters or situations)

Glossary

abbreviation Shortened form of a word that has come to be used in place of the whole word (*Mr., etc., NY*).

acronym A word formed from the initial letters of related words or word parts (*radar = radio detecting and ranging*).

adjust (as a strategic action) To read in different ways as appropriate to the purpose for reading and type of text.

adventure book A text in which the plot depends on the main character's overcoming danger and risk.

affix A part added to the beginning or ending of a base or root word to change its meaning or function (a *prefix* or a *suffix*).

allegory A narrative with an underlying meaning, often personifying abstract ideas, told to teach or explain something.

alliteration The repetition of the same initial consonant sounds of neighboring words or syllables.

alphabet book (ABC books) A book that helps children develop the concept and sequence of the alphabet by pairing alphabet letters with pictures of people, animals, or objects with labels related to the letters.

alphabet linking chart A chart containing upper- and lowercase letters of the alphabet paired with pictures representing words beginning with each letter (*a, apple*).

alphabetic principle The concept that there is a relationship between the spoken sounds in oral language and the graphic forms in written language.

analogy The resemblance of a known word to an unknown word that helps you solve the unknown word's meaning.

analyze (as a strategic action) To examine the elements of a text in order to know more about how it is constructed, and to notice aspects of the writer's craft.

animal fantasy A make-believe story in which personified animals are the main characters.

antonym A word that has the opposite meaning from another word (*cold* versus *hot*).

archaic words Words that are part of the language of the past and have specialized uses in language today.

assessment A means for gathering information or data that reveals what learners control, partially control, or do not yet control consistently.

autobiography The biography of a person written and narrated by himself or herself. See also *personal narrative*.

automaticity Rapid, accurate, fluent word decoding without conscious effort or attention.

base word A whole word to which you can add affixes, creating new word forms (*wash* and *–ing; washing*).

behaviors Observable actions.

biography A written history about a person's life or part of his or her life.

blend To combine sounds or word parts.

bold (boldface) Type that is heavier and darker than usual, often used for emphasis.

book and print features (as text characteristics) The physical attributes of a text (for example, font, layout, and length).

callout A nonfiction text feature, such as a definition, a quote, or an important concept, that is highlighted by being set to one side of a text or enlarged within the body of the text.

capitalization The use of capital letters, usually the first letter in a word, as a convention of written language (for example, for proper names and to begin sentences).

chapter book An early reading text that is divided into chapters, each of which narrates an episode in the whole.

choral reading To read aloud in unison with a group.

circular story A type of story in which a sense of completeness or closure originates in the way the end of a piece returns to subject matter, wording, or phrasing found at the beginning of the story.

closed syllable A syllable that ends in one or more consonants (*lem*-on).

comparative form A word that describes a person or thing in relation to another person or thing (*more, less; taller, shorter*).

compound word A word made up of two or more other words or morphemes (*play ground*). The meaning of a compound word can be a combination of the meanings of the words it is made of or can be unrelated to the meanings of the combined units.

concept book A book organized to develop an understanding of an abstract or generic idea or categorization.

concept words Words that represent abstract ideas or names. Categories of concept words include colors, numbers, months, days of the week, position words, and so on.

connecting strategies Ways of solving words that use connections or analogies with similar known words (knowing *she* and *out* helps with *shout*).

connotation The emotional meaning or association each word carries beyond the strict definition found in a dictionary.

consonant A speech sound made by partial or complete closure of the airflow that causes friction at one or more points in the breath channel. The consonant sounds are represented by the letters *b, c, d, f, g, h, j, k, l, m, n, p, q, r, s, t, v, w* (in most of their uses), *x, y* (in most of their uses), and *z*.

consonant blend Two or more consonant letters that often appear together in words and represent sounds that are smoothly joined, although each of the sounds can be heard in the word (*tr*im).

consonant cluster A sequence of two or three consonant letters that appears together in words (*tr*im, *ch*air).

consonant cluster linking chart A chart of common consonant clusters paired with pictures representing words beginning with each (*bl*, *bl*ock).

consonant digraph Two consonant letters that appear together and represent a single sound that is different from the sound of either letter (she*ll*).

consonant-vowel-consonant (CVC) A common sequence of sounds in a single syllable (*hat*).

contraction A shortening of a syllable, word, or word groups usually by the omission of a sound or letters (*didn't*).

content (as a text characteristic) The subject matter of a text.

conventions (in writing) Formal usage that has become customary in written language. Grammar, capitalization, and punctuation are three categories of writing conventions.

counting book A book in which the structure depends on a numerical progression.

critique (as a strategic action) To evaluate a text based on the reader's personal, world, or text knowledge, and to think critically about the ideas in the text.

cumulative tale A story with many details repeated until the climax.

cursive A form of handwriting in which letters are connected.

decoding Using letter-sound relationships to translate a word from a series of symbols to a unit of meaning.

dialect A regional variety of a language. In most languages, including English and Spanish, dialects are mutually intelligible; the differences are actually minor.

dialogue Spoken words, usually set off with quotation marks in text.

diary A form of personal narrative written in the first person and usually consisting of sequential, dated entries.

diction Clear pronunciation and enunciation in speech.

dimension (of a character) Traits, characteristics, or attributes that a character in fiction might have (brave, funny, selfish, friendly).

directionality The orientation of print (in the English language, from left to right).

distinctive letter features Visual features that make every letter of the alphabet different from every other letter.

draft (in writing) An early version of a writer's composition.

drafting and revising (in writing) The process of getting ideas down on paper and shaping them to convey the writer's message.

early literacy concepts Very early understandings related to how written language or print is organized and used—how it works.

editing and proofreading (in writing) The process of polishing the final draft of a written composition to prepare it for publication.

editorial See *opinion editorial*.

endpaper The sheets of heavy paper at the front and back of a hardback book that join the book block to the hardback binding; sometimes printed with text, maps, or design.

English language learners People whose native language is not English and who are acquiring English as an additional language.

essay An analytic or interpretive piece of writing with a focused point of view.

Exaggeration An overstatement intended to go beyond the truth to make something greater than it is.

expository text A composition that explains a concept, using information and description.

fable A fictitious story designed to teach a lesson, often with personified animal characters.

factual text See *informational text*.

fantasy An imaginative, fictional text containing elements that are highly unreal.

feature article A nonfiction text that focuses on one aspect of a topic.

fiction An invented story, usually narrative.

figurative language Language that is filled with word images and metaphorical language to express more than a literal meaning.

fluency in reading To read continuous text with good momentum, phrasing, appropriate pausing, intonation, and stress.

fluency in word solving Speed, accuracy, and flexibility in solving words.

folktale A traditional story, originally passed down orally.

font In printed text, the collection of type (letters) in a particular style.

form (as a text characteristic) A kind of text that is characterized by particular elements. Mystery, for example, is a form of writing within the narrative fiction genre.

formal letter A written communication, usually to a stranger, in which the form follows specific conventions (for example, a business letter).

free verse A poem whose rhythm (meter) is not regular.

friendly letter A written communication, usually to friends and family (for example, notes, invitations, emails).

functional genres A category of text in which the purpose is to accomplish a practical task. Friendly and business letters and directions are kinds of functional text.

gathering seeds (in writing) Collecting ideas, snippets of language, descriptions, and sketches for potential use in written composition.

genre A category of written text that is characterized by a particular style, form, or content.

grammar Complex rules by which people can generate an unlimited number of phrases, sentences, and longer texts in that language. Conventional grammar refers to the accepted conventions in a society.

grapheme A letter or cluster of letters representing a single sound, or phoneme (*a, eigh, ay*).

graphic text A simple or complex text in which the meaning is carried largely through a series of illustrations that depict moment-to-moment actions and characters' emotions. The illustrations are usually accompanied by speech balloons and narrative that describe action and create dialogue.

graphophonic relationship The relationship between the oral sounds of the language and the written letters or clusters of letters.

© 2011, 2008 by Gay Su Pinnell and Irene C. Fountas from *The Continuum of Literacy Learning, Grades PreK–2*. Portsmouth, NH: Heinemann.

guide words The words at the top of a dictionary page to indicate the first and last word on the page.

have a try To write a word, notice that it doesn't look quite right, try it two or three other ways, and decide which construction looks right; to make an attempt and self-check.

high-frequency words Words that occur often in the spoken and written language (*the*).

historical fiction An imagined story set in the realistically (and often factually) portrayed setting of a past era.

homograph One of two or more words spelled alike but different in meaning, derivation, or pronunciation (the *bat* flew away, he swung the *bat*; take a *bow*, *bow* and arrow).

homonym (a type of homograph) One of two or more words spelled and pronounced alike but different in meaning (we had *quail* for dinner; I would *quail* in fear).

homophone One of two or more words pronounced alike but different in spelling and meaning (*meat*, *meet*; *bear*, *bare*).

hybrid text A text that blends multiple genres in a coherent whole.

idea development (in writing) The craft of presenting and elaborating the ideas and themes of a text.

idiom A phrase with meaning that cannot be derived from the conjoined meanings of its elements (for example, *raining cats and dogs*).

illustrations (as a text characteristic) Graphic representations of important content (for example, art, photos, maps, graphs, charts).

imagery Descriptions, comparisons, and figures of speech that help the mind form forceful or beautiful pictures.

infer (as a strategic action) To go beyond the literal meaning of a text and to think about what is not stated but is implied by the writer.

inflectional ending A suffix added to a base word to show tense, plurality, possession, or comparison (dark-*er*).

informational genres A category of texts in which the purpose is to inform or to give facts about a topic. Nonfiction feature articles and essays are examples of informational text.

interactive read-aloud A teaching context in which students are actively listening and responding to an oral reading of a text.

interactive writing A teaching context in which the teacher and students cooperatively plan, compose, and write a group text; both teacher and students act as scribes (in turn).

intonation The rise and fall in pitch of the voice in speech to convey meaning.

irony A method of expression in which the usual meaning of words is the opposite of the thought in the speaker's mind.

italic (italics) A type style that is characterized by slanting letters.

label (in writing) Written word or phrase that names the content of an illustration.

label book A picture book consisting of illustrations with brief identifying text.

language and literary features (as text characteristics) Qualities particular to written language are qualitatively different from spoken language (for example, dialogue, figurative language, and literary structures such as character, setting, and plot in fiction or description and technical language in nonfiction).

language use (in writing) The craft of using sentences, phrases, and expressions to describe events, actions, or information.

layout The way the print is arranged on a page.

legend (as genre) A tale, usually from the past, that tells about a noteworthy person or event.

legend (as text feature) A key on a map or chart that explains what symbols stand for.

letter knowledge The ability to recognize and label the graphic symbols of language.

letters Graphic symbols representing the sounds in a language. Each letter has particular distinctive features and may be identified by letter name or sound.

letter (as genre) See *friendly letter* and *formal letter.*

letter-sound correspondence Recognizing the corresponding sound of a specific letter when that letter is seen or heard.

letter-sound relationships See *letter-sound correspondence.*

lexicon Words that make up language.

lists and procedures (in writing) Functional genres that include simple lists and how-to texts.

literary devices Techniques used by a writer to convey or enhance the story, such as figures of speech, imagery, symbolism, and point of view.

literary nonfiction Engaging factual texts that present information on a topic in interesting ways.

log (as genre) A chronological, written record, usually of a journey.

long vowel The elongated vowel sound that is the same as the name of the vowel. It is sometimes represented by two or more letters (c*a*ke, *ei*ght, m*ai*l).

lowercase letter A small letter form that is usually different from its corresponding capital or uppercase form.

maintain fluency (as a strategic action) To integrate sources of information in a smoothly operating process that results in expressive, phrased reading.

make connections (as a strategic action) To search for and use connections to knowledge gained through personal experiences, learning about the world, and reading other texts.

media Channels of communication for information or entertainment. Newspapers and books are print media; television and the Internet are electronic media.

memoir An account of something important, usually part of a person's life. A memoir is a kind of biography, autobiography, or personal narrative.

mentor texts Books or other texts that serve as examples of excellent writing. Mentor texts are read and reread to provide models for literature discussion and student writing.

metaphor A figure of speech that makes a comparison of two unlike things without using the words *like* or *as.*

modeled writing An instructional technique in which a teacher demonstrates the process of composing a particular genre, making the process explicit for students.

monitor and correct (as a strategic action) To check whether the reading sounds right, looks, right, and makes sense, and to solve problems when it doesn't.

monologue A long speech given by one person in a group.

mood The emotional atmosphere or tone communicated by an author in his or her work; usually established by details, imagery, figurative language, and setting.

morpheme The smallest unit of meaning in a language. Morphemes may be free or bound. For example, *run* is a unit of meaning that can stand alone (a free morpheme). In *runs* and *running*, the added *-s* and *-ing* are also units of meaning. They cannot stand alone but add meaning to the free morpheme. The *-s* and *-ing* are examples of bound morphemes.

morphemic strategies Ways of solving words by discovering meaning through the combination of significant word parts or morphemes (*happy, happiest; run, runner, running*).

morphological system Rules by which morphemes (building blocks of vocabulary) fit together into meaningful words, phrases, and sentences.

morphology The combination of morphemes (building blocks of meaning) to form words; the rules by which words are formed from free and bound morphemes—for example, root words, prefixes, and suffixes.

multisyllable word A word that contains more than one syllable.

multiple-meaning word A words that means something different depending on the way it is used (*run—home run, run* in your stocking, *run* down the street, a *run* of bad luck).

mystery A form of writing in which the plot hinges on a puzzling situation or event that is resolved by the end.

myth A traditional story originally created to explain natural phenomena or events.

narrative genres A category of texts in which the purpose is to tell a story. Stories and biographies are kinds of narrative.

nonfiction A text based on fact.

nursery rhyme A short rhyme for children, usually telling a story.

onomatopoetic words Words for which the pronunciations suggests the words' meaning.

onset In a syllable, the part (consonant, consonant cluster, or consonant digraph) that comes before the vowel (*cr*-eam).

onset-rime segmentation The identification and separation of onsets (first part) and rimes (last part, containing the vowel) in words (*dr-ip*).

open syllable A syllable that ends in a vowel sound (*ho*-tel).

opinion editorial A type of text in which the purpose is to state and defend an opinion, usually by an editor of a magazine, newspaper, or TV news show.

organization (in writing) The craft of arranging ideas in a written text according to a logical structure.

orthographic awareness The knowledge of the visual features of written language, including distinctive features of letters as well as spelling patterns in words.

orthography The representation of the sounds of a language with the proper letters according to standard usage (spelling).

parody A humorous imitation of a serious writing.

performance reading An instructional context in which the students read orally to perform for others; they may read in unison or take parts. Shared reading, choral reading, and readers theater are kinds of performance reading.

personal narrative A brief text, usually autobiographical and written in the first person, that tells about one event in the writer's life.

personification A figure of speech in which a lifeless thing or idea is spoken of as a living thing.

phoneme The smallest unit of sound in spoken language. There are approximately forty-four units of speech sounds in English.

phoneme addition To add a beginning or ending sound to a word (h + and, an + t).

phoneme blending To identify individual sounds and then to put them together smoothly to make a word (c-a-t = cat).

phoneme deletion To omit a beginning, middle, or ending sound of a word (cart − c = art).

phoneme-grapheme correspondence The relationship between the sounds (phonemes) and letters (graphemes) of a language.

phoneme isolation The identification of an individual sound—beginning, middle, or end—in a word.

phoneme manipulation The movement of sounds from one place in a word to another.

phoneme reversal The exchange of the first and last sounds of a word to make a different word.

phoneme substitution The replacement of the beginning, middle, or ending sound of a word with a new sound.

phonemic (or phoneme) awareness The ability to hear individual sounds in words and to identify particular sounds.

phonemic strategies Ways of solving words that use how words sound and relationships between letters and letter clusters and phonemes in those words (*cat, make*).

phonetics The scientific study of speech sounds—how the sounds are made vocally and the relation of speech sounds to the total language process.

phonics The knowledge of letter-sound relationships and how they are used in reading and writing. Teaching phonics refers to helping children acquire this body of knowledge about the oral and written language systems; additionally, teaching phonics helps children use phonics knowledge as part of a reading and writing process. Phonics instruction uses a small portion of the body of knowledge that makes up phonetics.

phonogram A phonetic element represented by graphic characters or symbols. In word recognition, a graphic sequence composed of a vowel grapheme and an ending consonant grapheme (such as *an* or *it*) is sometimes called a word family.

phonological awareness The awareness of words, rhyming words, onsets and rimes, syllables, and individual sounds (phonemes).

phonological system The sounds of the language and how they work together in ways that are meaningful to the speakers of the language.

photo essay An informational text that uses captioned photographs to convey its message.

picture book A highly illustrated fiction or nonfiction text in which pictures work with the text to tell a story or provide information.

plural Of, relating to, or constituting more than one.

poetic genres A category of texts in which the purpose is to use poetic form to explain feelings, sensory images, ideas, or stories. Free verse, traditional rhymes, and limericks are kinds of poetic genre.

point of view The way an author chooses to tell or narrate a story, such as through characters, events, or ideas.

portmanteau word A word made from combining two other words and meanings (*smoke* + *fog* = *smog*).

possessive Grammatical constructions used to show ownership (*John's, his*) .

pourquoi tale A legend told to explain why certain events happened (originally French).

predict (as a strategic action) To use what is known to think about what will follow while reading continuous text.

prefix A group of letters that can be placed in front of a base word to change its meaning (*preplan*).

principle In phonics, a generalization or a sound-spelling relationship that is predictable.

propaganda One-sided speaking or writing deliberately used to influence the thoughts and actions of someone in alignment with specific ideas or views.

publishing (in writing) The process of making the final draft of a written composition public.

punctuation Marks used in written text to clarify meaning and separate structural units. The comma and the period are common punctuation marks.

purpose (in writing) The writer's overall intention in creating a text. To tell a story and to inform or explain are two standard purposes for writing.

r-controlled vowel sound The modified or *r*-influenced sound of a vowel when it is followed by *r* in a syllable (*hurt*).

reader's notebook A notebook or folder of bound pages in which students write about their reading. The reader's notebook is used to keep a record of texts read and to express thinking. It may have several different sections to serve a variety of purposes.

readers theater A performance of literature, as a story, play, or poetry, read aloud expressively by one or more persons, rather than acted.

realistic fiction An invented story that could happen.

rehearsing and planning (in writing) The process of collecting, working with, and selecting ideas for a written composition.

report A text written to provide facts about a specific topic.

rhyme The ending part (rime) of a word that sounds like the ending part (rime) of another word (*mail, tale*).

rhythm The regular or ordered repetition of stressed and unstressed syllables in speech or writing.

rime The ending part of a word containing the vowel; the letters that represent the vowel sound and the consonant letters that follow it in a syllable (dr-*eam*).

root The part of a word that contains the main meaning component.

satire A literary narrative in which human failures are portrayed and ridiculed.

schwa The sound of the middle vowel in an unstressed syllable (the *o* in *done* and the sound between the *k* and *l* in *freckle*).

science fiction A form of fictional narrative in which real or imagined scientific phenomena influence the plot.

search for and use information (as a strategic action) To look for and to think about all kinds of content in order to make sense of text while reading.

segment To divide into parts (*to-ma-to*).

semantic system The system by which speakers of a language communicate meaning through language.

sentence complexity (as a text characteristic) The complexity of the structure or syntax of a sentence. Addition of phrases and clauses to simple sentences increases complexity.

series book One of a collection of books about the same character or characters and the different events or situations encountered.

shared reading An instructional technique in which the teacher involves a group of students in the reading of a particular big book in order to introduce aspects of literacy (such as print conventions), develop reading strategies (such as decoding or predicting), and teach vocabulary.

shared writing An instructional technique in which the teacher involves a group of students in the composing of a coherent text together. The teacher writes while scaffolding children's language and ideas.

short vowel A brief-duration sound represented by a vowel letter (*cat*).

silent *e* The final *e* in a spelling pattern that usually signals a long vowel sound in the word and does not represent a sound itself (*make*).

simile A comparison of two unlike things in which a word of comparison (often *like* or *as*) is used.

sketching and drawing (in writing) To create a rough (sketch) or finished (drawing) image of a person, a place, a thing, or an idea to capture, work with, and render the writer's ideas.

solve words (as a strategic action) To use a range of strategies to take words apart and understand their meaning.

sources of information The various cues in a written text that combine to make meaning (for example, syntax, meaning, and the physical shape and arrangement of type).

spelling patterns Beginning letters (onsets) and common phonograms (rimes) form the basis for the English syllable; knowing these patterns, a student can build countless words.

split dialogue Written dialogue in which a "said phrase" divides the speaker's words: "Come on," said Mom. "Let's go home."

strategic action Any one of many simultaneous, coordinated thinking activities that go on in a reader's head. See *thinking within, beyond, and about the text*.

stress The emphasis given to some syllables or words.

suffix An affix or group of letters added at the end of a base or root word to change its function or meaning (*handful*, hope*less*).

summarize (as a strategic action) Put together and remember important information, disregarding irrelevant information, while reading

survival story A form of adventure story in which a character or characters must struggle against nature or other people in order to stay alive.

syllabication The division of words into syllables (*pen-cil*).

syllable A minimal unit of sequential speech sounds composed of a vowel sound or a consonant-vowel combination. A syllable always contains a vowel or vowel-like speech sound (*to-ma-to*).

synonym One of two or more words that have different sounds but the same meaning (*chair, seat*).

syntactic awareness The knowledge of grammatical patterns or structures.

syntactic system Rules that govern the ways in which morphemes and words work together in sentence patterns. Not the same as proper grammar, which refers to the accepted grammatical conventions.

syntax The study of how sentences are formed and of the grammatical rules that govern their formation.

synthesize (as a strategic action) To combine new information or ideas from reading text with existing knowledge to create new understandings.

tall tale A fictional narrative characterized by exaggeration.

text structure The overall architecture or organization of a piece of writing. Chronology (sequence) and description are two common text structures.

test writing A functional genre required in schools.

theme The central idea or concept in a story or the message that the author is conveying.

thinking within, beyond, and about the text Three ways of thinking about a text while reading. Thinking within the text involves efficiently and effectively understanding what's on the page, the author's literal message. Thinking beyond the text requires making inferences and putting text ideas together in different ways to construct the text's meaning. In thinking about the text, readers analyze and critique the author's craft.

tone An expression of the author's attitude or feelings toward a subject reflected in the style of writing.

tools (as text characteristics) Parts of a text designed to help the reader access or better understand it (table of contents, glossary, photo captions, headings).

tools (in writing) References that support the writing process (dictionary, thesaurus).

topic The subject of a piece of writing.

understandings Basic concepts that are critical to comprehending a particular area.

viewing self as writer Attitudes and practices that support a student's becoming a lifelong writer.

visual strategies Ways of solving words that use knowledge of how words look, including the clusters and patterns of the letters in words (b*ear*, l*ight*).

vocabulary (as a text characteristic) Words and their meanings.

voice (in writing) The craft of creating a unique style.

vowel A speech sound or phoneme made without stoppage of or friction in the airflow. The vowel sounds are represented by *a, e, i, o, u,* and sometimes *y* and *w.*

vowel combinations Two vowels that appear together in words (m*ea*t).

vowel digraph Two successive vowel letters that represent a single vowel sound (b*oa*t), a vowel combination.

word A unit of meaning in language.

word analysis To break apart words into parts or individual sounds in order to parse them.

word boundaries The white space that defines a word; the white space before the first letter and after the last letter of a word. It is important for young readers to learn to recognize word boundaries.

word-by-word matching Usually applied to a beginning reader's ability to match one spoken word with one printed word while reading and pointing. In older readers, the eyes take over the process.

word choice (in writing) The craft of choosing words to convey precise meaning.

word family A term often used to designate words that are connected by phonograms or rimes (*hot, not, pot, shot*). A word family can also be a series of words connected by meaning (affixes added to a base word; for example: *base, baseball, basement, baseman, basal, basis, baseless, baseline, baseboard, abase, abasement, off base, home base; precise, précis, precisely, precision*).

wordless picture book A story told exclusively with pictures.

words (as a text characteristic) Decodability of words in a text; phonetic and structural features of words.

word-solving actions See *solve words.*

writer's notebook A written log of potential writing topics or ideas that a writer would like to explore; a place to keep the writer's experimentations with writing styles.

References

Fountas, Irene C., and Gay Su Pinnell. 2011, 2008. *Fountas & Pinnell Benchmark Assessment Systems 1 and 2.* Portsmouth, NH: Heinemann.

Use this system to determine reading levels, gain specific information about reader's strengths and needs, and document progress over time.

———. 2009. *Leveled Literacy Intervention.* Orange System (Levels A–C, Kindergarten); Green System (Levels A–J, Grade 1); Blue System (Levels C–N, Grade 2).

You can use these systems to align classroom teaching and intervention services. Leveled Literacy Intervention (LLI) *includes the professional book,* When Readers Struggle: Teaching That Works; a Program Guide, Lesson Guides, a *technology package, and fiction and nonfiction student books. The lesson guides provide specific help in implementing several lesson frameworks. The Guided Reading Continuum is an integral part of lesson plans. The Orange System provides 70 lessons to be used with 70 different titles; Green includes 110 lessons and titles; and Blue includes 120 lessons and titles. Each LLI system provides a complete range of resources, including children's books to support children who are struggling.*

———. 2009. *The Fountas & Pinnell Prompting Guide, Part 1: A Tool for Literacy Teachers.* Portsmouth, NH: Heinemann.

———. 2009. *The Fountas & Pinnell Prompting Guide, Part 1: Spanish Edition, A Tool for Bilingual Literacy Teachers.* Portsmouth, NH: Heinemann.

The two tools listed above provide specific suggestions for language that you can use to teach, prompt for, and reinforce effective reading behaviors.

———. 2006. *Teaching for Comprehending and Fluency: Thinking, Talking, and Writing About Reading,* K–8. Portsmouth, NH: Heinemann.

Use this book in your studies of the interactive read-aloud and literature discussions, shared and performance reading, and guided reading continua to skillfully teach meaning making and fluency within any instructional context.

———. 2006. *Leveled Books, K–8: Matching Texts to Readers for Effective Teaching.* Portsmouth, NH: Heinemann.

Use this book and the leveled books website, www.FountasandPinnellLeveledBooks. com, *with your studies of the Guided Reading continuum to analyze the characteristics of texts and select just-the-right book to use for guided reading.*

———. 2005. *Guided Reading: Essential Elements, The Skillful Teacher* (videotapes). Portsmouth, NH: Heinemann.

Use these videotapes with your studies in the interactive read-aloud and literature discussion and guided reading continua to see Guided Reading *in action. In the first part,* Essential Elements, *watch guided reading lessons as they unfold to see how teachers introduce a text, support students as they read orally and silently, discuss text meaning, use "teaching points" to reinforce effective reading strategies, revisit the text to extend meaning, and conduct word work as needed.*

In part two, The Skillful Teacher, *observe the planning and organizing behind guided reading and learn how to meet the needs of individual readers. You'll discover how to group students, select books, plan book introductions, support word solving, teach comprehension strategies, develop fluency, and take running records.*

———. 2004. *Word Study Lessons: Phonics, Spelling, and Vocabulary (Grade 3).* Portsmouth, NH: *firsthand.*

Use this book with your studies of the Guided Reading continuum to choose the lessons that align with your students' needs.

———. 2001. *Guiding Readers and Writers: Teaching Comprehension, Genre, and Content Literacy.* Portsmouth, NH: Heinemann.

Engage, inform, and inspire early readers and writers with this book that explores the essential components of a quality upper elementary literacy program.

———. 1996. *Guided Reading: Good First Teaching for All Children.* Portsmouth, NH: Heinemann.

Use this book for help with teaching guided reading lessons. Learn how to select and introduce texts, teach during and after reading, and assess student progress.

Pinnell, Gay Su, and Irene C. Fountas. 2011. *Literacy Beginnings: A Prekindergarten Handbook.* Portsmouth, NH: Heinemann.

A guide for supporting emerging readers, writers, and language users through play and exploration. Includes the Continuum of Literacy Learning, PreK.

———. 2009. *When Readers Struggle: Teaching That Works.* Portsmouth, NH: Heinemann.

Use this volume to help you design and implement effective intervention programs for children in grades K–3 who are have difficulty learning to read and write.

———. 2003. *Phonics Lessons: Letters, Words, and How They Work (Grades K, 1, and 2).* Portsmouth, NH: firsthand.

Use these books with your studies of the phonics and word study and guided reading continua to choose the lessons that align with your students' needs.

———. 1998. *Word Matters: Teaching Phonics and Spelling in the Reading/Writing Classroom.* Portsmouth, NH: Heinemann.

This book will help you design and teach for effective word-solving strategies.